AMERICAN POLITICS

Dr. Rodgir Cohen

Humanities
ACADEMIC PUBLISHERS

ISBN: 9781988557434

Published in the United States of America
Humanities Academic Publishers

Contents

CHAPTER 1

Key definition in Political Science

1.1. Governments and regimes

The term 'politics' is derived from the Greek word *politiká* which refers to the affairs of the polis. **Polis**, on the other hand, corresponds to the Ancient Greek city-states, the majority of which possessed an autarkic/self-sufficient governmental system. **Politics** is therefore primarily the process by which individuals develop, defend, and alter the general principles by which they live. For this reason, politics, in its daily use, is identified with the art of government and state affairs.

Relating politics to the activities of the state makes it necessary to distinguish between the **public sphere** and the **private sphere**. These ideas highlight the distinction between private and public interests in the strictest meaning. Beyond personal interests, the public sphere includes issues that affect the well-being of the entire society. Adversely, the private sphere is about personal concerns unrelated to the wider population. In this regard, libertarians and classical liberals draw a clear line between public and private matters. For instance, family life and business relationships are deeply embedded in the private sphere, and it is deemed improper for politics to directly meddle with these relationships.

However, some philosophies argue that the public and private spheres cannot be clearly divided. For instance, 'personal is political' is one of the most significant catchphrases of feminists. This catchphrase challenges the idea of the distinction between the public and the private sphere, contending that gender inequality in the public sphere has its roots in culture and family. The private domain is also rejected by Marxists, who argue that economic relations alone determine all aspects of political relations and institutions.

One of the key proponents of deliberative democracy, Jurgen Habermas, defines the public sphere as a social setting where a variety of viewpoints are presented, issues pertaining to general issues are debated, and communicative solutions to collective problems are found. Although this term is largely recognized, political philosophy will continue to dispute whether certain topics are public or private.

Being a social science and concerning the governance of our communities, the definition of politics is unavoidably connected to both conflict – a competition against opposing forces – and cooperation – the act of achieving goals through collective action. That is, human beings are social animals, but they have different wants, needs, and opinions, so they differ in the decisions about the **rules** by which they live. These latter are thus essential for any social system, since rules help to determine who will win or lose future power struggles without having to resort to violence.[1]

In contrast to the notion that politics is a form of conflict resolution, some authors associate politics with the production and distribution of resources, values, and social statuses. This type of comprehension is also known as power politics. Power politics de-idealizes and redefines politics as a simple struggle for power. There is no such thing as legitimate politics in this regard, but there are winners and losers. Marx, for instance, does not view liberal democracy as a legitimate political system, but rather as an ideological deception manufactured by capitalists to defend their class interests. This is why, in a broader context, anarchists consider all governmental power to be illegitimate. This radical rejection

---

[1] Roller, E. (2005), *The Performance of Democracies: Political Institutions and Public Policy*. Oxford University Press, Oxford.

of politics is not shared by the majority of political scientists. Moreover, the legitimacy of political authority is regarded as a fundamental theme in political science.

Therefore, politics is a **process** and not an outcome: due to the inescapable presence of diversity and scarcity, not all conflicts in society can be resolved, so the process of setting rules can create disputes among the population. These disputes are at the basis of two essential concepts to understand politics: **authority** and **power**. The latter can be defined as the ability to influence others, so it may not necessarily be political, while the former is a form of **legitimate** power, which means that authority is itself the right to exercise power. That is, individuals acknowledge that society requires a form of common agreement to ensure that rules are upheld, so politics is connected to exercise of authority, such that Easton defines it as the "authoritative allocation of values."[2] Yet, to reach this agreement, it is essential that human beings cooperate one with another up to the point that political power can also be defined as "acting in concert" as done by Hannah Arendt[3].

Following a discussion of what politics is, it is necessary to quickly define political science. Experiments, observations, and inferences that can be repeated are the cornerstones of scientific inquiry, which seeks to provide robust explanations for observed and hypothesized phenomena. Thus, **political science** is defined as the social science that examines politics by means of the empirical method. In this view, the term 'political science' refers to an approach to the study of politics that is empirical in nature and is devoid of any value judgments. This method is the product of **positivism**. This highlights the clear divide that exists between the fields of political science and political philosophy, which is analogous to the gap that exists between empirical and normative analysis.

---

[2] Easton, D. (1976). "Theoretical approaches to political support.", Canadian Journal of Political Science, 9 (3), pp. 431-448.
[3] Phillips, J. (2013), "Between the Tyranny of Opinion and the Despotism of Rational Truth: Arendt on Facts and Acting in Concert.", New German Critique, 40 (2), 97-112.

In this sense, science asks "what is it?" but philosophy asks, "what ought to be?" The disciplines of political science include, for example, what democracy is and the extent to which countries have democratic standards relative to one another. To argue why democratic regimes are superior to other types of regimes, however, is undoubtedly a question of political philosophy. Since it would be pointless for political scientists to analyze democracy apart from its normative claims, it is not always possible or desirable to maintain a clear distinction between political science and political philosophy. The importance of the collaboration between political science and philosophy becomes clearer when we revise the legitimacy problem of political authority.

The concept of legitimacy is essential to understand what **the State** – the current prevalent form of political organization of our societies -- is, since Max Weber defines it as a "human community that (successfully) claims the monopoly of the legitimate use of physical force within a given territory."[4] This means that other actors may use violence, but the state is the only actor legitimized to do so. To exercise its power, the State power must be organized, and in order to decide who is in charge of allocating citizens' different values, societies need a form of **government,** namely a system or an organization for exercising authority over a body of people.

This argument describes the state as a legal monopoly of power; nevertheless, it does not elaborate on the source of the legitimacy of power. Weber recognized three sorts of political legitimacy, based on history and customs (traditional authority), charismatic authority, and a system of formal, legal rules (legal-rational authority). Modern societies, according to Weber, are increasingly defined by the exercise of legal-rational authority and a sort of legitimacy that derives from respect for formal and typically legal rules.

Contemporary democratic political authorities are examples of rational-legal authority. In democratic societies, the ability to shift political

---

[4] Weber M. (2004 [1919]), The Vocation Lectures. "Science as a Vocation". "Politics as a Vocation", Ed by David Owen D. and Strong T.B., Hackett Publishing Company, Cambridge.

authority through elections is historically quite exceptional. During the Middle Ages, when it was believed that God granted dynasties the right to govern, it was not feasible for political power to be transferred by elections. The power to rule is personified by the assertion that the right to rule belongs to a dynasty or charismatic leader. Believing that the authority to rule is personal is predicated on the concept that ruling is not a scientific or rational practice, but rather an assertion of personal abilities and traits. This political assumption also explains the aristocratic and hierarchical organization of traditional societies. Modern democratic countries, on the other hand, adhere to the idea of political equality and do not assume that the peaceful transfer of power through elections will result in treason or political instability. On the contrary, it is claimed that democratic political decision-making systems will serve the common interests of society, hence denying individuals personal right to rule. Since governance is a rational practice, the transfer of political power via elections is regarded as a usual political procedure.

Politics produce different kinds of governments according to the level of control and authority exercised by the government over its population. At one end of the spectrum, the government makes all decisions about how individuals live their lives, and citizens are powerless to push back. On the other end, there is an anarchic system where individuals make the decisions for themselves, and the government does not exist. Hence, governments can exercise this authority in different ways, and the form of government, or the set of rules that regulate the operation of a government, are defined as the political **regime.** This latter defines only a form of government and must not be misunderstood with its negative connotation, namely regime as an authoritarian political system that restricts the people's liberties.[5]

The difference between 'government' and 'regime' is important. For example, the United States federal government is composed of the three

---

[5] Dietrich, S. and Bernhard M. (2009). "State or regime? The impact of institutions on welfare outcomes." *The European Journal of Development Research*, 28 (2), 252-269.

main branches (**legislative**, **executive** and **judiciary**) and draws its powers from the Constitution, the President and federal courts. With the elections, citizens decide which party (**Democratic Party** or **Republican Party**) they want to direct these branches and who should be the President. Instead, regime defines the political institutional framework of the country. Examples of regimes can thus be "**democracy**," "**authoritarian**," or "**totalitarian**." The United States system of governance, namely its regime, is a **democratic republic** style, and this does not change with the elections. Elections are made to select – and to replace – governments while they cannot change regime type. Hence, regardless of whether Republicans or Democrats win the elections, the United States regime will remain a democratic republic. It is commonly acknowledged that republics are fundamentally classified into parliamentary and presidential systems. However, a parliamentary form of government can also exist inside a constitutional monarchy, as in the United Kingdom. The political regime of the United Kingdom is a **constitutional monarchy** with a parliamentary **form of government**.

Overall, we can find four main types of regimes: democracy, theocracy, autocracy, and totalitarianism. To identify the type of a political regime, we can take into account three fundamental factors: the political decision-making procedure, the source of sovereignty, and the extent of the official ideology. Democracy's etymology comes from the Greek word *demos* ("the people") and *kratos* (power), and this implies that any democratic system must be based on a **popular sovereignty**, namely the principle for which the authority of the state and its government are created and sustained by the consent of its people, who are the source of political power.[6] This sovereignty can be exercised in two main forms.

First, in a democracy as self-government, citizens can be directly involved in politics and make the rules that govern themselves, as it was in the case in Ancient Athens, Greece. Today, direct democracy can be recreated in several ways, from deliberative assemblies to direct decisional

---

[6] Held, D. (2006), *Models of Democracy*, Stanford University Press, California.

means such as referendum, or the initiative process. The method by which citizens can become directly involved on a single issue by voting directly on an issue and proposing new laws or amendments to a state constitution is referred to as a **referendum**.

Second, modern democracy does not necessarily require a direct involvement in politics by the whole populace. Democracy can also assume the form of a **republic**, namely a form of government in which the people hold the power, but they rule indirectly by means of their representatives. This form of **representative democracy**, supported by Madison in his *Federalist Papers*,[7] is adopted in the United States and defines a regime where politicians rule society according to the constitutional law on behalf of the citizenry, but where the people still retain power due to democratic procedures such as **elections**, **party system**, and the **division of powers**. However, this form of government is not necessarily democratic, since there could be republics where citizens do not hold sufficient institutional means to control the elites ruling the country.

In this regard, liberal democracies and illiberal democracies can be distinguished. Liberal democracies are constitutional democracies. It is not sufficient that states have written or unwritten constitutions to qualify as constitutional states. Constitutionalism seeks to protect the rights and liberties of individuals against the state by restricting political power through the separation of powers and checks and balances. Governments that do not successfully satisfy this political objective cannot be called constitutional government. For instance, Iraq under Saddam Hussein and contemporary Iran both have written constitutions. However, we do not classify these countries as constitutional government.

Additionally, we can categorize illiberal democracies within themselves. According to the annual Democracy Index produced by the Economist Intelligence Unit, for instance, the categories of regimes include full democracy, flawed democracy, hybrid regimes, and authoritarian

---

[7] Madison J. (1982 [1788]), *The Federalist Paper by Alexander Hamilton*, James Madison and John Jay, Bantam Books, New York.

regimes. Attempting to categorize regimes in an unorthodox manner reveals that it is extremely challenging to build democracy with all of its institutions. In general, democracies with strong democratic histories in Western Europe and North America are classified as full democracies, while countries with significant flaws in their democratic institutionalization are classified otherwise. Countries such as Brazil, Argentina, and India, in which democratic politics have not been fully established despite holding regular and fair elections, are examples of flawed democracies. Countries such as Paraguay, Mexico, and Ecuador, where elections are not fair and competitive, the media is controlled by the political authority, and civil liberties are not guaranteed, are referred to as hybrid regimes, even if they hold regular elections. These countries can be classified as illiberal democracies because they have moved away from the democratic ideal.

Authoritarian regimes are those without democratic political institutions, and political pluralism is either absent or heavily restricted. Many of the nations that fall into this category are dictatorship. There may be some formal democratic institutions, but in practice, democracy is more of a form than a substance. If elections take place at all, they are not held under democratic principles. There is a dismissive attitude toward violations of civil freedoms and abuses of those rights. In most countries, the media are either owned by the state or are under the authority of groups with ties to the government. Both criticisms of the government and general expressions of opinion are subject to widespread censorship. The judicial system is not free from outside influence.[8] This category may contain Russia, Venezuela, and Saudi Arabia.

In this regard, it is important to underline the difference between an authoritarian and a **totalitarian** regime. The former restricts only certain liberties of the population; it may also accept certain independent organizations and it does not necessarily rely on a strong ideology to influence the people's values. On the contrary, **totalitarianism** aims at

---

[8] Economist Intelligence (2021). Democracy index 2021: the China challenge, UK, p. 68.

controlling every aspect of citizens' life and does not accept any independent organization.[9] As mentioned by Benito Mussolini, father of Italian **fascism**, in a totalitarian state there is "all within the state, none outside the state and none against the state."[10] Traditional societies cannot support totalitarian regimes. By utilizing all state structures and institutions, an incredibly powerful government is able to keep every structure and even every individual of the society under surveillance and control. Totalitarian regimes possess an ideology, such as Marxism-Leninism, Fascism, or National Socialism, which is required to produce a perfect society, as well as the ability to monitor and manage this ideology. It is very difficult for a totalitarian regime to form and consolidate in the absence of these two capabilities. While there are still several authoritarian regimes in the world, North Korea is the last totalitarian regime left.

Finally, a regime can also be a "**theocracy**," namely a political system where the government is controlled by religious officials who are regarded as divinely guided. Such government leaders are members of the clergy, and laws are not based on political constitutions but rather on religious law. This form of government was typical of early civilizations, and while the **Enlightenment** has rendered this regime obsolete in Western societies, some theocracies still exist in the Middle-East, such as in Saudi Arabia and Iran.[11]

1.2. Theories of power

While 'government' and 'regime' are terms that define the way political power is organized within a certain state, different theories exist concerning the way scholars believe power should be framed, of which we can find four main paradigms. First, there is the **pluralist theory**, for which,

---

[9] Curtis, M. (1979), *Totalitarianism*, Transaction Publishers, New Jersey.
[10] Ibid.
[11] Cosgel M.M. & Miceli T.J, (2013), "Theocracy", *Working papers 2013-29*, University of Connecticut, Department of Economics.

if elected, representatives manage to represent equally the different interests present in our societies. Their rule could be both democratic and respecting the people's liberty. As an academic explanation **pluralism** developed after the end of the Second World War and reached its height during the 1950s and 1960s, periods of economic and political development for Western societies characterized by low social conflict.[12]

During this time, scholars stressed the beneficial consequences of social diversity for politics, advocating for constitutional ways of accommodating this diversity on public policy issues. In this framework, group interest is the building block of politics, since this helps citizens develop their political skills and understand how democracy necessitates bargaining and compromise. For this framework to work properly, no group must be blocked from competing on equal terms with another one, and any category of people who share an interest must have the chance to form a group. Therefore, **pluralists** believed that electoral competition creates a *polyarchy*, namely a government of minorities where elections are competitive. In this system, diverse groups have the opportunity to make themselves heard effectively in the political system with politicians relying on the electorate's support for their re-election.

Considering politics as the result of the mediation between the requests of competing groups, pluralists hold that representative procedures ensure the representation of a large number of influential groups, thus avoiding the concentration of power in the hands of few individuals, which was the theoretical pillar of the second paradigm, namely the **elitist scholars**. This literature developed with Italian sociologists such as Gaetano Mosca[13], Roberto Michels[14] and Vilfredo Pareto[15], but later

[12] Dryzek J.S., Dunleavy P. (2009), *Theories of the Democratic State*, Palgrave Macmillan, Basingstoke.

[13] Renzo S. (1952). "Note on Gaetano Mosca.", *The American Political Science Review*, 46.2 (1952), 603-605.

[14] Michels R. (1915), *Political Parties: A Sociological Study of The Oligarchical Tendencies of Modern Democracy*, Hearst's International Library Company, New York.

[15] Pareto V. (1935), *A Treatise on General Sociology*, General Publishing Company, Memphis.

developed also in the United States thanks to scholars such as Charles Wright Mills.[16] This philosopher maintained that the common man cannot control politics, since power is centralized in the hands of a political **elite** that makes the fundamental decisions for everyone. Therefore, Mills defined elites as: "those political, economic and military circles which, arranged in a complex and stratified order, make decisions of at least national importance."[17]

Mills noticed that in the American society of his time, the greatest power existed in the economic, political, and military spheres.[18] These elites determined the direction of the state and reduced all minor institutions to below these top powers. Moreover, each sector extended and thickened its relations with the others, so there was a strong interdependence between them. The members of these elites could also be considered as a single whole since they behaved in a benevolent way among themselves and had common interests with similar social origins. Therefore, despite the theory that democracies should spread political power equally, these elites ruled centralized power in their hands.

The power of the elites is connected to the third paradigm, namely the **bureaucratic theory**. This view relies on Weber's famous theory for which bureaucratization was intertwined with the development of the **territorial state** and the **capitalist economy**.[19] That is, the development of mass citizenship increases both the quantitative demands on the state administration, and the qualitative demand for uniformity of treatment, which can only be met by a **supra-local** administrative system, operating on the basis of impartiality between persons. Hence, bureaucracy is a distinctive feature of the modern world because it constitutes an efficient structure of power and of administration over a large territory.

---

[16] Mills C.W. (1956), *The Power Elite*, Oxford University Press, Oxford.
[17] Ibid.
[18] Ibid.
[19] Lutzker, M. A. (1982), "Max Weber and the analysis of modern bureaucratic organization: Notes toward a theory of appraisal.", *The American Archivist*, 45 (2), 119-130.

This process influences also the structure of democratic systems, since bureaucratization reduces the importance of the parliament in favor of the party, its leaders, and of specialized agencies. For example, the bureaucratic theory suggests that in the United States, those within agencies like the EPA, CIA, and the FBI, are the ones who have the real power within the nation. That is, '**democratization**' did not lead to a great dispersal of power to the masses, even though this does not mean that parliament has become obsolete. Rather the opposite: certain democratic processes have become essential in politics, such as the selection of leaders by electoral competition, the provision through Parliament of a forum for public debate and review of policy, and a mechanism for removing leaders in the event of a serious loss of confidence.[20]

Finally, the last paradigm connected to political distribution of power is the **social movement theory**. This theory explains how social mobilization occurs, under which forms it manifests, and which political consequences it may have. This paradigm became particularly influential in the 1960s, when many in both the United States and Europe began to see civic protests as a means to improve politics. At first, these protests puzzled scholars because studies relied on a **deprivation theory** which taught that protests were a result of social sufferance, while social movements in the 1960s were the result of an increase in social welfare. Furthermore, answers to this puzzle created differences between American and European sociology.[21]

On the one side, American theories relied more on structural approaches that examined which social and political contexts enabled or restricted protests. Among the factors that increased political movements, scholars underlined features such as an increased access to political decision-making power, an instability in the ruling elites, and a lower

[20] Waters T, Waters D (2015), *Weber's Rationalism and Modern Society: New Translations on Politics, Bureaucracy, and Social Stratification*, Palgrave Macmillan, London.
[21] Morris, A. (2000), "Reflections on social movement theory: Criticisms and proposals.", *Contemporary Sociology* 29 (3), 445-454.

ability of the state to repress these actions. Moreover, resource mobilization was of particular importance, since the more organized a community, and the more material, moral, cultural and human resources it possessed, the more likely a protest was to begin.

On the other side, the European strand focused more on social-constructivist approaches that focused less on social-class and material explanations, to argue instead that current protests are different from past labor movements based on social-class, since social movements are now based on post-material features as collective identity, gender, and sexuality. On top of that, recent scholars such as Goodwin and Polletta argued that emotions, construction of meaning and agency, play a significant part as well in leading to the formation of social movements.[22]

As described by these paradigms, power is not organized in the same way in each country and this has significant consequences, not only for the people's political power, but also for one of the pillars of any political system, namely the people's liberty.

1.3. Types of liberty

Overall, two main conceptions of liberty have dominated the political debate, namely Isaiah Berlin's division between a "**negative liberty**" and a "**positive** (or **organic) liberty**."[23] Negative liberty, which is the absence of external constraints on one's actions, includes civil and political rights such as freedom of speech, life, private property, freedom from violent crime, freedom of religion, habeas corpus, a fair trial, and freedom from slavery. Positive liberty requires the agent to take an active part in gaining control of themselves, since it claims, "I am free to the extent that I achieve self-mastery." Positive liberty mainly focuses on answering the question: "By whom am I ruled?" Therefore, the positive desire to

---

[22] Buechler, S. M. (1995). "New Social Movement Theories", *The Sociological Quarterly*, 36(3): 441-464.

[23] Berlin I. (1958), *Two Concepts of Liberty*, Oxford University Press, Oxford.

govern myself is connected to the belief that it is essential to determine who is making the political decisions to assess if citizens are free or not. Hence, the main question on which this conception of liberty is framed is: "What does it mean to be free to govern myself?"

First, self-mastery entails that individuals must be a *subject* and not an *object*, namely a self-directed doer able to make decisions by herself and not something moved by external forces. Being a subject is important because only insofar as I am able to conceive policies and goals of my own (and I am afterwards able to realize them), can I consider myself a self-mastered human being. Otherwise, I will just be an object, a mere 'thing' directed by others according to their needs. In this framework, I am free to the degree that I can realize my own will, while I am enslaved to the extent that I cannot do so.[24]

On the contrary, **negative liberty** is the concept describing individuals having a personal sphere that must not be constrained by any external interference – a space within which they can act unobstructed by others. Conceiving freedom in terms of non-interference, it becomes essential to understand which hindrances damage personal liberty and which could instead be accepted. The negative liberty scholars' answer to this dilemma has a pivotal social component, since they maintain that citizens are unfree if others prevent them from doing what they could otherwise do. Individuals are then politically unfree when – and only when – they are prevented from attaining a goal by another human being: the wider the area where they are not hindered by other human beings in exercising their choices, the freer they are[25].

At first glance, it may seem simple to guarantee this liberty in a framework where all coercion is conceived as bad because it represses human desires. Total freedom lacking coercion. However, the fact that we live in social systems, where personal liberties are inevitably connected, creates disputes among scholars regarding how many "bads" we ought to impose

---

[24] Berlin I. (2002), *Liberty*, Oxford University Press, Oxford.
[25] Berlin 2002; 171-177.

to avoid larger evils. The problem is then how wide each individual's personal sphere should be, since if everyone was given unlimited freedom, we would live in a chaos where the will of the stronger would prevail over that of the weaker. In a negative liberty framework, the argument is thus: the line between the area of private life and that of public authority should be drawn to have the maximum degree of non-interference compatible with the minimum demands of social life.

Thus, the negative liberty solution differs from the one given by positive liberty. Whereas the latter aims to put authority directly in the hands of the citizenry, the former focuses on finding a minimum area of personal freedom that cannot be violated by anyone, and by this means, they aim to block authority. Hence, these two views focus on two different aspects of power: whereas positive liberty scholars focus on the *source* of the power in the hands of those ruling the social system, negative liberty scholars address the problem of the *intensity and amount* of power that rulers ought to have.

How should therefore negative freedom be restricted? Wouldn't that result in a chaotic order if everyone attempts to do whatever they please? For example, can press freedom involve publishing inaccurate information about another person? According to Mill, a person's freedom is justified if it does not violate the rights and liberties of others. The term for this is the harm principle. You can specialize in martial arts as you like, but you cannot beat anyone other than in self-defense. Individuals who are free to choose in a free society will have competing interests and objectives. This needs numerous legal norms for conflict settlement. In this regard, free societies are also characterized by the strict enforcement of the law. However, the rules of law here are intended to expand individuals' negative freedoms. In contrast, the purpose of the laws in a non-free society is to restrict negative liberties.

The primary criticism of positive freedom is that it is unclear what it means to be free from the influence of others and our own inner constraints. For instance, one of the primary justifications for compulsory public education is that ignorant persons are incapable of making wise decisions. In this regard, proponents of positive freedom claim that via education, individuals may make better decisions. Due to the impossibility of separating educational content from ideologies and conceptions of the good life, especially in the social sciences, there is a risk that public education may become a form of ideological indoctrination. The primary reason communist regimes such as the Soviet Union are regarded as totalitarian is their attempts to entirely eliminate individual preferences. Radical communist indoctrination might be viewed as a radical manifestation of the positive conception of freedom.

In light of this, libertarians take a firm stand against positive freedom arguments. However, modern social democracies are acutely conscious of the contradiction between negative and positive freedom. Consequently, social policies aiming at fostering the development of human capacities strive not to limit individual preferences with preconceptions of the good life.

Berlin's division has yet been criticized by the republican conception of liberty as non-domination, whose origins can be found in Rome and later in the commonwealthman tradition, with books such as *Cato's Letters* by Trenchard and Gordon[26] or Madison's essays in the *Federalist Papers*. This ideal centers around the threat of having to live at the mercy of another, since it maintains that liberty involves **emancipation** from any **subordination** under **domination**. That is, it is important to determine when a party 'A' is actually dominating party 'B.' According to Philipp Pettit, the answer is that 'A' is dominating 'B' if – and only if – the former practices interference at will and with impunity, thus posing an arbitrary imposition on the latter's life.[27]

Republican liberty as non-domination has two main features. First, liberty is the opposite of slavery, and even if the master were to be benign, 'living at the mercy of another' is considered a great evil to avoid. Second, if the interference is not arbitrary, but controlled by the interests and

---

[26] Trenchard J., Gordon T. (1971), *Cato's Letters*, Da Capo, New York.

[27] Pettit P. (1997), *Republicanism: A Theory of Freedom and Government*, Clarendon Press, Oxford.

opinions of those affected, it is not a form of domination. This view cannot be represented by Berlin's dichotomy. On the one hand, the fact that I am free from the mastery of another individual has no direct connection with the achievement of my self-mastery. On the other hand, republicanism focuses on a different X from which we should be free than the one chosen by negative liberty scholars, since the latter think that X should be "interference," whereas the former maintain that it ought to be "mastery."[28]

For this reason, there are two main differences between non-domination and non-interference. First, if one individual is subjected to a master, even though she does whatever she likes, thus enjoying non-interference, she is still a slave, since it is the opportunity to interfere at will that gives the dominating power to the master, despite whether or not the master will eventually use it. The problem of non-interference is even though the master may let the slave decide freely under some conditions, the slave will never be free. Conversely, non-domination grants greater security to personal freedom, since the master cannot interfere with the individual in any case.[29]

Second, interference may occur without people being rendered thereby unfree, since no domination exists if one interferes with my liberty but does so according to my will. Conversely, non-interference entails that every interference limits people's set of choices of some degree, and as such it constrains their freedom. Some interferences in people's lives are thus acceptable, especially if a third party interferes in a relationship where A dominates B to defend and free the latter. This aspect is central in relation to the rule of law, since it entails that a proper law is a non-mastering interferer if it does not compromise the people's liberty. On the contrary, in a non-interference framework, the fact that each law is an interference creates a difficult puzzle for the state, since its actions are seen as an inevitable constraint on an individual's set of choices.

---

[28] Pettit 1997; 52-61.
[29] Pettit P. (2012), *On the People's Terms: A Republican Theory and Model of Democracy*, Cambridge University Press, Cambridge.

Political Ideologies

Ideology is typically employed in a pejorative way in everyday language. To imply that a particular conduct or notion is ideological is to imply that it is the result of a biased, radical, or dogmatic attitude, rather than a result of careful examination. However, political ideologies are only partially coherent and comprehensive in terms of political ideas, theories, and actions. In political theory, concepts are not spontaneously created. Each problem or claim has a rich history and numerous sources from which it draws. In this regard, in order to evaluate and give significance to political theories and even actions, it is vital to comprehend the paradigm to which these concepts and behaviors are tied.

Thus, political ideologies are intellectual traditions that provide empirical and normative ideas and claims on human nature, historical evolution, and political-social systems that are only partially coherent. It is assumed that the intellectuals, who are presumed to be part of a ideological tradition, approach humanity, society, politics, and economics with at least some fundamentally shared assumptions and methods. In this regard, it is feasible to connect the concepts of philosophers to particular political beliefs.

This part will provide responses to the following questions: Who are the most influential thinkers within an ideological tradition? What are the essential principles and ideas of a particular ideology? What are the several schools of thought that arose from the same ideology at different points in history? What fundamental characteristics unite or distinguish these schools of thought? What influence have ideologies had on political systems in the past, and what are their projected future implications? What are the effects of ideological movements in multiple countries and what kind of diversity may be found in these ideas?

Through the transition from feudalism to capitalism in the modern age, three primary ideological traditions have emerged: liberalism, conservatism, and socialism. Nevertheless, we can also add minor ideologies such as anarchism, nationalism, fascism, feminism, and green ideology. Although the divide between major and minor ideologies is somewhat arbitrary, it gives a clear framework for analyzing the inter-relationships and conflicts between various ideologies. Even if minor ideologies have their own conceptual vocabulary and political purposes, they are tied to large ideologies in a certain manner. Nationalism, for example, can be classified based on major ideologies, such as liberal nationalism, conservative nationalism, and anti-colonial nationalism. Nationalisms with diverse traits do not mean that nationalism is not an ideology on its own, but it would be impossible to make sense of these distinct varieties of nationalism without a strong reference to major ideologies. Due to space constraints, only the major ideologies will be discussed in this chapter.

Liberalism

Liberalism is distinguished from other ideologies by its acceptance of individual freedom as a fundamental value and its argument that the government should be limited by the constitution to defend individual freedom. The primary tenet of this ideology is the concept of limited government. Philosophers like Jeremy Bentham, Immanuel Kant, Charles-Louis de Secondat Montesquieu, Alexis Tocqueville, Adam Smith, John Locke, and John Stuart Mill are a few people who made significant contributions to the growth of liberal thought beginning in the seventeenth century. Philosophers like Friedrich August von Hayek, Robert Nozick, and Ludwig von Misses were a few of the names that fueled liberal philosophy in the 20th century.

Types of Liberalism

There are three major liberal currents: classical liberalism, modern liberalism, and libertarianism. The fundamental policy distinctions between the various liberal currents relate to how the government governs relationships between the individual and society.

Classical Liberalism

The primary framework of liberalism is **classical liberalism**, which is the first of these. The values of traditional liberalism, which came into existence in the seventeenth century, include fundamental human rights, limited government, the rule of law, and free markets. John Locke and Adam Smith are two influential founders of classical liberalism. Smith created the concept of economic liberalism while Locke created political liberalism. The primary concern of classical liberals in the 17th and 18th centuries was on defining the constitutional monarchy and the institutions of the market economy that were beginning to form in England and refining these developments. The main issues that unite the classical liberals of this era are that political power should derive its legitimacy from the consent of the people, that the violation of the fundamental rights and freedoms of individuals by the state is immoral, and that free markets are an important guarantor of wealth and freedom. On the other hand, the classical liberals of the 19th century were focused on the social, political, and economic challenges generated by the economic inequities that were a natural consequence of representative democracy, fast social transformation, and widespread market economy. On the other side, liberals of the 20th century fought against the "threat" posed by communist regimes produced by socialist revolutions on constitutional democracy and the market economy. During this time, when economic problems and economic systems dominated the discourse, liberal economists' influence in liberal thought rose to the forefront.

On a methodological level, it is possible to divide classical liberalism into two major categories: natural law theorists and utilitarians. Locke is the most influential advocate of the natural law tradition. Locke, a social contract theorist, argues that natural rights are inherent. This implies that human rights existed prior to the establishment of both society and the state. If individuals possess human rights before society and the state, neither social practices nor state-established norms can violate these rights. From this perspective, Locke maintained that the political sovereign cannot exist without the consent of the individuals who comprise the political community and that once the government has emerged, the political authority is once again accountable for preserving the rights of these individuals. As is evident, Locke's political theory is predicated on moral assumptions. One could claim that the United States Constitution was drafted in accordance with Lockean ideals.

In contrast, utilitarianism evaluates rules and behaviors based on their outcomes. In this view, utilitarianism can be divided into two categories: classical utilitarianism and rule utilitarianism. Bentham created the classical utilitarian theory. Bentham argues that empirically unprovable normative assumptions, such as natural law theory, are superstitious and that humans should be viewed as utilitarian animals that seek pleasure and avoid pain. Bentham maintains that the policy with the greatest good for the greatest number of people is always the correct one, regardless of the nature of the pleasure or pain involved. The utilitarianism of Bentham contributed to political equality by promoting the principle of one person, one vote. Bentham was unable to provide a clear solution for preventing the tyranny of the majority, or the majority's seizure of the rights of minorities. After Bentham, who did not distinguish between pleasures and pains qualitatively, Mill asserted that there are qualitative distinctions between 'utilities'. Mill highlighted these distinctions in the following aphorism:

> It is better to be a human being dissatisfied than a pig satisfied; better to be Socrates dissatisfied than a fool satisfied. And if the fool, or the pig, is of a different opinion, it is only because they only know their own side of the question.

Rule utilitarianism, on the other hand, examines whether laws and institutions have produced positive results throughout history for the common good, as opposed to accumulating utilities. By reviewing the historical growth process of British political history, Hume argues that the laws and institutions that made England superior to other nations arose as a result of the maintenance of excellent institutions rather than the outcome of pure utility calculation. Hayek is the most influential advocate of rule utilitarianism in the 20th century.

Rule utilitarianism is also used to justify the unequal results of free markets. Production and consumption relations in the market based on private property and voluntary exchange create material inequality in terms of their results. Justice in the market economy and liberal political system, in general, is based on equality before law. Application of general, abstract and equal legal rules to individuals without discrimination constitutes the basis of the classical liberal idea of justice. The formal features of the law are to ensure that the rules do not serve a specific purpose or group.

However, the equal application of the rules does not mean that the results of social and economic transactions will be egalitarian. On the contrary, since equality before law opens a wide area of freedom to individuals, it causes individuals to gain unequal income and even social status. Thus, the market economy does not serve predetermined collective ends. Rather, individuals conduct market transactions for their own purposes, and each individual's pursuit of maximizing his own interests within the rules is considered justified. In this respect, it is uncertain in which direction the relations of production and consumption will develop in a market economy and cannot be directed towards collective goals in principle.

Governments usually intervene in the market economy with monetary and fiscal policies, and labor regulations. These interventions ultimately serve collective purposes. However, social justice policies that try to provide material equality will disrupt the structure and functioning of the market. Comprehensive interventions in the market economy will also deteriorate the wealth creation expected from the free markets and the level of individual freedom will decrease. The increase in economic planning means the decrease in individual planning, and the expansion of the public economy means the shrinkage of the private economy.

Classical liberals establish a causal relationship between individual freedom, the rule of law, and free market economy. Therefore, they argue that the rule of law and freedom cannot be institutionalized in countries where there is no robust market economy. For example, in communist planned economies, there are no general, abstract, egalitarian rules, and economic production and consumption are governed entirely by a chain of command. In this respect, communist countries do not have a rule of law in the Western sense. Therefore, classical liberals perceive comprehensive market interventions or destruction of the free markets primarily as a threat to individual freedom and argue that extensive direct interventions in the market economy will also destroy the rule of law. A classic example of such an argument can be studied in Hayek's Road to Serfdom.

Modern Liberalism

The notion of **social liberalism/modern liberalism**, which has existed since the middle of the nineteenth century, is the second movement to emerge within liberalism. In contrast to classical liberalism, this perspective places obligations on the state in some particular areas and promotes democratic participation, social and economic rights, and the notion of equality. Prominent philosophers in this school of thought include Thomas H. Green, John Stuart Mill, and John Rawls. Modern liberal philosophers, on the one hand, maintain the political values and civil rights championed by classical liberalism, while on the other, they argue that the unrestricted market economy treats disadvantaged individuals in society unfairly and hinders their potential personal growth. Modern liberals assign the state an active role in regulating economic and social connections to promote social justice and preserve social equality. Social policies such as unemployment benefits, union rights, price controls, and social health care aid are among the new responsibilities imposed on the state by modern liberals.

As mentioned above, classical liberals view the state as an umpire who enforces the rules uniformly to all members of society. In contrast, modern liberals view the state as the protector of its citizens. It is considered that disadvantaged individuals cannot change their social and economic conditions and do not always know what is best for them when left alone. For this reason, the state is granted broad authority over social and economic matters, and efforts are made to achieve the social goals set by politicians.

In addition to mistrust in the market economy and faith in the state, modern liberals view the unequal power relations established by private property as unfair. Consequently, material inequalities should be eliminated to some extent so that individuals can successfully exercise their civil and political rights and achieve self-fulfillment. Later papers by Mill are known to provide such defenses. However, A Theory of Justice by John Rawls, released in 1971, remains the primary source of liberal perspectives on social justice today.

According to Rawls, social and economic inequality can be justified if it benefits society's most disadvantaged members the most. Therefore, even while Rawls acknowledges that there are justified inequalities, he strictly conditions these inequalities and ascribes a social purpose to them. The demand for justice has collective ends that are independent of market processes, according to modern liberals who support social justice. For instance, market forces alone should not determine what happens to disadvantaged groups who lack marketable skills or who struggle in the markets. Governments must support these collective ends as a necessity of social justice by redistributing income, values, and status to ensure that societies have social goals that go beyond those that emerge from the markets. Insufficient service of private education, for instance, is one of the reasons why public education is compulsory. In this regard, people who did not have a good education because of unfavorable environmental circumstances cannot be held accountable for the negative social and economic circumstances they found themselves in. Therefore, modern liberals argue that others in society have a moral obligation to assist those who are disadvantaged in society owing to factors beyond their control.

Libertarianism

The **libertarianism** that emerged in the 20th century is the third concept to emerge within liberalism. The state is regarded as a night watchman in this view, which was established by philosophers like Robert Nozick and Ayn Rand, and it calls for the government excludes from all spheres of social, economic, and political life. The libertarian concept holds that it is vital to leave the provision of all services, including those related to infrastructure, education, health, and social security, to the **free markets** at large, except for those related to security and justice.

Libertarianism is a political theory that originated in the United States, particularly during the second half of the 20th century. Libertarians, who think that individual liberty and the right to property are necessary conditions for a good society, require that all human relationships be based on consent. According to **the principle of non-aggression**, the only legitimate use of force is self-defense. Libertarianism is quite similar to Lockean classical liberalism; however, libertarians defend social and economic problems from the standpoint of property-based individual freedom in a more comprehensive manner than Locke did. Libertarianism is a political ideology created in opposition to the welfare state's nanny state conception, i.e., the conception of politics that claims guardianship over individuals.

In this context, individuals cannot be coerced to support social causes such as social justice or the greater good. Libertarians argue that the government's taxation of its citizens in the name of programs such as welfare expenditures, economic efficiency, or cultural development represents an unfair income transfer. For instance, libertarians contend that the government should not seek to advance the arts. They believe that art enthusiasts should cover their own expenses with their own funds. They think that no one can be obliged to accommodate another's artistic preferences. Similarly, it is ethical for individuals to voluntarily assist others. When the government or others compel individuals to provide social assistance, libertarians argue, individuals are compelled to sacrifice themselves for the benefit of others. For libertarians, this is equivalent to slavery or serfdom.

Conservatism

Although its origins can be traced back to antiquity, conservatism as a political ideology evolved throughout the modern era. It is possible to identify conservatism as an attitude or attitude among numerous philosophers and eras. In addition to ideologies such as liberalism and socialism, however, conservatism as a distinct political ideology was molded by criticisms of Enlightenment philosophy on the philosophical level and the French Revolution on the social and political level. In this framework, conservatism, which is a contemporary political philosophy, has had various thought traditions, significant political movements/parties, and a substantial social base till the present day.

Although the concept's intellectual roots were established in the 18th century, it was not used as a distinct political position or ideology until the first part of the 19th century. Notable conservative philosophers include Edmund Burke, Joseph Maistre, Adam Müller, Robert Nisbet, Hanry Sidwick, Michael Oakeshott, and Roger Verman Scruton. It should not be assumed, however, that the concept has the same meaning everywhere. Temporally and geographically distinct articulations of conservatism have occurred. In contrast to the liberal content of Anglo-American conservatism, the authoritarian content of Continental European conservatism has increased. In the 20th century, conservatism was divided between paternalism, which favored reformist and interventionist programs, and liberalism, which somehow adopted free market principles. Discussions on the position of conservative political philosophy on the scale of authoritarianism-liberalism and totalitarianism-pluralism, as well as the various intellectual currents that evolved in this context, continue to exist today.

Types of Conservatism

There is a significant difference between authoritarian European Conservatism and liberal Anglo-American Conservatism. Moreover, paternalist conservatism, which advocates and implements interventionist measures, contrasts with the pro-free market neo-conservatism that emerged in the 1980s.

Continental Conservatism and Authoritarian Conservatism

Continental European conservatives reject both the Enlightenment and the French Revolution, along with all of their social and political ramifications, out of deep-seated hate for both. It is a counterrevolutionary and reactionary political ideology that advocates the rule of the traditional elite and yearns for the Middle Ages. In contrast to other conservative ideologies that value authority, hierarchy, and order, they promoted authoritarianism and autocratic governments. Defending authoritarianism is distinct from highlighting the importance of authority. This political tradition, often known as **authoritarian conservatism** in this regard, demonstrates little support for liberal democratic ideas. So much so that it justifies the obligation of loyalty even to a terrible ruler, despite individual liberty, rights, participation, and so on.

Authoritarian conservatives continued to promote hierarchical and autocratic systems throughout the 19th century, and conservative elites in Germany and Italy supported movements and organizations that opened the way for Mussolini and Hitler throughout the first half of the 20th century. Authoritarian conservatives, who rejected the limitation of political power through constitutions and parliamentary institutions, also supported power patterns such as Bonapartism and Peronism, which combined authoritarianism with a commitment to economic and social welfare to create a plebiscite dictatorship. These regimes combined populism with an authoritarian emphasis on obedience, discipline, and national unity to preach a sort of conservative nationalism. At this time, it is essential to consider the gap between authoritarian conservatism and fascism. Although they are distinct philosophies, when authoritarian conservatism is taken to its extreme, fascism is nourished. The existence of a conceptual framework is possible.

In contrast to the Anglo-American tradition, thinkers, and arguments within the German conservative thought point to conservatism with a higher dose of authoritarianism.

Liberal Conservatism and Anglo-American Conservatism

Although it shares some conceptual underpinnings with authoritarian conservatism, Anglo-American conservatism has significant ties to liberal ideas. This tradition, which was inspired by anti-rationalist philosophers such as Adam Smith, David Hume, and Adam Ferguson, is empiricist, evolutionist, and liberal. Anti-rationalism is the belief that society cannot be ruled and understood by abstract rules based on pure reason. Individuals' behaviors are governed by their emotions, ambitions, and instincts; in the context of social connections, the reason is secondary to these passions. Edmund Burke, who is considered to be the creator of liberalism, was a Whig, and Adam Smith shared his ideas on ethics and economics to a great extent. This 'liberal' character will become apparent when this fact is explored. As a liberal conservative, Burke criticizes the Enlightenment's fundamental rationalism but accepts John Locke's empiricist epistemology. In contrast, abstract rationalism asserts that society may be recreated from scratch using just abstract rational principles. In this regard, liberal conservatism opposes the French Revolution fiercely, while supporting the British and American revolutions. It advocates 'moderate', 'balanced,' and parliamentary government.

There is no contradiction between traditional social order advocacy and market economy advocacy under the liberal conservative framework. As Burke views market laws as natural laws, he rejects all forms of economic intervention. Burke opposes authoritarian conservatism with his advocacy of limited government. But Burke attributes limited government to the political and social traditions of Britain. In this view, he does not consider the limited government to be an application of abstract liberal principles Liberal conservatives do not adopt particular liberal concepts and institutions as a unified whole and pragmatically incorporate them into their ideology.

Paternalist Conservatism and Neo-Conservatism

Paternalist conservatism, which advocates interventionist policies, can be observed in the policies of Benjamin Disraeli in England, the welfare statist policies of Lord Randolph Churchill, and the practices known as "moderate middle way" or "mixed system" after World War II. **Interventionism** refers to the active involvement of public institutions in addressing social problems caused by economic inequality. The term one-nation conservatism is also used to refer to this concept. Beginning in the period of Disraeli, conservatives projected that increasing industrialization, urbanization, and inequality would divide England into two distinct nations, the "rich" and the "poor" and promoted reformist/interventionist measures to combat this threat.

In this context, conservative governments expanded the voting rights of the lower classes, improved working and housing conditions, and enacted social reforms designed to shield individuals from the detrimental effects of the market economy. The objective of these paternalist interventionist policies is not to expand positive freedom, eliminate hierarchy, or establish social equality; rather, it is to prevent changes that could undermine hierarchy and organic social structure by means of state intervention. **Paternalism** refers to the governmental treatment of individuals in a manner comparable to a father's exercise of control inside the family. Just as a father makes judgments for his children based on his experience, knowledge, and authority, so too does the government know and apply what is beneficial for individuals. Conservative paternalism is primarily motivated by concern about the radicalization of the lower classes. During the post-World War II period, Christian democratic parties in a number of European countries embraced similar interventionist tactics. During this period, Christian democratic parties, which had begun to abandon their authoritarian views, advocated for political democracy, social reforms, and constitutional government, and sought to implement a social market economy and Keynesian welfare policies in opposition to the free market economy.

Neo-conservatism, which reconciles with the market-centered arguments of neo-liberalism and rejects the interventionist policies of paternalist conservatism, rose to popularity during the 1980s as part of the
New Right program that formed in response to the crisis of the Western
welfare state. During this time period, the neo-conservative notions of
authority, tradition, national identity, and law and order, which were
combined with the neo-liberal notions of market economy, economic
efficiency, and individualism, advocated for market deregulation and
political authority. Neoconservatism, which condemns welfare state
policies by incorporating them with socialism, advocates for the restoration of law, order, and discipline that have been eroded by the revival
of traditional values and moral principles. In this context, this entails
strengthening the family, enhancing penalties, and reinforcing national
identity. Within this context, it should be highlighted that especially
American neo-conservatism supports the interventionist foreign policies
and 'order of the world' of the United States.

Socialism

In chronological order, socialism is third among the major political ideologies. Socialism prioritizes collective action, shared property, and social
equality. As a modern ideology, its primary objective is to expose the
negative aspects of capitalism and propose alternatives to it. It views capitalism as exploitation and seeks the ways to abolish this exploitation or,
if this is not possible, to at least mitigate its effects. It is precisely these
formulations that give rise to various socialist concepts. At one extreme
of the spectrum of socialists are radical revolutionary socialists who seek
to demolish the market economy, eliminate private property, and replace
the capitalist system with a communist regime. On the other hand, there
are moderate socialists who, despite their critique of the market economy, do not demonstrate a revolutionary approach, accept liberal values
occasionally, but suggest democratic formulas to establish equal opportunity for everyone to realize liberal objectives.

Socialism should be viewed as a spectrum that includes these two extremes. The welfare state policies in countries where moderate socialists were powerful show that this idea found a serious and practical application. However, instances where the most radical socialists gained power include the Soviet Union, China, Eastern Europe, Cuba, Vietnam, and North Korea. In the majority of the countries listed, socialism as an economic order has vanished or suffered a significant setback. Similarly, the social welfare policies shaped under the impact of socialism are the subject of severe criticism and heated debate. Despite these negative developments and the fading of socialism's power as an economic option, it remains the most significant topic of political and cultural criticism. For this reason, people/parties that uphold the socialist tradition and/or accept socialist ideas remain among the most formidable alternatives to power in a number of nations, particularly democratic nations.

Types of Socialism

Despite the fact that Marxism has mostly dominated the socialist tradition, I will discuss the pre-Marxist socialists briefly here. In addition, I will provide a quick analysis of democratic socialism and social democracy outside of Marxism.

Utopian Socialism

Since the commencement of the Industrial Revolution and the growth of the factory system, some philosophers have attacked the capitalist system for being inefficient, wasteful, irrational, or unfair. Beginning in the 1800s, these complaints became the distinguishing characteristics of a particular political attitude. In particular, people such as Comte Henri de Saint-Simon and Charles Fourier in France and Robert Owen in England became the forerunners of pre-Marxist socialist theory and the leaders of an anti-capitalist political movement with followers who committed to a particular program of action. Their works were widely read, their speeches attracted big audiences, and the concept of social-ism spread to distant nations such as America. Within the context of the history of socialism, this process correlates with the first phase between the Napoleonic Wars and the 1848 upheavals. Not content with merely criticizing the current state of society, the people cited go on to advance their own ideas and plans for how society ought to be. In accordance with these ideas, each of the philosophers will provide a detailed vision of the perfect society of the future, revitalizing their own image.

This period in socialism's history is known as utopian socialism. This naming was attained by Karl Marx and the Marxist tradition in the years that followed. The justification for such naming is the Marxist tradition's evaluation of the ideas of the named individuals. Therefore, 'utopian socialists' hope for a general social transformation in which individual-ism, competition, and the dominance of private property are abolished, without recognizing the necessity of class struggle and without valuing the revolutionary role of the proletariat in the socialist transformation. In addition, the fact that earlier socialist movements were referred to as utopia and viewed as consisting of benevolence is tied to Marx and his followers' insistence that their socialism is 'scientific'. Because Marx's point is that he found the laws of social transformation, unlike the social-ist tradition that came before him.

The abolition of capitalism is the most essential element shared by the utopias proposed by Simon, Fourier, and Owen. Each describes the capitalist system as wasteful, unjust, and unplanned. They seek a planned society that is efficient and egalitarian. As with capitalism, this society will eliminate the minority of non-workers who own the means of pro-duction and live in comfort and luxury. The ownership of the means of production was viewed as the method to achieving this objective, and it was believed that the majority of working people would live a happy life if they owned the means of production. From a methodologi-cal standpoint, St. Simon, Fourier, and Owen are attempting to build a brand-new science of human nature. Here, significant emphasis has been focused on the moral/ideological domain as the decisive foundation for all other elements of human behavior; an effort has been made to turn this discipline into a legitimate science that will answer the problem of societal cohesiveness. In accordance with these efforts, the existing moral, religious, and political ideology is regarded as the greatest barrier to the adoption of the newly revealed harmony rules.

Another defining characteristic of the anti-capitalist reaction exemplified by Simon, Fourier, and Owen is that it is an 'emotional' reaction to the poor working and living conditions brought about by the industrial revolution. This emotional aspect diminished the degree of realism and application of their proposed remedies. Utopian socialists know where they want to go, but their ideas on how to get there are unclear. Since these names lack a sufficient understanding of the historical dimension of social development, they believe that social disorders can be eliminated quickly by adopting and implementing their imagined ideal orders. When appealing to people's consciences and minds, they expect the ruling classes and administrators to accept new (socialist) social organizations. This led to the view that 'revolutionary' goals might be reached through 'evolutionary' means as a result of the belief that economic problems could be solved with economic remedies without a major change in the political structure. The evolutionist perspective observed here involves the notion that it will be sufficient to attract the powerful or wealthy by convincing them of the correctness and beauty of the new system, leaving the remainder to their common sense. However, the interests of the parties on the opposing side of this expectation necessitate the continuation of the current order, rendering the proposed ideas unrealistic.

Marxism

In the second half of the 19th century, Karl Marx's theories began to significantly influence socialist ideology and movements. While Marx's critical analysis of capitalist society laid the theoretical foundations for the political movement that bears his name, it has been influential in a wide range of fields, from justice to political economy, humanism to the relationship between the individual and society, and methodology to philosophy.

Marx's method might be referred to as historical materialism or dialectical materialism. The simplest definition of dialectics is the emergence of synthesis from the interaction between thesis and anti-thesis. The synthesis combines the best features of the thesis and the antithesis that formed it. Until a synthesis is reached, the reconciliation process between thesis and antithesis will be repeated numerous times throughout the vast expanse of history. Regarding this, materialism is the belief that all things are either composed only of matter or are ultimately dependent on matter for their existence and nature. It is possible for a materialistic philosophy to grant spirit a secondary position, yet the vast majority of materialism denies the existence of spirit or anything non-physical.

Marx believed that the **mode of production** is the only factor that determines everything about society. The material mode of production comprises of **production forces** and **production relations**, which Marx refers to as the **base**. The forces of production consist of **means of production** and **labor power**. Production relations define social formations and classes. Marx asserts that all social structures developed throughout history have been molded by **class struggle**. **Class**, on the other hand, refers to the economic position of a certain group in the mode of production. If you own the means of production, you are a member of the exploitative class, whereas if you are paid for your labor, you are a member of the exploited class. This explanation analysis, for instance, the class relationship between lords and serfs in feudal society and between bourgeois and proletariat in capitalist society.

However, history is not stationary and is inevitably in progress. This materialist historical progress is shaped by class conflict. The conflict between exploiting and exploited classes results in a social revolution that alters the social, political, and economic order. The exploiting class is the thesis, the exploited class is the antithesis, and the newly emerging social structure is the synthesis within this account. The emergence of the bourgeois class during feudalism and the conflict between aristocrats and the bourgeois gave rise to capitalism, a new social structure. Similarly, the conflict between capitalists and proletariat within the capitalist system will result in a revolution and pave the way for the formation of socialism. Additionally, the socialist system will be the end of history. Because, once the proletariat has eliminated the capitalists, a classless society will be built, and the conflict between thesis and antithesis will be resolved. Because workers would also control the means of production under socialism, exploitation, and class struggle, and ultimately historical progress will cease to exist.

The idea of the superstructure is one of the most massive implications of historical materialism. According to the superstructure theory, the base determines all social institutions and traits, including the legal and political system, morality, religion, social practices, literature, art, and culture. The superstructure's role is to ensure the ongoing reproduction of this exploitative order because the main purpose of the base is to promote class exploitation. Therefore, Marx despises and opposes all bourgeois ideals, including democracy, human rights, and the rule of law. The same reasoning underlies Marxists' vilification of artistic and literary works that do not advance the cause of the working class. The liberal social, cultural, and political system known as the superstructure was created in the capitalist society to conceal the bourgeoisie's class interests from the working class. By creating the illusion that the capitalist order is just, the superstructure primarily aims to prevent the proletariat from developing **class consciousness**, which is synonymous with revolutionary awareness.

Marx and the Marxists did not contribute to the political ideas that developed under these systems because they saw the superstructure, or social and political system, as the bourgeoisie's **ideological apparatus**. Marx, for instance, lacks a personal philosophy of justice. The primary cause of this is that Marx saw politics to be a transient, historical process. Although he believes that exploited workers are not treated fairly in capitalist production relations, he did not provide a universal notion of justice. The universal cannot be historical, hence this cannot be the case. In this setting, rather than asserting theories on its own, Marxist political terminology primarily presents itself as a critique of capitalism. Marx's theory of the state is intimately tied to this intriguing Marxist perspective. The state, a superstructure apparatus, ensures the perpetuation of class exploitation as its primary function. However, when the extractive institutions vanish in the socialist society, the state will whittle away. Marxists have been willing to criticize modern theories, which they allege to be capitalist, rather than making original contributions to political theories, on the grounds that the state will eventually disappear.

A significant dispute has emerged over this shortcoming in Marxist theory, particularly in light of the totalitarian nature of the political structures erected by communist governments. Socialist writers employed the ideas of real socialism, or, to put it another way, actually existing socialism, to explain the distinctions between the Marxist ideal of socialism and communist regimes before the fall of the Soviet Union. The elimination of private property and the market economy prompted communist regimes to develop a comprehensive and extensive bureaucratic organizational system. This bureaucratic administration's failure to deliver the prosperity, equality, and freedom promised by Marx has given rise to a prolonged argument between communist and anti-communist writers.

The problem of **alienation** is another topic that weighs heavily on Marx's thoughts in relation to capitalist economic relations. Marx argues that all social classes in capitalist society experience political and social alienation that is founded on economic alienation. Labor is the source of alienation. People must work and produce in order to survive, and because this activity generates **surplus value**, the connection between man and nature is transformed into a dialectical one where the two parties interact and influence one another. In this instance, capitalism also creates a dichotomy between individuals and the outcomes of their effort. Because manufacturing activities are no longer a process of liberation through which people realize themselves, and people are no longer the masters of their products. People are subject to outside factors that prevent them from realizing their own freedom and creativity, and these forces also have control over their work. Thus, in terms of alienation, the outcome of capitalism for the proletariat is that it is alienated from the products it produces, the actual production process, all of its potentials as a human being, and other workers who are its own friends.

Democratic Socialism and Social Democracy

Democratic socialism or revisionist socialism is a nineteenth-century ideology that asserts socialist ideals may be accomplished through democratic politics without the need for revolutionary violence. Eduard Bernstein and Karl Kautsky are prominent democratic socialist theorists. These philosophers, who first sought to achieve socialism in a revolutionary manner similar to that of Karl Marx, came to believe that socialism could be achieved without revolution, particularly when the working class gained political rights through workers' parties. Democratic socialism has multiple origins. One of these sources is the nineteenth-century European social justice policies that sought to promote material equality through the transfer of wealth. The first instance of democratic socialism can be shown as German social welfare state. German welfare state intended to construct an order based on equality by distributing wealth to vast populations at the end of the 19th century. In England, Fabianism, another source of democratic socialism, evolved. Fabianism, an intellectual rather than political movement, sought to gradually replace the capitalist economy with a system of public production. Fabianism, which opposed the revolution, maintained that socialism could be established in England by democratic means, with the education of elites and the general public about socialism, on the grounds that socialism is a scientific fact.

Rapidly developing in the first half of the 20th century, workers' parties played a crucial role in the transition of democratic socialism into a powerful popular movement. After World War II, however, the workers' parties, following the example of the German Social

Democratic Party, abandoned the goal of abolishing private property entirely. Instead, they adopted a welfare state model characterized by dominant public production and social democratic policies aimed at achieving material equality.

In this respect, democratic socialism and social democracy can be distinguished. The legal and political position of private property is not up for debate in contemporary Western social democracies, which are founded on competitive markets. Instead of supporting egalitarian principles through public production, welfare governments redistribute tax-funded budgets in accordance with social objectives. Social democracy cannot be founded on the anti-property and anti-market ideals of democratic socialism in contemporary democracies.

There are also claims that democratic socialism and democratic decision-making processes have significant flaws. It is not always possible for socialism to be compatible with its values, goals and democratic decision-making processes. In a democracy, political decisions are made by simple majority vote. In this regard, it is always feasible for the majority to deviate from socialist principles. In response to this argument, democratic socialists claim that the purpose of democracy is to ensure equality of power in society and that equality of power cannot be achieved without material equality. In this regard, they contend that only socialist principles can form a genuine democracy.

Regarding the ideology of social justice, democratic socialism and social democracy have another intricate link. Modern liberal philosophers significantly formulated the principles of social justice that provided the welfare state with political justification. Although contemporary liberal authors have advocated several extensive collectivist systems, they have framed their theoretical arguments and policy proposals inside a liberal political framework. Social democracy owes more to modern liberals than democratic socialists, at least in terms of the theory of social justice. In this context, the concept of the third way is an intriguing example of how workers' parties' conceptions of social democracy have evolved. This third way is shown as an alternative to "top-down" state intervention and free-market capitalism. It is widely associated with the government of Tony Blair and "new" Labor in the UK, but it was also influenced by the Administration of Bill Clinton in the USA.

During the early years following 1945, concepts and programs associated with social democracy had the greatest possible impact. They were promoted by socialist parties, as well as occasionally liberal and conservative ones, and the ultimate result was the expansion of economic and social intervention in the majority of Western governments. As a result of this, social democracy is frequently praised for having successfully tamed the unpredictability of capitalism while also bringing about more economic growth and greater social cohesion. However, the progress of social democracy took place concurrently with the "long boom" of the post-war period. When the "long boom" ended during the recessions that occurred in the 1970s and 1980s, the fundamental contradiction that exists within social democracy (between preserving the market economy and promoting equality) was brought to light. As a consequence, a significant number of people have moved away from the conventional social democratic stances in favor of ideals and policies that are more oriented toward the market economy. On the other hand, in the same way that the shortcomings of the social democratic pro-state position opened up opportunities for the New Right in the 1980s, developing reservations about the pro-market attitude of the New Right may open up new prospects for modernized or new social democracy.

The persistence of the concept of a third way reveals a profound disappointment with free market capitalism and state socialism. Politicians who advocate for **third way** make an effort, in essence, to develop a non-socialist critique of an unfettered free market economy. Concern about the arbitrary and frequently immoral consequences of market competition continues to be a primary criticism leveled against capitalism, despite the fact that the philosophical and ideological premises upon which this critique is based are constantly evolving. From this vantage point, the problem with capitalism is that it poses an ongoing danger to the cohesiveness of society as well as its overall stability.

Third way theorists, on the other hand, are opposed to socialism for two reasons. First, they feel that collectivization and planning are unable to give a workable alternative to the free markets. Second, they believe that socialism is associated with a planned economy. Politics that take a "third way" are criticized heavily, mostly for two reasons. The first argument is that the concept of a third way is nothing more than a populist slogan that has no basis in either political or economic reality. The second argument is that third way ideas are fundamentally inconsistent due to the fact that they are unable to consider alternatives to the capitalist model of economic organization.

CHAPTER 2

Politics and Economic Models

2.1 Politics and economics

Why would the discussion of economic models and politics occur intertwined?

The first answer to why these two fields are connected is that human beings are a social species. That is, each individual defines her own needs and desires in cooperation with others, so we must find a way to socially organize these relations. If we lived in a world where resources are infinite, this would not be necessary, since all citizens could just fulfill any of their desires as they please. However, in our empirical world **scarcity** plays an essential role. This refers to the fact that human and non-human resources are finite and society is thus only capable of producing a limited amount of goods.[30] In short, there are not sufficient resources to produce all the wares that people desire or want to consume. For this reason, societies have to find a way to redistribute the limited amount of goods and wares at their disposal. This is the role of **economics**, which is defined as the process for deciding who gets the material resources and how they get them. Hence, economic goods are those wares that are relatively scarce and need to be allocated according to a certain criterion.

---

[30] Hahnel R. (2003), *ABCs of Political Economy. Modern Primer*, Pluto Press, London.

In democratic systems, the reelection of governments is directly related to economic performance. Although there is no absolute rule, any administration will wish to hold elections during a period of economic expansion and rising income levels. This is because economic growth and stability is one of the most influential elements in shaping voter preferences for political parties. Voters hold governments accountable for economic performance as a result of their direct or indirect influence over the economy. The performance of national economies is frequently determined by political decisions including monetary and fiscal policy and economic regulations. In this regard, political decisions influence economic decisions and economic output.

An economy is the sum of all exchanges, or all ongoing buying and selling, in an area. While all economies today are built around goods, services, and money, they differ radically from one another. Each country's economy can have structural differences according to how wealthy its citizens are, how wealth is distributed among the population, and the technology by which wealth is produced. Structural differences in economies can profoundly change countries' political decision-making processes, voter behavior and expectations, and even political regimes.

In addition, some economic indicators can provide data on the functioning and success of the political system. For example, GDP and per capita income are the most commonly used data to categorize the socio-economic status of countries. The gross domestic product (GDP) is an estimate of the total value of completed products and services produced within the borders of a country over a specific time period, often one year. Popularly, GDP is used to measure the size of an economy. For example, as of 2021, the GDP of the US is $25.2 trillion, that of the UK is $3.2 trillion and that of India is $3.4 trillion. While these ratios are often seen as a by-product of the level of industrialization of countries, they only yield more meaningful political results in terms of GDP per capita. In this respect, the annual per capita income in the US is 69 thousand dollars, in the UK it is 47 thousand dollars and in India it is around 2,400 dollars. Therefore, when measuring the level of development of countries, it is more accurate to examine national income per capita rather than GDP.

Per capita income in developed economies is much higher than in developing countries. For example, while the GDPs of the UK and India are close to each other, the population of India is 1.14 billion people, while the population of the UK is 68 million people. These figures show that economic productivity in India is extremely low compared to the UK. According to the Fraser Institute's annual Economic Freedom of the World report, countries with high per capita income are those with a developed market economy and a robust liberal democracy. So how rich a country's citizens become is clearly directly related to its politics.

In addition to the per capita national income, the GINI coefficient is an important economic indicator that is used when measuring the degree of development of countries. The GINI ratio is an extremely valuable indicator of the prevalence of income inequality in a population. Predictably, countries with more comprehensive social welfare systems have GINI coefficients that are lower than those of other nations. For instance, economic disparity in Northern European nations is significantly smaller than in the United States.

Moreover, there is a direct relationship between the institutional framework in which political decisions are made and the institutional framework in which economic decisions are made. In this respect, we cannot analyze political values in isolation from economic models. For example, individual freedom can only exist in a political regime based on a sound market economy. As the famous monetarist economist Milton Friedman pointed out, individuals who do not have any use rights over economic resources cannot have control over their lives in line with their priorities and goals. This is why classical liberals and libertarians always emphasize the direct relationship between private property and individual liberty. For example, should the market of readers or government bureaucrats decide which books should be published or not? The more discretion governments have over economic resources, the less discretion individuals have over their own lives and plans.

Certainly, it is possible to argue that individual liberty is an exaggerated political goal and that equality should be politically favored. However, it would be a contradiction to place a high value on individual liberty and at the same time advocate the abolition of private property. Similarly, the rule of law is in many ways related to free markets. The decentralized decision-making processes required by the market economy necessitate abstract, general, equal rules of law. Therefore, the rules of law on which a market economy is based grant immunity to individuals and limit the discretionary power of the government. In contrast, a centrally planned economy would be largely governed by orders and directives in line with the social goals set by politicians and bureaucrats, and the immunity rights of citizens would be largely eliminated.

As political values evolve, so do economic models. It is logical, for instance, that the concept of economic and social human rights has come into conflict with free market economies, particularly following World War II. The majority of economic and social rights relate to goods and services that cannot be provided on the market or cannot be produced in adequate quantities. When these commodities and services, which can be defined in a variety of ways and to varying degrees, are deemed justifiable, direct state interference in free markets and private wealth is required. A progressive tax policy, for instance, may only be justified in light of social objectives. In this regard, the scope, breadth, and institutions of the welfare state will dictate directly the structure of the market economy.

The link between political values and economic models can be extended to definitions of political regimes. For example, before the collapse of the Soviet Union, what constituted a "real" democracy was a heated debate among political scientists. During this period, constitutional or liberal democracies were heavily criticized. Socialist writers argued that true democracy could only be established in communist societies, claiming that material inequality, especially in capitalist countries, made democratic rule impossible.

This discussion on democracy is very informative as it clearly demonstrates the relationship between political ideals and economic models.

It is now widely accepted that a democratic government requires regular and competitive elections and at least two political parties. In the Soviet Union, however, it was not possible to have a second political party and it was illegitimate to have alternative politics outside the communist party. The elections that were held were not expected to conform to universal standards in any way. However, it could be argued that only in a classless society would government serve collective purposes and true political equality be possible. By calling Western democracies formal democracies, the formal conditions of liberal democracy were devalued by socialist writers. For this reason, the idea that the Soviet Union, a one-party dictatorship, had built a true democracy could be debated in academic circles for years.

As demonstrated by the preceding illustration, there is a close relationship between our evaluations of economic models and our political ideals. This is a complex process in which the political and economic meanings we give to concepts are linked, as opposed to a one-sided relationship in which one determines the other in an absolute manner. Analyzing this topic is a field of study for both political science and political economy. The link between economic models and political systems contains both descriptive and normative features in this regard.

Before proceeding to analyze the main economic models and related political debates, it is important to define the political economy. The study of the political meanings of economic models often requires the use of political economy methods. The term "political economy" has been around for a long time, and throughout that period it has taken on a wide variety of meanings. Political economy, according to Adam Smith, is the study of how to best direct a country's resources to maximize its ability to create and distribute wealth. Marx was interested in the impact that controls over the means of production had on the course of history. The term "political economy" has been used with competing definitions during the majority of the 20th century. The relationship between economics and politics has been seen as both a field of study and a research strategy at different times. Even the approach to methodology was split in two: the economic approach (also known as public choice) focused on the rationality of individuals, and the sociological approach focused on the larger institutions that shaped that individuals' behavior.

Political economy, in its broadest definition, is the economic study of government and politics. Therefore, rather of being a singular method, it is a set of related methods. This method integrates many of the concerns of political sociologists because institutions are no longer neglected and are often the target of the inquiry. Politics becomes the study of political economics since political behavior and institutions are themselves academic fields. Methodologies previously used only in the field of economics are now integral to political science. In most cases, the individual serves as the unit of analysis.

2. 2. Political Economic Approaches in Historical Perspective

Economic policy was not an essential political problem in the closed autarchic economies of the Middle Ages, which were founded on economic self-sufficiency. Nonetheless, since the move from autocratic economies to modern economies open to international commerce, the means by which nations enhance their national wealth have become a significant economic concern. In contrast to the medieval age, when continual economic expansion was not expected, economic growth is now one of the primary objectives of political powers in the modern era.

2.2.1. Mercantilism

In this regard, mercantilism was the first kind of political economy to arise. During the 15th and 17th centuries, mercantilism effectively connected national wealth to export surpluses. The more a country exports goods and services, the better, but importing goods and services is as undesirable. This economic policy grants governments the authority to directly and broadly intervene in the production and consumption processes. In order to sustain economic growth, governments have devised vast regulations governing what individuals produce, how they produce, and what they consume.

Mercantilism led to economic protectionism. Since goods and services coming from abroad were considered harmful to the national economy, the goods to be imported were strictly listed. Except for these lists and the persons and firms appointed by the government, imports were prohibited. In the national economy, the government granted monopoly powers to various individuals and firms in order to give these producers an advantage in the international market. For example, sectors that had not yet developed in the national economy were called infant economies and these sectors were completely protected from foreign trade. International trade is considered a zero-sum game. This means that international trade is not based on mutual interests, but on a winner-take-all game/ zero-sum game. For this reason, mercantilism is also known as economic nationalism. Because the goal of international trade was determined as national interests.

This perspective has significant flaws. In a world where all nations embrace mercantilist policies, international trade and economic cooperation between nations are severely constrained. When countries perceive each other as economic adversaries, antagonism and sometimes conflict are inevitable. According to the famed French economist Frederic Bastiat, "when goods don't cross boarders, soldiers will." Therefore, mercantilism ultimately led to economic expansionism via wars and invasions. Specifically, mercantilists, who deprived themselves of the opportunity to influence natural resources and international markets through trade, attempted to achieve their economic objectives through colonialist practices.

Especially when the economic history of modern Europe is analyzed, it is clear that the economic warfare created by mercantilism resulted in global catastrophes. Among the economic reasons of World Wars I and II, it is simple to recognize economic nationalism's role in interstate conflicts. After World War II, the common market was the most crucial measure to avoid another war in Europe. Europe's adoption of a free trade strategy to prevent economic nationalism from generating conflicts between large industrialized economies was no accident. In this regard, the European Union is built on a policy of international free trade that was intended to combat the issues posed by economic nationalism.

2.2.2. Adam Smith and Invention of Free Markets and Minimal Government

The publication of Adam Smith's *An Inquiry into the Nature and Causes of the Wealth of Nations* in 1776 was the most significant intellectual cause for the change from mercantilist policies to free trade in Europe. Smith argued that the increase in the division of labor and specialization was the primary cause of the wealth of nations. This claim, which initially appears to be a technical matter, conceals broader economic and political arguments. But first, let's explore what type of efficiency is indicated by the division of labor.

Smith elaborated on the advantages of dividing production processes and assigning them to different people in order to maximize output and efficiency. The notion behind the "division of labor" concept was that if a worker specialized in performing a single activity, he would inevitably increase his speed and precision in carrying it out. Once the thought process was eliminated and the numerous manufacturing actions became second nature, it was possible to increase output. He, for instance, claimed that ten workers could manufacture 48,000 pins each day if each of the 18 specialized duties was assigned to a specific worker. The average production per worker each day is 4,800 pins. But without labor division, a worker would be fortunate to produce even one pin per day.

The productivity gains from the specialized division of labor that Smith observed in just one pin factory are enormous. When we apply this division of labor to an industry, to a national economy and even to international markets, we increase the scale of the division of labor enormously. One could argue that the productivity gains that would result from an increased division of labor at the national and international level are beyond the imagination of 18th century readers. In this respect, contrary to mercantilism, international trade cannot be a zero-sum game. On the contrary, it is argued that a global economy in which production processes are supported by international division of labor and specialization can generate previously unimaginable productivity gains.

To achieve the efficiency envisaged from the international division of labor, governments must abandon their interventionist and regulatory policies on national economies. Who will thereafter oversee the production and consumption processes? Smith contends that the price mechanism will drive production and consumption processes far more effectively than the government. At the junction of the supply of goods and services that producers are able and willing to produce and the demand for goods and services that consumers are able and willing to consume, prices are established. If producers and consumers are allowed to freely exchange on national and international markets, then production and consumption levels are naturally established. Smith used the metaphor of the "invisible hand" to describe the price mechanism in order to demonstrate that the price-setting process does not require government involvement.

Consequently, although Smith appears to be discussing the division of labor, which is a strictly technical production process, this is in fact a profoundly political subject. If the magnitude of the division of labor is the primary predictor of productivity and if price levels can be established without direct government interference, then it is likewise incorrect for political forces to claim political authority through economic nationalism. This is because politicians and bureaucrats are unaware of which commodities and services serve the national interest. Given the dynamic structure of international trade and the fluctuating supply and demand relationships of the global economy, the knowledge on which commodities and services should be produced and which should be imported is in constant flux.

If it is not a meaningful claim that the processes of production and consumption should be directed by governments in the national interest, then by whom and for what purposes should economic processes be directed? Smith simply but forcefully states that the processes of production and consumption should be driven by individuals seeking to maximize their own self-interest. Human beings are by nature utilitarian in economic matters. But in a well-functioning market, economic utilitarianism is not harmful to society as a whole, but rather beneficial. In the market, individuals have to satisfy the needs of others in order to satisfy their own needs. In markets where we depend on each other for the mutual satisfaction of our needs, everyone pursues his or her own self-interest while actually serving the interest of the general public. Smith supports this claim with the following example[31]:

> It is not from the benevolence of the butcher, the brewer, or the baker, that we expect our dinner, but from their regard to their own interest. We address ourselves, not to their humanity but to their self-love, and never talk to them of our own necessities but of their advantages.

If individuals following their economic interests in free markets are the most essential elements in the process of wealth creation, what role do governments play in the economy? Smith suggested that the government should enforce contracts and grant patents and copyrights to encourage inventions and new ideas. In addition, he believed the government should provide public works, such as roads and bridges, that individuals could not provide. Surprisingly, he desired that users of these public works pay proportionately for their use. Smith also maintained that tax rates should not be excessively high and that wages could only be increased through capital accumulation and labor productivity growth. These responsibilities assigned to the government by Smith are today known as minimal government.

Smith also opposed British imperialism by stating that Britain's expenditures and wars to hold on to the American colonies were much

---

[31] Adam Smith, Wealth of Nations, Book 1, Chapter 2.

higher than the revenues it obtained from the colonies. Similarly, he opposed the monopoly powers of the East India Company, which managed Britain's eastern trade, and argued for the institutionalization of free trade and voluntary exchange between countries. He argued that importing what countries produce expensively and exporting what they produce cheaply would promote mutual interests and strengthen peaceful relations of dependence between countries. Imperialism, on the other hand, would fuel war and conflict.

Smith's ideas on international trade inspired the British economist David Ricardo to develop the law of comparative advantages a century later. Although individuals, firms or countries have the potential to produce different goods, in order to benefit from the efficiency of the division of labor, individuals, firms or countries should produce the goods and services that they are most advantageous in producing. Therefore, they should give up the production of other goods and services. Ricardo's theory is essential for comprehending globalization because it gives a solid theoretical foundation for the notion that free trade across nations is advantageous for all parties.

With the industrial revolution in England in the 1830s, the international division of labor and the theory of comparative advantages found wide application for the first time in history and opened the doors to a global economy. **The Industrial Revolution** was a period of scientific and technological advancement in the 18th century that changed predominantly rural, agrarian cultures into industrialized, urban ones, particularly in Europe and North America. Due to the development of new technologies and techniques in textiles, iron production, and other sectors, goods that were once carefully fashioned by hand began to be mass-produced in factories by machines.

Today, the global economy based on the law of comparative advantages has developed beyond the predictions of these philosophers. Supranational corporations, supranational trade organizations and international trade law have played important roles in the functioning of the global economy beyond the dreams of Enlightenment philosophers.

2.2.3. Marxism as a Classical Economic Theory

Smith's explanation reveals that the basic axioms assumed to drive human behavior have far-reaching political implications. Marx, as a critic of capitalism, based his fundamental assumption about individuals on the assertion that human nature is not fixed. Since the economic infrastructure determines the actions of individuals, axiomatic claims centered on individuals are incorrect from the start. Instead, he stresses the systemic elements that influence individual behavior. In this regard, Marx's citation of technology as a structural component is particularly intriguing. Marx asserts that every economic age has its own technology. The industrial revolution would not have been feasible without the steam engine, but capitalism enabled not the singular use of machines, but their systematic application in the factory system. Marx believed that the use of machines by capitalists lowered worker pay, created a new proletariat, and oppressed the existing proletariat.

Marx, on the other hand, admired the wealth generated by the Industrial Revolution and believed that this technological knowledge could be effectively utilized for the benefit of the working class in a socialist economy. Marx holds that there is no correlation between technological productivity and market-based institutions such as private property and contract law. In contrast, whereas under capitalism technology is a weapon of worker exploitation and alienation, it would serve the working class in a socialist society.

Therefore, there is no need for practical knowledge disclosed by market processes other than technological expertise. Since technological knowledge can only be converted into an efficient method of production within the division of labor and specialization that occurs on the market, the use of technology cannot rely just on technical knowledge, according to Smith. It is only relevant in the institutional context in which the technology will be utilized. Marx, however, believed that technological knowledge could be easily transferred from the capitalist system to the communist system in order to assist the working class.

According to Marx, the idea that human needs are subjective is also wrong. For it is not possible to argue that needs are determined through market processes or that the products demanded in the market are necessarily human needs. The goods and services on the market are commodities produced for profit and the link between them and objective human needs has been broken. Add to this the claim that it is the labor of workers that gives the value of goods and services, and the basic presuppositions of a socialist economic system are revealed. Since labor is the main criterion of value, capitalists or market processes and rules have no contribution to the production of value. Therefore, there is no need for capitalists or market processes to produce value.

Marx is therefore not concerned with questions of what, where, when and how to produce. Such problems are only a problem of chaotic market processes, and under socialism, there will be no problem of how to allocate scarce resources among diversified needs. Once capitalism is abolished, production processes based on technical knowledge to meet objective human needs will be established by the collective management of the working class.

As can be shown, the vast contrasts between Smith and Marx have simple origins in human action. During the 19th century, economists abandoned the objective labor theory of Smith and Marx in favor of the subjective theory of value. I shall explore the controversy that the subjective theory of value produced for socialist economic planning in the section on planned economies.

2.2.4. Neoclassical Economics

The classical school of economics assumed that the market value of goods and services was determined by the labor used in their production. This was called the labor theory of value. Marx even accused capitalists of exploitation of workers, since workers produced goods and services with their labor while capitalists had surplus value without using any labor. But if the prices of goods and services in the market have nothing to do with the labor spent on them, does Marx's claim of capitalist exploitation still hold?

Before drawing political conclusions from economic theory, let us start by explaining the theory of diminishing marginal value. An early assumption of neoclassical economics was that consumer utility, not production cost, is the most significant factor in establishing the value of a good or service. Based on the works of William Stanley Jevons, Carl Menger, and Léon Walras, this method was established in the late 19th century. The law of diminishing marginal utility states that the more an item is used or consumed, the less satisfaction is derived from each additional unit utilized or consumed.

Therefore, market prices are determined by the preferences of individuals and businesses and have no direct relationship with labor. Individuals and businesses engaged in market transactions are called rational agents, and their preferences are reasonable under specific conditions. Agents who are rational maximize their utility based on their priorities and market conditions. Traders participate in a competitive bidding process with other traders in order to create transactions that involve the purchase and sale of items. These transaction prices serve as signals to other producers and consumers, encouraging them to realign their resources and activities along lines that will yield greater profits. It is claimed that these market transactions involving rational agents will enable the markets to reach equilibrium.

Neoclassical economics attempted to mathematically explain Smith's economic theory with certain axiomatic presuppositions based on rationality. The set of concepts presented by neoclassical economics, especially after the 1950s, has been used not only to explain economic behavior but also to explain all kinds of social phenomena. For example, in addition to sociological, psychological or cultural explanations of family life, the economic explanation of family life can also be explained with neoclassical economic terminology. It is possible to come across studies that explain the evolutionary development of family structure with economic theory.

However, besides economics, politics is the field where neoclassical economics has been utilized the most. In this framework, the evolution of public choice theory and new institutional economics is crucial to political theory. By eliminating moral justifications from political research, public choice theory attempts to transform politics into a purely positive science. The objectives of politicians and bureaucrats, for instance, are not to serve the public interest and devote themselves to public service, but rather to maximize their personal priorities. In this scenario, the sole objective of politicians is re-election, whilst bureaucrats seek to maximize their budgets. James Buchanan, one of the founding fathers of public choice theory, describes this strategy as "politics without romance." Buchanan has made significant contributions to the field of political science, particularly in exposing the arbitrariness/randomness of democratic decision-making processes.

New institutional economics is mostly concerned with politics. New institutionalism, made famous by Douglass North's work, explores the formation of political institutions by adapting rational choice theory to the concept of institutional equilibrium. Rather than the propagation and adoption of liberal values, North describes the evolution of liberal democracies in Europe as a process of power struggle among political elites finding an equilibrium.

Axiomatic presuppositions about how individuals act directly affect political analysis. The fact that neoclassical economics expresses its theories in a mathematical language has increased its prestige among social sciences and political debates have been increasingly influenced by economic theory. In this context, objections to neoclassical theory have also been directly related to the perspective on politics.

2.2.5. Keynesian Economics and Government Intervention

The most important criticism of neoclassical economics comes from John Maynard Keynes. Keynesianism was the main source of criticism of free markets, especially after the Depression of 1929. According to Keynes, the claim that individuals are rational and that markets always move towards equilibrium is largely false. In reality, individuals act on wild instincts, not rational calculations, and may make many economically harmful decisions in the face of economic uncertainty as a reflex of self-preservation. For example, in a time of economic uncertainty, if consumers save more than the market needs instead of consuming, panic may start in production processes, leading to unnecessary closures of businesses. In this case, a deflationary pressure arising from the abundance of products could disrupt the structure of markets and the economy would inevitably shrink.

Keynes argued unequivocally that markets do not always reach equilibrium on their own and that the products and services generated in markets do not automatically clear. Consequently, what should governments do when irrational panic spreads throughout the markets? Budget equilibrium and free markets are the foundation of conventional fiscal theory. However, when the economy begins to shrink due to uncertainty in the absence of a fundamental cause, it will not be possible for the market to self-correct and reach maximum capacity utilization and full employment. For this reason, Keynes encourages governments to provide money to the public, particularly in times of crisis, through the use of fiscal policy, i.e., by substantially boosting public expenditures. Thus, individuals will contribute to the expansion of production processes by investing cheaply acquired money in the market. In accordance with Keynesianism, monetary growth through fiscal policy will have a multiplier effect on the economy. Monetary growth will boost aggregate demand, and the money flowing in the economy will increase national revenue by a greater amount than the amount spent.

During the Covid 19 pandemic, it is not surprising that governments around the world have prioritized Keynesian fiscal policy. Governments, who covered the income demands of those who were unable to work during the pandemic by printing unbacked money, are now attempting to contain inflation by implementing restrictive monetary policies. If governments are so competent at stabilizing the market, the Smithian concept of minimal government will have little relevance.

Historically, the most important reason for the popularity of Keynesian policies was the Great Depression and the World War II that followed. These two major social crises created a state of great uncertainty and led to a period in which not only governments but also citizens demanded more government intervention in the economy. With the rapid development of welfare states in Europe after World War II, a consensus for social democracy emerged. That is, right and left-wing parties and the majority of the population strongly supported government redistribution of income through social policies.

The concept of market failure explains one of the most significant points of the social democratic consensus. Failure of the market has two distinct meanings. The first is associated with the idea that market agents have no social purpose and maximize their individual utility. Aside from the goals pursued in the market, society may have several necessities that should be supplied not by the invisible hand of the market, but by the visible hand of the government, i.e. by central planning. For example, providing everyone with a sufficient income to live humanely or providing appropriate health care for all. It is argued that such social objectives are too crucial to be left to the uncertain production and consumption processes of the market.

The second is based on a critique of Keynesian arguments for the economic efficiency expected from free markets. Managed/regulated markets are demanded instead of free markets and Big government is proposed instead of minimal government. This is defined by the belief that state intervention, especially in the form of social welfare, can expand freedom by protecting individuals from the social ills that threaten individual existence. The famous Beveridge Report, released in the UK in 1942, called for state intervention against the following five ills that plague society: want, ignorance, idleness, squalor and disease.

2.2.6. Monetarism

The great economic expansion of the 1950s and 1960s is considered a great success of Keynesian policies. However, the stagflation of the 1970s greatly shook the intellectual hegemony of Keynesianism. Stagflation is a situation of high inflation accompanied by economic stagnation. In stagflation, the general level of prices continues to rise as the economy continues to shrink despite monetary expansion. Unemployment, loss of real income and fear of the future lead citizens to question the ability of governments to manage markets. The most prominent thinker to criticize Keynes during this period was the American economist Milton Friedman.

In addition to the phenomenon of stagflation, the 1970s also saw the side effects of the comprehensive welfare state, such as bureaucratic inefficiency, social inertia and corporatism preventing governments from making policy. The main problem with Keynesian fiscal policy was the realization that governments did not have as much control over the effects of monetary policy as they thought they did. The economic growth generated by monetary expansion in the short run misdirected the consumption and savings behavior of consumers and the investment behavior of producers in the long run. In particular, the trade-off between short-term needs and long-term investments became inefficient as price signals were distorted by inflationary pressures.

Moreover, people' investments in private markets have declined as a greater proportion of their income has been eroded by rising taxes and inflation. The drop in private investment caused by an increase in public expenditures is known as the crowding-out effect. As opposed to Keynes' multiplier effect, the crowding-out effect inhibits the expansion of markets. In addition, as Friedman demonstrated, the fact that government interventions have little effect on the velocity of money circulation enables monetary expansion to generate inflation rather than economic development over the long term.

Likewise, Austrian economist Friedrich von Hayek, a prominent critic of Keynes and socialism, opposed state intervention, believing that market processes were too complex for governments to regulate. Hayek argues that extensive government intervention distorts the price mechanism and the price signals that assist market agents in making production and consumption decisions. Due to the complexity of labor division and specialization in contemporary markets, there is no technological and fixed data to guide trade processes. This information must be determined by market players during exchange processes. In contrast, government interventions misdirect these exchange mechanisms, resulting in unintended negative outcomes.

In addition to Keynesian critiques, public choice theorists' attacks on the welfare state have contributed significantly to the changing intellectual climate. Public choice supported market-based economic policies by refuting market failure arguments with the government failure argument. The argument for government failure challenges the capacity of governments to attain specified social goals. Therefore, market failure for a product or service does not inherently warrant government intervention. Instead, the proper investigation should establish whether market-based or bureaucratic solutions should be implemented. Theorists of public choice frequently prefer market-based approaches to bureaucratic ones.

The economic crises of the 1970s, combined with the intellectual triumph of libertarian economists such as Friedman and Hayek, paved the way for the birth of the political program known as the New Right in the UK and the US. Margaret Thatcher in the UK and Ronald Regan in the US launched a new wave of liberalization and free trade around the world with a strong return to traditional free market economic policies. The emphasis on reform of the welfare state, low inflation, private sector efficiency, and balanced budgets led to a revival of classical liberal policies. By critics, these economic policies are also known as neoliberalism.

2.3. Abstract Models of Economic Systems

The analysis of the relationship between economic systems and political institutions is basically based on the definitions of two competing economic systems, capitalism and socialism. However, an important problem with this analysis is that while the abstract principles of capitalism and socialism can be more or less agreed upon, it is not possible to find a pure application of these two forms. Moreover, authors may choose to define these economic systems according to their ideological positions. Hence the debate on different types of capitalism and socialism. They are much more useful analytical tools when these concepts are assumed to be ideal types.

2.3.1. Capitalism

Capitalism is usually defined as an economic regime where enterprises and/or private citizens own the means of production and where employers pay a wage to their employees to manufacture goods with the purpose of afterwards selling them to produce profits. Even though these general traits are usually largely accepted in the literature, there is not a specific definition of capitalism that is unanimously accepted, so it is difficult to trace back its origins. If one argues that capitalism is simply the most natural way to allocate resources within an economic community, then it has always existed and it is an intrinsic feature of human beings. That is, human beings' nature is made of the will to enrich oneself or her community, so capitalism has always existed and will always exist. Yet, others argue that capitalism is not related to human beings' nature, but it rather developed as a result of specific economic phenomenon, such as the development of agriculture, or slavery in ancient societies. Hence, capitalism is a precise historical feature that has not always existed and it will not necessarily last forever[32].

That said, there is a widespread agreement concerning the fact that capitalism is an economic system where production is not planned by a central government, but it is dictated by laws of **demand and supply** – defined as the economic relationship between the amount of a

---

[32] Weingast B., Wittman D.A. (2006), *The Oxford Handbook of Political Science*, Oxford University Press, New York.

commodity that producers want to sell at a certain prince and the quantity consumers wish to buy - in the market economy. The term **market** is thus central to capitalism, and it refers to decision making of multiple individuals about what to buy or sell, which creates different levels of demand and supply.

This is also how price is determined, since **prices** represent the equilibrium point at which the quantity of goods supplied by producers equals the amount required by consumers. More in detail, prices represent the compensation – usually measured in a certain currency - given by consumers to producers in return for one unit of goods or services. Prices are thus influenced by different factors that do not remain constant over time, such as production costs, demand of the product and availability.

While this standard definition of capitalism is correct, it does not explain why we need a definition of capitalism other than that of a free market economy. For example, according to Ludwig von Mises, a prominent free market advocate "The market economy is the social system of the division of labor under private ownership of the means of production". Mises's description of the market economy and the preceding explanation of capitalism are approximately identical. In this regard, it is important to keep in mind that the discussion on capitalism is a value-laden ideological debate. This is because socialists have a negative connotation to capitalism and assert that it is an exploitative economic system. Marx's decision to place capitalism rather than liberal democracy at the core of his critique arises from his belief that liberal democratic institutions are the product of the economic system.

The advocates of the market economy, on the other hand, adopt and use the word capitalism, but use it more as a slogan in the ideological debate against socialism. There are also thinkers who define capitalism as a separate process within the market economy. For example, according to Craig Parsons,[33] "Capitalism is when people who own money (known as

---

[33] Craig Parsons, 307, Introduction to Political Science

"capital") make more money without directly doing the labor to produce goods or services. They make their money by owning businesses that make a profit, investing their money in someone else's business and getting a return on that investment, or charging interest on loans to others. Capitalists make profits on their capital."

It is also possible to follow the debates on the definition of capitalism in the varieties of capitalism. If the production and consumption of goods and services are realized entirely through market prices, it is possible to call it free-market/laissez faire/enterprise capitalism. Although it is not possible to see an ideal free-market capitalism, the first example that comes to mind is the USA. However, it is possible to identify which countries are more free-market based on international indexes of economic freedom. According to the Heritage Foundation's 2022 Index of Economic Freedom, the top 10 countries with the freest markets in the world are as follows: Singapore, Switzerland, Ireland, Luxembourg, New Zealand, Taiwan, Estonia, Netherland, Finland and Denmark. The US ranked 25th in the mostly free category. Interestingly, Netherland, Finland and Denmark, which are considered to be important social states, are in the top 10.

For free-market capitalists, capitalism is not just a model of wealth production. Capitalism is the foundation of modern civilization and liberal values such as individual liberty and the rule of law can only exist in a capitalist system. Moreover, even if capitalism creates economic inequality, the mass production on which capitalism is based increases the material wealth of the masses in a way that no other economic system can match. According to Mises, the consumer is sovereign in capitalism. Consumer sovereignty is based on the fact that the goods and services to be produced are ultimately formed by consumer preferences and that most of the production consists of the daily needs of the ordinary consumer rather than luxury goods. Moreover, the perception of luxury consumption is constantly changing due to the efficiency created by capitalism. For example, the use of cars, computers, or cell phones are no longer luxuries but basic necessities in capitalist societies.

However, it is also possible to come across definitions such as social capitalism and state capitalism. The first country that comes to mind in the context of social capitalism is Germany with its "social market economy" established after World War II. In addition to Germany, Austria and most Scandinavian countries can also be included in this category. This economic model is based on the concept of a social market, which is an attempt to reconcile market competition with the need for social cohesion and solidarity. In a social market economy there is no need for excessive state interventionism. An analysis of the economic freedom index reveals that most social democracies have competitive markets. However, trade unions are often represented by works councils and participate in annual rounds of industry-wide wage negotiations. This connection is supported by comprehensive and well-funded welfare programs that provide social guarantees to workers and other disadvantaged populations.

The concept of state capitalism is sometimes used in the literature to describe the economic model of some countries. In these countries, especially investment activities are directed by various bureaucratic organizations and investors' access to capital can be determined as a result of various political processes. In countries lagging behind in industrialization, it is observed that governments identify various strategic sectors for economic development and rapid industrialization and make planned investments in these areas. The political regimes of these countries are not always liberal democracies. The fact that there are examples of countries where capitalism does not intersect with liberal democracy is a prominent feature of state capitalism from time to time.

Japan, South Korea, Taiwan, Singapore, and Hong Kong are among the East Asian nations that are defined by state capitalism. The defining feature of these nations is their export-oriented economic policies. Their primary purpose is to dominate select international markets, not to strengthen domestic startups. Samsung or the chemical sector in South Korea and Taiwan's high-tech manufacturing are instances of successful state capitalism. Important practices in Japan include the lifelong employment strategy and comprehensive employee benefits.

From this short review, it is evident that capitalism is not a monolith, but rather manifests itself in political science with multiple facets and manifestations. As aforementioned, all scholars agree that capitalism is the economic regime where capital goods belong to private citizens, but since the way it is organized has differed significantly over time, there have been different visions related to what capitalism actually is. Due to this difficulty in defining what capitalism precisely is, there has never been an academic agreement on its 'political economy', but rather many different perspectives on some specific questions related to its ethics, equality and morality. More pertinent to the economy, there has always been a debate on how much we ought to regulate markets.

On the one hand, there are those sustaining a **Laissez-faire/free-market capitalism**, for whom capitalist markets should be completely free from any economic interventionism such as subsidies and regulations. This view is based on two pillars. First, on an integral conception of freedom as non-interference for which individual economic liberty must not be curtailed by the state's intervention. Second, that markets are capable of self-regulating and that best results are thus achieved when the market is left to its spontaneous order.[34] Hence, there is no space for government intervention in the economic sector. Laissez-faire developed in the 18th century, but this view is still influential, since **neoliberalism** - one of current the dominant economic paradigms - has drawn from it most of its structural features.[35]

On the other hand, most scholars acknowledge that we should have forms of **regulated capitalism** to control markets in a certain way, even though decision-makers should mainly be individuals rather than public agents as the government. In this system, individuals may decide they want the government to step in to regulate behaviors that are not in the public interest and to fix externalities created by economic liberty. As

[34] Hill, L. E. (1964), "On Laissez-Faire Capitalism and Liberalism'.", *The American Journal of Economics and Sociology*, 23 (4), 393-396.
[35] Ganti, T. (2014), "Neoliberalism.", *Annual Review of Anthropology*, 43, 89-104.

for previous features, the spectrum of "how much" government ought to intervene is wide and can be differently connected to capitalism. Yet, another important economic theory, socialism, maintains that it is not a matter of regulating capitalism, since we can reduce capitalism's problems only insofar as governments keep total control of the economy.

2.3.2. Socialism

Socialism is defined as an economic system where there is a social ownership of economic means of production, together with a planned market economy. According to Marx, forms of planned and public economy can be traced back up to primitive human-gatherer societies, but it is only with the modern era that this theory proposed itself as the alternative response to capitalism.[36] This latter commodifies land, means of production and work to create profit, but this can be seen as opposite to the fabric of society. Some scholars thus started pointing out that the problem of capitalism was private property, since they maintained that even if we control and 'tame' private property with social justice, the fact that some individuals own the means of production unavoidably leads to the exploitation of those who do not own them.[37]

Capitalism was thus seen as contrary to "objective" human needs such as creative work, diversity, solidarity and satisfaction of needs. As a response, socialism aimed at structuring an economic system more compatible with these objective economic needs. At first, socialism was more a utopian ideal. Analyzing workers' poor conditions, some scholars – such as Shaker's Christian socialism or the Hutteriti in the United States - maintained that the source of workers' problems was that they were working in large factories exploited by their employers. On the contrary, the solution was to be found in small communities that would have

---

[36] Saitta, D. J. "Marxism, prehistory, and primitive communism.", *Rethinking Marxism*, 1 (4), 145-168.

[37] Brenkert, G. G. (1979), "Freedom and private property in Marx.", *Philosophy & Public Affairs*, 122-147.

resolved material scarcity by structuring societies on a commune spirit. Hence, this first period lacked a proper economic theory and was mainly based on utopian ideas.[38]

The first glimpses of an economic theory that promoted equality as a way to achieve a meritocratic society arose with the anarchist Pierre-Jospeh Proudhon, or with anti-capitalist scholars such as Robert Owen and Charles Fourier.[39] Yet, it was Henri de Saint-Simon who first coined the term "socialism" as the alternative system to capitalism who could have granted equal opportunities to the people.[40] Finally, socialism became a proper economic theory thanks to the famous work of Karl Marx and Friedrich Engels "Das Kapital" (Capital),[41] where it is possible to find the basis of the main socialist economic concepts. Since Marxist economic theory has been explained under the previous headings, Marx's views on the crisis of capitalism will be briefly mentioned here. For Marx, capitalism is not only based on exploitation, but is also inherently unstable.

The accumulation of capital is crucial to the instability of capitalist economic growth. Capitalism is inherently led to continuously accumulate wealth by gaining from investments' returns and by profiting from workers' surplus value. For this reason, capitalism must continuously find new markets and opportunities to expand itself worldwide and to repeat the accumulation process. Capital accumulation cyclically finds social and economic barriers that lead to periods of crisis which often result in further centralization of the means of production in the hands of fewer capitalists. The constant concentration of capital in the hands of

---

[38] Bestor A. (2018), *Backwoods Utopias: The Sectarian Origins and the Owenite Phase of Communitarian Socialism in America, 1663-1829*, University of Pennsylvania Press, Pennsylvania.

[39] Prichard, A. (2013), *Justice, order and anarchy: The international political theory of Pierre-Joseph Proudhon*, Routledge, London.

[40] Simon, W. M. (1956), "History for utopia: Saint-Simon and the idea of progress.", *Journal of the History of Ideas* 17 (3), 311-331.

[41] Marx K. (2019 [1867]), *Das Kapital (Capital) A Critique of Political Economy*, Benediction Classics, Oxford.

a smaller capitalist will make class conflict and exploitation much more intolerable and obvious. For this reason, it is argued that the beginning of the socialist revolution will arise from this internal contradiction that capitalism cannot overcome.

In this framework, class conflict is an inherent characteristic of the economic system that according to Marx could be fixed only with a revolutionary movement aimed at the abolishment of private property so as to favor public property as the means of production. After Marx, other scholars not necessarily connected to socialism – such as J.S.Mill and J.M.Keynes – acknowledged that capitalism was unstable and that if the economic system was to 'tame' social conflict and to produce better results both in the different economic fields and in the market, it required some form of public intervention.[42] This debate on the connection between public intervention and market liberty has been a central feature of political economic debate over the last century, even though there currently are almost no countries framed on an integral socialist model.

Nowadays, we identify a **socialist economy** as a system where commodities are produced directly to be used, rather than to be sold to create profit. A central feature of the socialist economy is that it is **'planned'** which means that economic inputs are assigned directly by using resources to produce value according to the needs. This is opposite to what happens in a market economy where value is assigned indirectly by letting the market and economic cycles decide the inputs. A planned economy requires the public ownership of the means of production, even though this varies from a complete ownership by the state (statism) to mixed forms of ownership by workers' cooperatives and a common property by all society.

Socialist industries do not encompass hierarchical relationships, but should be based on workers' self-government where each worker has the

---

[42] Taylor Q. (2016), "John Stuart Mill, Political Economist: A Reassessment", *The Independent Review*, 21 (1), 73-94.

same decisional power over collective decisions as others.' Yet, most historical examples of socialist countries, such as the Soviet Union or Yugoslavia, framed the management of their factories on a rigid bureaucracy that implemented the will of the state, thus leading to the debate related to whether or not such states were actually economically socialist or "collectivist bureaucrats."[43]

Aim of socialism is thus to 'neutralize' the capital by tying investments and capital to a social planning aimed at eliminating the economic cycle and the overproduction crisis typical of economies that rely on private property. In this way, socialist theorists maintain that workers could obtain more equality, freedom to access the resources they need to live and they would not be exploited of the value produced by their work. Over the last century, there have been several attempts to implement socialist economy in practice, even though most of them encompass certain capitalist features such as salaries given to employees and forms of partial free market.

Most of the social historical examples were structured on an economy planned by a central government who decided the kind and number of commodities that had to be produced, as it was the case in the Soviet Union, in the Vietnamese socialist republic or in Cuba. This economic regime reached its peak in the 80s, when almost 1/3 of the total world population lived underneath such economic regimes, even though all these economies together generated only 15% of world's GDP. However, with the dissolution of the Soviet Union in 1991, countries steadily changed their economies to more liberal forms, such that nowadays only a few countries – Cuba, North Korea, China – adopt this economic regime and aside from North Korea, this socialism is more liberal than the centrally planned version of the Soviet Union.[44]

---

[43] Verdery, K. (1996), *What was socialism, and what comes next?*. Princeton University Press, Princeton.

[44] Sabry, M. I. (2017), *The Development of Socialism, Social Democracy and Communism: Historical, Political and Socioeconomic Perspectives*, Emerald Group Publishing, Bingley.

An interesting example of the socialist economic model in theory and practice is market socialism. As Mises argued, an important source of the inefficiency of the socialist economic model is the absence of any mechanism to provide information about the relative scarcity of goods and services. In market economies, prices indicate how relatively scarce goods and services are in the market. For example, if the price of a good rises rapidly, other things being equal, it is understood that this good has become scarce in the market and entrepreneurs start producing it to make a profit. Similarly, if the price of a good is falling, this price movement informs entrepreneurs that no more of that good should be produced. Since economic resources can be used to produce many different goods and services, how these economic resources are allocated among different goods and services is governed by the spontaneous ordering of the price mechanism in the market.

When socialists abolish private property and free exchange, they also abolish the price mechanism. In real life, however, socialists have faced the reality that limited resources cannot be allocated smoothly among supposedly objective needs. Ignorance of the relative scarcity of goods has led to the creation of many shortages in socialist economies, often leading to the production of many goods and services that cannot be demanded. Problems of interregional transportation of goods have been characterized by a similar problem of ignorance.

Some socialist economists who recognized this problem, notably the Polish socialist economist Oskar Lange, developed the theory of market socialism. The basic idea was to create a market for the exchange of raw materials and to obtain price information on these economic resources. Part of this model was also applied in Czechoslovakia. There are some important problems with market socialism. First, if the market is more efficient than central planning, why is the production of other goods and services managed by bureaucratic mechanisms? Second, in the face of constantly changing economic conditions and demands, it is recognized that the socialist economy cannot adapt its production processes to new conditions and needs. There does not seem to be a sound justification given by market socialists for why a comprehensive welfare state based on a market economy should not be preferred over this system.

For these reasons, Mises argued that economic planning is impossible in socialist economies. Although socialists found the production processes in a market economy irrational and chaotic, they could not provide a satisfactory answer to the fundamental economic problem of how to allocate resources between goods and services in a centrally planned economy. Marx argued that this problem was only a problem of capitalism and assumed that socialism would not have the problem of inability to produce. But in theory and in practice the problem of scarce resources clearly exists.

CHAPTER 3

American Political Culture

3.1 American Political Culture

Political culture is a set of *shared* ideas, values, and beliefs that define the role and limitations of government and people's relationship to that government. Political beliefs and values are the primary elements that determine the political priorities and responses of citizens. Therefore, solely a rational cost-benefit analysis cannot be used to assess voter behavior and explain political phenomena. We can consider political beliefs and values that manifest political culture as the political personality of the average voter. These political values, which are commonly held by the average voter, are the primary determinants of a nation's political character. In fact, citizens evaluate political events based on these traits, and political reality can only be defined in relation to these values. In this regard, it may be difficult to demonstrate that political reality exists apart from political culture.

In addition to official norms, political culture consists mostly of unwritten practices and traditions. These practices and traditions are culturally transferred from generation to generation through socialization and are frequently referred to as "habits of the heart." Rather than studying and adopting them objectively, new generations frequently view reality in terms of these values. For instance, despite the fact that the

American Constitution is a legal document that must be obeyed, Americans also see it as quasi-sacred. Therefore, amending the American Constitution is not merely a matter of Congressional politics. Any change to the Constitution requires the genuine support of the American people.

President Roosevelt's attempt to increase the number of Supreme Court judges in 1937 is an intriguing example of a proposed constitutional amendment. At the height of his popularity, when the Supreme Court began to block some of Roosevelt's crucial New Deal legislation, he requested Congress for permission to increase the number of Supreme Court justices. The request of President Roosevelt provoked indignation across the nation. Opponents' primary concern was that this meddling in the legal system would compromise judicial independence. Roosevelt's request was denied with the support of the Democrats following a lengthy debate. Even the Democrats opposed the idea of President Roosevelt.

Even a prominent leader like President Roosevelt was not permitted to compromise judicial independence following the Great Depression of 1929. However, as time passed, Supreme Court justices realized they could no longer oppose social security legislation. Following Roosevelt's proposal, the New Deal laws were implemented without significant legal opposition.

The political culture that contributes to the stability of the political system should not be susceptible to significant change. However, profound economic crises and social upheavals can serve as catalysts for changes in political culture. In the instance of the Supreme Court, the American public's ambivalence between judicial independence and social security laws resulted in the formation of a new political mindset. With minor adaptations, the American political system has been able to stabilize itself in the face of significant social crises.

In many ways, the political culture of the United States diverges significantly from those of its Western relatives. American political culture is built upon values that limit the power of government. The emphasis on limited government originates from the United States being the first modern republic with a written constitution. The written constitution is an American invention in this regard. Before the United States, the estab-lishment or even survival of a truly democratic republic across a broad geographical area was deemed unachievable by the majority of European political elites. Despite the fact that the United States engaged in a civil war over a century after its foundation, the country emerged from this conflict with enhanced political equality.

The direct foundation of a democratic system in the United States, without the establishment of a monarchical rule, separates it from other nations in which democracy is founded through revolutions or reforms. This distinction is typically referred to as the American exceptionalism. On the other hand, the Constitution of United States and American practices of self-government did not appear out of thin air. The Constitu-tion of America is in part a redesign of political institutions founded on the rational principles of separation of powers and the rule of law, which matured in England following the Glorious Revolution, to fit the Ameri-can federal system. For instance, the Constitution of America borrows heavily from the Instrument of Government issued by Oliver Cromwell, the leader of the Parliamentary army after the first English civil war, and the Bill of Rights issued in 1689 following the Glorious Revolution.

As will be shown in greater detail in the coming chapters, British political theory, especially John Locke's theories of natural law and social contract, are also essential components of American constitutional draft-ing. Furthermore, the first colonies founded in North America at the start of the 17th century created representative governments with approval from the British government. By the end of the eighteenth century, all colonies were autonomous through their representative governments. Such procedures cannot exist outside of British political philosophy and the British political tradition.

Certainly, the American political system and culture are markedly unlike from those of the British in certain areas. Despite its parliamen-tary components, the political system and social structure of England were aristocratic. The conservatism and traditionalism of British aris-tocracy clashed with the American people's rigorous egalitarianism and

dedication to liberal rational ideals. The originality of the American political system enabled the establishment of a state founded on rationalism
and principles of self-governance as opposed to a political creed founded
on myths and traditions. Before the American Revolution, despite all the
experience with limited government and liberal thought, the concept of
a limited government based on rational liberal principles was considered
a utopian vision. After the American Revolution, however, the majority
of intellectuals eagerly backed the French Revolution.

"Taxation without representation is slavery" was one of the slogans
that symbolized the drastic split with political and social equality between
the American colonies and Britain, and possibly the rest of the world.
Following Britain's imposition of direct taxes on Americans following the
Seven Years' War between Britain and the French-led union, this slogan
gained popularity. The introduction of direct taxes on top of those for-
merly imposed mostly through transactions was viewed by the American
colonists as a great injustice. American colonists, viewing themselves as
equal Britons, believed that direct taxes could only be enforced with their
consent. However, the British could not comprehend why the sovereign
state's right over its subjects was being questioned.

While it was widely acknowledged that taxation was a sovereign right,
the American colonists internalized the notion that a legitimate government could only be founded on consent more than any other society.
Americans did not anticipate that the concept of consensual government
would emerge gradually in an aristocratic culture. For them, consent-
based government was a moral imperative, and failure to implement this
idea meant the end of liberty and even servitude. Ordinary taxes for
another political community were a just and necessary reason for American colonists to rebel. Clearly, no other civilization would have interpreted taxation without representation as slavery during this time period.

As is evident, the distinct contrasts between the American and British political cultures prevented them from understanding one another.
In addition, the British Empire failed to appreciate the reason and commitment of those who resisted it. Thomas Jefferson charged the British

monarch with abusing his authority and stated that the king had failed to fulfill his responsibilities to his subjects. According to Jefferson, the king unfairly restricted the colonists' trade relations, taxed them without their consent, and deprived them of self-government. As meaningful and justifiable as Jefferson's resistance to the king was, the American rebellion was utterly pointless and unjustifiable in the eyes of the British ruler. In Democracy in America, Alex de Tocqueville observed that the American notion of democracy pointed to the emergence of a new type of society based on political and social equality. While this type of social structure appeared to come naturally from the American experience, it was revolutionary for the rest of the world.

However, the American political culture is woven together from political narratives that are vastly different across the nation. Every state has unique stories and a history defining the political narrative. We also see many instances when states do not get along or cooperate, and in these instances, cultures clash. Take, for example, the American Civil War, arguably the darkest and bloodiest hour in the country's history. That conflict represented an enormous fracturing in the political culture. The Union states maintained one set of beliefs on slavery, tariffs, suffrage, and government power, whereas the Confederates held diametrically opposite views. For years, the United States was divided on the most fundamental aspects of political culture, and it culminated in war. It was a loss of social cohesion that led to widespread suffering. This is one of the most critical reasons for studying the topic of American political culture and developing a better understanding of its dynamic input and output functions.

It is impossible to provide a tangible understanding of the American political culture. The political culture is unembodied and unspoken. Disparate views abound, especially with things based on personal experiences and exposure to other cultures. Those who have not traveled or met many people from other countries are more likely to think that the beliefs they share are objective reality, not just one set of many optional sets of narratives. In the political science subfield of comparative politics, scholars research other countries and discover widely different values on everything from group identification to suspicion of government, to tolerance of outside cultures. Examining these differences is one the primary methods researchers use to analyze societies objectively, avoid ethnocentrism, and disseminate information for learning purposes.

Political culture is easiest to recognize when one steps outside of it. Being inside of a political ideology or system can keep a person from seeing the 'big picture' of the political system. Political culture gives people a common set of assumptions about the world and a common political language within which they can agree. Let us now examine the essential values of American political culture and the historical events that gave rise to a new type of society in greater detail.

3.2 Fundamentals of American political culture

Three fundamental political values have been dominant in the United States since the colonial period: freedom, equality, and self-government. Let's begin with the American conception of liberty. Individual liberty is the predominant conception of freedom in the American political system. Individual freedom, as described in the first section, refers to negative freedom or freedom of choice. Individual liberty is a fundamental principle of all modern democracies. According to Freedom House's 2021 Global Freedom Report, the United States got 83 out of a possible 100 points, placing it below a number of advanced liberal democracies. Considering that the study is based on the criteria of political rights and civil freedoms, it is important to remember that the emphasis on freedom in American politics does not always reflect the truth.

However, the American political emphasis on individual liberty is clearly based on Locke's idea of natural rights. Individuals do not need society's or the consent of the people to exercise their inalienable natural rights, according to Locke. Consequently, natural rights are rights asserted against the government and society. The public sphere includes matters that extend beyond the limits of natural rights, and the government's authority over the individual is restricted to this carefully defined public sphere.

Locke's theoretical claims have significant implications for the formation of American politics on a daily basis. For instance, two of the most prominent political debates in the United States are gun control and abortion rights. Conservatives are individuals who oppose gun regulation, whereas progressives are those who support abortion rights. However, both camps frame their arguments in terms of individual autonomy. In other words, it is simpler to garner public support if your political arguments are framed in terms of individual liberty.

This emphasis on individual liberty does not necessarily result in the development of legislative laws consistent with this theory, but it does result in the establishment of a robust political discourse among the people. It is rare to identify any nation where the concept of individual liberty is as deeply embedded as it is in the United States. For instance, the emphasis in Hollywood movies that the government supports public services via income taxes may lack political relevance in a great number of other nations. By paying taxes for public services, voters expect a check on the government.

This emphasis on taxation also reinforces the implication that the government's authority to govern is derived directly from the people. Even the anarchist American author Henry David Thoreau refused to pay taxes because he opposed the Mexican-American War, which began in 1846, on moral grounds. This political activism, referred to as civil disobedience, is fundamentally American. Individual liberty is an extreme reflection of the notion that moral standards can arise from the individual and that individuals can oppose government activities they do not morally approve of.

The second most important value of American political culture is equality. What is the origin for the concern for equality in modern political culture? In 19th century France, the motto of "liberte, egalite, and fraternite" (liberty, equality, and fraternity) became a chief concern after the violent French Revolution. Philosophers like Jean-Jacques Rousseau and

Maximilien Robespierre emphasized equality as an important ingredient in forming a social contract between members of society. Equality paves the way for the possibility of thriving democratic republics.

Equality can be divided into four main categories: equality before law, social equality, political equality and economic equality. Equality before law, defined, expresses that all citizens enjoy the same privileges, statuses, and rights in the eyes of the law. Social equality means that all individuals enjoy the same lawful status in society. Social equality is where the political/social hierarchy is free from institutional nobility. This would bar the existence of titled privileges such as those of barons or archdukes who inherit special benefits when they are born. Civil servants in the government are elected or appointed based on the law rather than heredity. Political equality is the means that every citizen has the same political rights and opportunities. This includes **suffrage** (voting) but it also includes the right to **due process** (trial by jury, right to an attorney). Although America has a dark history of universal suffrage being denied to anyone other than white landowning property owners, the United States has made great strides to create political and social equality for all people. Equality also is considered to be economic equality. Economic equality focuses on the differences in wealth. Social critics scrutinize wealth/income inequality out of concerns for justice and the loss of quality of life for those with less wealth. Others counter this by claiming that some inequality is unavoidable and that equality under the law is the only thing worth safeguarding. At any rate, the issue of equality, social, political or economic, retains an important point of divergence in today's political culture.

As described by Tocqueville in Democracy in America, Americans would rather be equal under slavery than unequal under freedom. This is why the rhetoric on equality has such a profound effect on Americans. A poorly justified claim of privilege, for instance, is perceived as an assertion of superiority, leading to severe criticism. The recent controversial affirmative action policy is an intriguing example of how Americans view equality. Opponents of affirmative action reject the positive privileges demanded by affirmative action for underprivileged communities on the grounds that they generate inequity between individuals. However, proponents of affirmative action claim that they demand it in order to alleviate the current impacts of systemic discrimination against particular communities. In other words, affirmative action is required to eliminate a social inequity produced by prior discrimination. In this regard, ideologically distinct parties explain their policies using the same collection of concepts.

Democracy is the third prominent political value in American political culture. Democracy is a decision-making process by which individuals register their preferences for their rulers (and the policies they promise). A democracy is a government which citizens rule directly and make government decisions themselves. In a democracy, the citizens have power over their government's decision making.

Is the United States considered a democracy? Yes, in some sense, but it is important to maintain precision of terms. With some exceptions (see the next section), the United States is not what you would call a "direct democracy," but rather a constitutional republic or representative democracy. Aristotle was one of the first to use the term "republic," which accounts for the United States and most countries in western civilization today. Under this model, citizens participate in politics by voting on representatives (members of Congress, the Senate, the President) who are expected to carry out the general will of those they govern. Elected officials, even your local mayor or councilmember, have a fiduciary responsibility to govern with the best interests of the people in mind. They are held accountable electorally. If they fail to satisfy their constituents, or are found guilty of a scandal, they run the risk of getting voted out of office.

In a democracy, the use of referendum can allow citizens to have direct access to creating a democratic state. A referendum is an election in which citizens vote directly on an issue. This is a way to employ "direct democracy." California passes laws and removes people from office with this method. An example of this, in 2020, was Proposition 17. This gave citizens the opportunity to vote on a referendum regarding voting rights for convicted felons released on parole. In that instance, it passed with 58% of Californians voting in favor.

In a democracy, we would assume a social, political, and economic equality amongst the people. Equal opportunity is the idea that every American has the same chance to influence politics and achieve economic success regardless of their race, gender, or class. It is the American dream that anyone can pull themselves up by their bootstraps, rich or poor, and have the same opportunities as anyone else. In the American political culture, the attitudes, beliefs, and assumptions that we create give order and meaning to public life. In a democracy, the American political culture gives Americans the ability to disagree but remain united ultimately.

Americans appear to have a natural inclination for democratic government, which can be viewed as an extension of the values of freedom and equality. However, in a democratic government, freedom is viewed as a result of equality. In other terms, freedom is the state of not being ruled by another individual. This is why democracies oppose the expert rule and place a higher value on political equality than technical expertise. Therefore, they feel that a government comprised of equals is superior to a hierarchical one ruled by the most knowledgeable individuals.

Political equality in the United States is founded on the adoption of the idea of one person, one vote. Nonetheless, equality and non-domination prevail in the representative democracy of the United States. In spite of the fact that decisions are taken more slowly in representative democracies than in authoritarian regimes, and that decisions can always be questioned, the fact that citizens can change and criticize their government is regarded as more significant than the shortcomings of democracy. The superiority of democracy over other kinds of government is almost indisputable in the eyes of Americans.

However, democratic government and limited government are not necessarily compatible. Ultimately, democratic decisions are determined by a majority vote among citizens of equal status. Democracy is a procedure for making decisions. Not always are democratic outcomes consistent with individual liberty or even equality. The violation of minority rights in democracies is a prime illustration of this issue. Therefore, the American democracy is a constitutional democracy based on the principle of limited government. So, constitutional government based on individual rights is essentially an American invention.

The right to "life, liberty, and the pursuit of happiness" is a strong embodiment of Locke's theory of limited government in the Constitution of the USA. In this regard, limited government is a result of the other three political ideals. American democracy should also be evaluated separately from democracies without a real constitution. American democracy is a liberal democracy in the conventional sense. The Constitution exists in order to avoid the self-destruction of democracy and to safeguard the natural rights of individuals. In this regard, the concern that democracy can become corrupted is firmly embedded in American political culture.

Thus one can assume that American political culture is defined by the concept of limited government. **Limited government** is the political philosophy of a government limited in power. This is a key concept in the history of liberalism. **Liberalism** is a school of thought derived from the Enlightenment, found particularly in thinkers such as John Locke, Adam Smith, and David Hume. One might notice the similar sounding of the words "liberty" (from the Latin "*libertas*", meaning freedom from despotic control) and "liberal" (meaning free from restraint in speech or action). Each of these terms, in their most classical sense, refer to freedom and an aversion to external coercion. Locke and his adherents, like Thomas Jefferson, wrote in a time when many began to bring into question the legitimacy of the old, sometimes despotic, European monarchies.

The perception of individualism that dominates American political culture is one of the primary reasons why the system of limited government is so well-established in the United States. Individualism refers to moral individualism in this context. Moral individualism acknowledges that all humans are moral beings, i.e., they are capable of moral judgment. Again, we can defend this claim using Locke as support. While Locke argues that every individual is rational, he also implies that individuals can independently discover the natural law that maintains social order. In this situation, rational individuals can use their reason to determine the right action and limit their behavior in accordance with these moral principles. Obviously, these universal moral principles require codification and full implementation by positive law. Individuals are capable of respecting the rights of others, however, when rights are clearly defined and legally guaranteed.

Due to the government's well-defined and effective protection of individual rights, it is therefore possible for a social order to emerge through a contract between free individuals. Locke contends that natural law rules are negative claims. Therefore, the only legal obligation individuals have to one another is to respect each other's rights. In this regard, it is not surprising that positive claims are significantly less prevalent in American politics than in European democracies.

Negative rights claims ultimately support value pluralism. Value pluralism rejects a hierarchical ranking of individuals' political, religious, etc. values. Certainly, some values are favored over others, but the favored values are expected to be well-reasoned and few in number. This is where limited government and value pluralism intersect. The government uses coercion to implement its policies. This implies that every government policy must adhere to a particular hierarchy of values. If the government intervenes extensively in social and economic life, it will do so in accordance with a hierarchy of values.

In a communist regime, for instance, there are no individual values but only collective ones. The role of the state is to implement these hierarchical collective values in social and economic life. Nonetheless, because liberal democracies embrace value pluralism, they must reject state intervention in a number of areas. The United States emphasizes value pluralism more than its Western counterparts, at least in terms of discourse. The American opposition to the welfare state is the political arena in which value pluralism is most obviously reflected in American politics. Since the welfare state must pursue policies based on equality of outcomes, the imposition of certain value hierarchies becomes inevitable as welfare states expand. For instance, public education severely restricts the opening of private educational institutions and the ability of schools to design their own curricula. Public health care provides an analogous case study. In this context, we can evaluate the debates regarding the absence of public health care in the United States.

In American society, we hold the expectation that people will provide for their own forms of retirement and social welfare. Other countries, such as Great Britain, embrace community and communitarianism, insisting that people be protected by the government. For those people who prefer to have a social democracy, or community-focused democracy, the public interest is best served when all of society uses the government as a mechanism to take care of its citizens through things such as universal healthcare and a social welfare system. In the United States, with individualism, it is not the government's responsibility to provide for full coverage of one's retirement, wellbeing, or employment.

3.3 American Political Ideologies

America has several different political ideologies. In modern times, it may feel like the competing political ideologies are polarized and in constant disagreement. **Ideologies** are the competing narratives we create to explain those disagreements. Typically, ideological division in the United States has been along economic terms, disputes between conservatives and liberals. Sometimes the disputes involve social dimensions as well though.

In the American political spectrum, **conservatives** on the right call for less regulation of the economy (lower taxes, freer trade, unrestricted competition). Conservatives are Americans who believe in reduced government spending, personal responsibility, traditional moral values, and a strong national defense. It is common to see conservatives known as "right wingers." However, conservatives or conservative presidents do not always follow the policies required by the conservative discourse.

For example, Ronald Regan and George W. Bush significantly increased public spending. Donald Trump, on the other hand, suspended the Transatlantic Trade and Investment Partnership, the planned free trade agreement between the European Union and the US. Trump's policy choice was widely supported by the conservative voters.

Liberals are the second political group in the American political spectrum. **Liberals** on the left call for more government regulation (like social welfare programs, universal health care, and free preschool programs). Liberals value cultural diversity, government programs for the needy, public intervention in the economy, and individual's right to a lifestyle based on their own social and moral positions. Modern liberals may differ from the Locke's classical emphasis on negative liberty, but they still emphasize positive liberty, couched within a need to safeguard society with economic safety nets. For example, a modern liberal would be socially-libertarian on something like drug possession, preferring not to criminalize it, but would seek state intervention on economic measures such as Social Security, a regulatory safety net.

Starting in the 1960s and 1970s, however, other non-economic issues started to motivate voters—issues like racial desegregation, civil rights, women's rights, including reproductive rights, prayer in school, and reducing crime. These issues split Americans along a political dimension much like a vertical line. When you combine the horizontal, economic ideological dimension with the vertical, social ideological dimension, you get four ideological categories that are important for understanding American politics today.

3.4 A closer look at American ideologies

American ideologies are distinct along economic lines. American **economic conservatives** are those that believe in the narrative that the government that governs best, governs least. Proponents of this ideology want to see the government provide less oversight on fiscal policy. An example of a political ideology that believes in less oversight is libertarianism.

Libertarians believe that respect for individual freedom is a central condition of justice. They believe that human relations should be based on mutual consent. Libertarians advocate a free society based on cooperation, tolerance, and mutual respect. Libertarianism states that each of us should be allowed to live our own lives as long as we do not violate the rights of others. They believe that individuals cannot be forced to take any action in the name of the collective good, such as economic stability, better cultural development, etc. Libertarians also believe that we should not use force except in self-defense. This principle is called non-aggression. Libertarians also uncompromisingly advocate a free-market economy and minimal government. They tend to favor policies like gun rights, reproductive rights, civil rights, assisted suicide, and legalized marijuana. Most want only as much regulation of the economy as it would take to keep competition fair and the market from tanking. Robert Nozick, author of *Anarchy, State, and Utopia*, gives the model of a "night-watchman" state, where the government exists only for the most basic functions. It would go no further than minimal governance such as police, courts of law, and a small military. This model omits most state intervention into economic and social matters. Some libertarians reject the legitimacy of the state altogether. This type of libertarianism is called **anarcho-capitalism**.

Although the US is not the most libertarian country in the world, some libertarian principles have become common sense for Americans. Things like the consensual nature of social cooperation and the need for the strict protection of the private sphere are commonplace social assumptions for Americans. However, libertarianism and conservatism are not the same things.

In terms of state intervention in social and economic life, American conservatives differ from libertarians. In practice, numerous conservatives demand various forms of government intervention. The most significant difference between libertarians and conservatives is in foreign policy. Conservatives frequently support US military foreign interventionism and typically do not oppose limiting individual rights in the name of combating terrorism or the war on drugs. In addition, the conservative belief that Judeo-Christian principles should have some influence in politics is diametrically opposed to the libertarian perspective on secular politics. For instance, homosexuality-related restrictions cannot be associated with libertarianism.

The progressives are those who are on the most extreme left end of political ideology. **Progressives** are those who are the farthest to the left on the political continuum. Social democrats, left-wings, and left-libertarians are those who believe in an even stronger role for the state in creating equality. Progressives represent various shades of leftist politics. Left-libertarians, for instance, share the same beliefs as libertarians regarding civil rights and pluralism. However, many post-Marxist groups do not embrace libertarian principles under any circumstances. Progressives share a commitment to social justice, universal healthcare, gender equality, labor rights, environmentalism, and opposition to big corporations. For instance, the Occupy Movement, which began in 2011, is a global progressive political movement against economic and social inequality.

Progressives made a substantial impact in America around the turn of the 20th century under the leadership of presidents like Theodore Roosevelt and Woodrow Wilson. This was during a time when the United States saw an expansion in population, industrialization, and urbanization. Progressive critics, like Upton Sinclair, believed that this coincided with an increase in corruption, business monopoly, and worker exploitation. The response to this was the creation of several new government bureaucracies such as the Food & Drug Administration (FDA), the United States Department of Agriculture (USDA), the Federal Trade Commission (FTC), and the passage of the 16th Amendment, which enabled the income tax. This would eventually go on to include the Prohibition of alcohol with the 18th Amendment. The biggest takeaway from this era was the bipartisan (Republicans and Democrats) embracing of a more hands-on and active approach to governance.

Social issues are a source of division between conservatives and liberals as well. **Social conservatives** put a priority on the government preserving a traditional social order. Social conservatives include several groups who believe that their vision of the social order (that is, how people should live their lives) is absolute and want to put it into law. Social conservatives receive some of the intellectual foundation for their views in the works of the Irish philosopher/statesman, Edmund Burke. Burke, as opposed to Rousseau, was more suspicious of the concept of social contract because he thought it would lead to the disintegration of tradition and customs. Social conservatives seek to enact protective laws for maintaining social norms but are wary of what they consider to be the "social engineering" of social liberals.

Social liberals have concrete ideas about what they think is right and don't mind stepping on civil liberties if necessary to realize them. The social liberal doesn't always gain many adherents because it pushes the limits of Americans' limited government, individualistic culture. There are some occasions, however, when social liberals can make an impact. Whenever a perceived crisis gains public visibility (i.e., the Vietnam War or the Civil Rights Era), social liberals may have a chance to persuade the public to vote to enact legislative changes that contradict the prevailing social milieu. Exceptional circumstances notwithstanding, since we tend towards limited government, Americans distrust the government and place limits on the authority the government can exercise over people.

Evidently, political culture manifests itself in numerous forms. You have probably encountered friends, family, and opponents who represent some or all of these viewpoints. It is not difficult to see how the competing sub-cultures might clash as they did during the American Revolution, the American Civil War, the Civil Rights Era, and perhaps today as federal, state, and local elections continue to be contentious. With this framework for comprehending political culture, we can learn about the current political context. What are the major points of contention between social conservatives and social liberals? How do they fuel the debate over the hot-button political issues (war, abortion, drug restrictions, education costs, etc.)? Can we reconcile these cultural differences without incurring violence and civil wars? How do individualists and communitarians get along under the umbrella of the same government? Understanding political culture is a useful way to make sense of the various political forces at play in American civic life.

CHAPTER 4

Federalism

What is federalism? Federalism is the division of governmental power among the various public jurisdictions. In antiquity, government was much more unitary or "top-down" in its execution and delivery. Before power-sharing arrangements became common, political systems had been either unitary systems or confederal systems. Power was usually exercised in a *one-way direction.* A **unitary government** is a national polity governed as a single unit. The idea is to have the central government exercising all or most political authority. Most of the world's governments (nearly 90 percent) are unitary. A strong central government lends power to subnational governments, who cannot make and execute policy on their own. Unitary governments can create or abolish subnational units of governments. Federal governments typically cannot. The U.S. national government, for example, can't decide that Wyoming would be much better as a part of Montana, or that two Dakotas is just one too many. A **confederation** is a group of independent states or nations that yield some of their powers to a national government. A confederation, in which a group of states are equal partners in a government, aims to prevent a strong central government from dictating to its members, it also means nobody's in charge. A Confederation differs from a unitary government by the way the subsidiary states much more sovereign authority. During the period of American history when the country was governed under the Articles of Confederation (1781 to 1789), the individual states had more autonomy but also less cohesion with neighbouring states. Critics of that regime claimed that the absence of a weak central government left the young republic vulnerable to crises without mediation or judicial arbitration. Shay's Rebellion, a tax revolt that took place in Massachusetts, was considered the crisis that ended the United States' attempt at confederate governance.

America turned away from a unitary government style and tried a Confederation style of government for 10 years. The United States has used the federal form of governance since 1789 and the ratification of the United States Constitution. American federalism is not just the division of powers between the federal government and the states but is further nuanced by local governments. In U.S. federalism, for example, states have the ability to regulate trade within their borders, but only the federal government can regulate commerce that crosses state borders. National governments usually retain the sole ability to provide for national defence and the conduct of foreign relations, whereas both the states and the national government can create traffic and environmental laws. Both levels have the ability to raise revenues and spend money, while only national governments can address topics relating to international trade. Larger nations sometimes turn to federalism to manage widespread territories, such as the United States, Canada and Australia.

In American Federalism, some of the powers that the federal government possesses it also shares with the states. These are called **concurrent powers**. Federalism is a system of implementing public policy across multiple layers of government. The process of testing and spreading ideas across multiple levels of government from federal, state, and local levels is known as diffusion. **Diffusion** is the spreading of policy ideas from one city or state to others. An example of diffusion comes whenever local governments borrow policies. If New York City were to construct an ordinance that fined litterers $100 per offense, and San Francisco copied and administered the same policy, then it was a diffusion of New York City's original concept.

4.1 The Federalist Papers and Federalism

The Federalist Papers are a collection of 85 newspaper editorials written in support of the Constitution under the pseudonym of Publius, whose real identity was three Federalists: Alexander Hamilton, James Madison, and John Jay. The word 'federalism' does not appear in the Constitution of the United States. It has been adopted and became manifest within the governmental structures as inspired by The Federalist Papers. James Madison, writing as Publius, addressed the concept of Federalism in The Federalist Papers.

There are many different topics in The Federalist Papers. In Federalist No. 39, Madison defines "republic" and establishes three rules which must apply:

1. What is the foundation of its establishment? Only the possess *ultimate* sovereignty over the government.

2. What are the sources of its power? The elected officials chosen by the people should not break the rules or abuse their power.

3. Who has the authority to make future changes? When someone is chosen to rule the country, he or she should only be in that position for a certain amount of time and must be held accountable (through impeachment if necessary) if found to have committed high crimes or treason.

The republic defined by Madison consists of the different elements of the government leadership. A Madisonian republic is a system of government as defined by these three stipulations where the citizens elect representatives to make decisions for them. This constitutes most civic officials within the three branches of government: the executive, the judicial, and the legislative. There are still some offices that are *not* directly accountable to the people. This includes justices on the Supreme Court of the United States as well as United States senators prior to the passage of the 17th Amendment. Federalists like Madison believed that there needed to be a balance of direct election (popular vote) versus internal appointment by informed elites.

Madison, along with the other framers, was aware of two methods of arranging the government: confederate or federal. The Articles of Confederation was the country's original attempt at confederacy, which was a loosely assembled body of state governments prior to the ratification of the Constitution. The second version of government is called federal, national, or consolidation. It is also known as a unitary system.

Madison's essays proposed a five-component model for the American federal system. The first component was the method of ratification. The establishment of the Constitution was not a mere proclamation or decree by central authorities. Rather it was voted upon by the various member states before becoming the supreme law of the land. The second component was the sources of power for national officers. Here Madison emphasized how the bodies of Congress (House & Senate) as well as the presidency should arise. The presidency, for example, would be subject to direct election by the people, but administered as a function of the states through the Electoral College. The third component considers the apportionment of representatives based on the census. This determines how many representatives there are per state. This third component was the establishment of the representative as a national officer. The people thus gained a national representation. The fourth component referred to a fixed number of senators; two per state. People are not represented in the Senate, the states are. The Senate reinforces the federal nature of the Constitution. Madison's fifth component was the power of the presidency. The president's power is derived from elections and governed through the Electoral College system. As was mentioned before, the popular vote of the citizens is involved with determining the president, but it is the Electoral College (based on the size of the state and its apportionment of senators and representatives) that ultimately elects the president.

4.2 Federalist Paper 10 and Factions

Federalist No. 10 was published on November 23, 1787, under the pseudonym "Publius." It addresses the question of how to reconcile citizens with interests contrary to the rights of others or the interests of the greater community. During the late 18th century, the concept of factions bothered the founding fathers. Madison saw factions within society as inevitable due to the nature of man. As long as humans hold differing opinions, have differing amounts of wealth, and own differing amounts of property, they will continue to form alliances with people who are most like them. The result is that they may work against the public interest and infringe upon the rights of others. Madison warns against these dangers.

Federalist No. 10 continues a theme begun in Federalist No. 9, "The Utility of the Union as a Safeguard Against Domestic Faction and Insurrection." Scholars and jurists contend that Federalist 9 and Federalist 10 are an authoritative interpretation and explication of the Constitution. The question of faction undergirds the development of modern interest groups and the role in which minority groups are protected from majority opinions.

In addition to the problem with factions, Federalist No. 10 continues the discussion of the question broached in Hamilton's Federalist No. 9. Hamilton there addressed the destructive role of a faction in breaking apart the republic. The role in which people form groups and allegiances dictate how effective a republic will be. The question Madison answers, then, is how to eliminate the negative effects of factions. Can a faction exist without the consequences to the republic? Madison defines a faction as many citizens, whether amounting to a minority or majority of the whole, who are united and actuated by some common impulse of passion, or of interest, adverse to the rights of other citizens, or to the permanent and aggregate interests of the community. In Madison's definition, he identifies the most serious source of faction to be the diversity of opinion in political life which leads to dispute over fundamental issues such as what regime or religion should be preferred.

Distribution of property was at the core of the debate during Madison's time. At the heart of Madison's fears about factions was the unequal distribution of property in society. The reality of property ownership was that some people owned property and others owned nothing, and Madison felt that people would form different factions that pursued different interests based on such a gap in ownership.

Recognizing that the country's wealthiest property owners formed a minority and that the country's unpropertied classes formed a majority, Madison feared that the unpropertied classes would come together to form a majority faction that gained control of the government. This fear of the minority rising became part of the framing of the American Constitution. Specifically, Madison feared that the unpropertied classes would use their majority power to implement a variety of measures that redistributed wealth in a disordered fashion. In short, Madison feared that a majority faction of the unpropertied classes might emerge to redistribute wealth and property for populist purposes and to the dismay of the ruling class, which would inevitably result in conflict.

4.3 Madison's Arguments for Faction Limitation

Madison first assessed two ways to limit the damage caused by factions: remove the causes or control the effects. He then described the two methods of removing the causes of factions: first, destroying liberty, which would work because liberty is to faction what air is to fire. The second option would be to create a society of homogeneous opinions and interests, which is difficult but not impossible. Madison particularly emphasized that economic stratification prevents everyone from sharing the same opinion. He concluded that the damage caused by factions can be limited only by controlling the effects.

Madison further contended that a person may offer two ways to check majority factions: (1) prevent the existence of the same passion or interest in a majority at the same time or, (2) render a majority faction unable to act. Madison concluded that a small democracy cannot avoid the dangers of a majority faction because small size means that undesirable passions can very quickly spread to a majority of the people, which can then enact its will through the democratic government without difficulty. A republic is different from a democracy because its government is placed in the hands of delegates, and, as a result, can be extended over a larger area. The idea is that, in a large republic, there will be more fit characters to choose from for each delegate.

4.4 Federalist 51 and Checks and Balances

The notion of checks and balances became fundamental in the formation of government. Federalist No. 51 is titled: "The Structure of the Government Must Furnish the Proper Checks and Balances Between the Different Departments." It was another essay by James Madison. This document was published on February 8, 1788, under the pseudonym Publius. Federalist No. 51 addresses a means by which appropriate checks and balances can be created in government and advocates a separation of powers within the national government One of its most important ideas, an explanation of check and balances, is the often-quoted phrase, "Ambition must be made to counteract ambition." In government, it is well known that people will seek to be self-promoting. Madison's idea was that the politicians and the individuals in public service in the United States would all have proclamations and ideas that they would work hard to enact-- this is true for Madison's time as well as now. The solution to ensure that laws and strong ideas were not enacted by a small group of partisan individuals was to use a federalist system where each level of government had different branches, each branch having the authority to impact the operation of the other branches. One of the primary ways that Federalist Paper 51 was able to encourage checks and balances was to tie it to the concept of liberty and an aversion to centralized tyranny. The concentration of power into one branch or level of government is antithetical to liberty. Whenever one branch or institution (of any sort) gets too much power, they become corrupted and tyrannical. As Lord Acton reminds us: "power corrupts; absolute power corrupts absolutely." Checks and balances can be a remedy to the corruption of power.

The system of checks and balances, as espoused by Madison and philosophers like John Locke and Jean-Jacques Rousseau, was designed to allow an independent function of the various branches of government within certain constraints. For example, the legislative branch would draft laws that would have to be signed (or vetoed) by the president. The Supreme Court could strike down the laws if deemed unconstitutional. The president appointed members of the court, but only by an approval vote of the Senate. It was a way to avoid allowing any one branch to gain too much influence and power.

4.5 Changes in Federalism Over Time

The balance of power between states and the national government changes over time. Because the balance of power between state and national government was clearly left open to some interpretation by the founders, it left a lot of power to the Supreme Court for interpretation. Looking at federal/state power relations over time, we can see two trends:

1. Changes like industrialization, urbanization, and advances in science and technology have led citizens to look to the government at all levels for assistance, protection, and security.

2. There is an undeniable shift of power over time from the states to the national government, particularly since the culmination of the Civil War, but some of it as early as the ratification of the Constitution.

There have been some key moments where power has shifted from the states to the federal government. John Marshall's tenure as Chief Justice of the Supreme Court (1801–1835) marked a drastic shift of power from the states to the federal government. **Marshall** was the third Chief Justice of the Supreme Court. He believed in the Federalist vision of a strong national government. One of the ground-breaking cases heard under his tenure was *Marbury v. Madison*. **Marbury v. Madison** (1803) gave the Supreme Court the power of **judicial review** to determine if congressional laws, state laws, or executive actions are constitutional. This ground-breaking change in the role of the judiciary extended the role of checks and balances to the judicial branch with stronger enforcement.

A second key moment that shifted the power from the states to the federal government was the extension of the "Necessary and Proper Clause" in *McCulloch v. Maryland* (1819). The result of this case allowed that clause to be interpreted broadly to include many powers that were not in the Constitution.

The third key moment that shifted the power from the states to the federal governments was *Gibbons v. Ogden*. The extension of the Interstate Commerce Clause and the right to regulate commerce emanating from *Gibbons v. Ogden* (1824) opened the door to federal regulation of commerce, broadly understood to mean most forms of business. The landmark decision in which the Supreme Court of the United States held that the power to regulate interstate commerce, granted to Congress by the Commerce Clause of the United States Constitution, encompassed the power to regulate sea navigation.

4.6 Federalism: Then and Now

Nowadays, advocates of national power tend to be Democrats whose ideology leads them to believe, like the Federalists, that national power is not a threat to individual liberties. Republicans tend to be more like the Anti-Federalists in their distrust of national power and their preference for keeping important decisions at the state level. Republicans have long advocated *devolution*, or the returning of power to the states. Their enthusiasm for that position changes somewhat when they are in control of the federal government. When Republicans control Congress and the executive, many of them are less wary of the reach of the national government because it is doing their bidding. Similarly, when Democrats are out of power, they look to the states to enact their agendas. Today the battle over federalism seems to have less to do with its old framework of limited government versus big government and more to do with the battle for power between two highly polarized parties.

During the first 150 years of the United States, the country practiced something called Dual Federalism. **Dual Federalism (1789-1933)** is when you have a clear division of governing authority between national governments and state governments. One example of this is layer cake federalism, which is when you have a clear division between the authority of the state government.

During the 1930s, President Franklin D. Roosevelt's New Deal programs involved a strengthening and combination of federal/state functions. This included new regulatory agencies such as the Tennessee Valley Authority (TVA). This concept became known as Cooperative Federalism. **Cooperative Federalism (1933-1981)** is the mingling of governing authority between different levels of government. Cooperative federalism featured a much larger role for the federal government, with more money flowing to the states, along with marching orders to go with the cash. States became conduits for federal policy, with federal matching funds there to entice the states to administer programs such as welfare.

President Ronald Reagan (1981-1989) changed how American federalism operated. It was coined **New Federalism**. **New Federalism** was a version of Cooperative Federalism but with less oversight by the federal government. It left more control to the state and local levels. New Federalism was characterized by the administering of Block Grants from the federal government to local governments. This was a way of transferring federal funds to local jurisdictions.

During the Obama administration, President Barrack Obama became known for Progressive Federalism in 2009. **Progressive Federalism** known as modern federalism is when the national government has broad goals but relies on local and state innovation to make sure they are met. Sometimes the federal government has pushed programs onto the states (pay for it yourself). At other times, the federal government has attempted to dictate to the states (the Defense of Marriage Act, No Child Left Behind, the continued criminalization of marijuana and hemp). The Feds have given states money via block grants with few restrictions, categorical grants with lots of restrictions, and revenue sharing with no restrictions. Typical federal funding still often involves matching funds for a specific purpose.

4.7 Tools Used in Modern Federalism

The modern tools used in federalism today are tied to the types of funding and programs that the federal government grants the state governments. One type of tool used by the federal government to fund state programs is a block grant. A **Block grant** gives funds that come with flexibility for the states to spend the money as they wish within broad parameters. Block grants were first introduced in 1966 as a channel for the federal government to give money to specific areas they wanted to improve. These examples in the 1960s included transportation and education. A second tool used by the federal government to fund the state governments is a categorical grant. A **categorical grant** is a grant of money with specific instructions on how it is to be spent. Finally, a third type of funding tool used by the federal government is an unfunded mandate from the federal government to the states. An **unfunded mandate** is when Congress will tell the states to do something but provide no funds for administering the policy. Unfunded mandates include local, state, and federal requirements not in synergy. For the unfunded mandate, there are federal laws or regulations that the local or state government must pay in order to enact a new law.

As one can tell, federalism has taken many shapes and forms in our country's history. There has been a general decline in the influence of the states, but the institutions of government remain similar to what was conceived by the founders of the Constitution. The United States has evolved considerably since the Articles of Confederation and the old debates over the various Federalist Papers. Things are different and they will undoubtedly change more with the passing of time. What will be the future for federalism and power sharing in America?

4.8 American Federalism- Who Really Is In Charge?

American federalism reflects a strong distrust of centralized government. This fundamental distrust of centralized power, along with the perhaps grudging admission that some of it was necessary, led to both the division of federal power into three branches, and the division of power between the states and the national government. So who has the power? The U.S. Constitution does seem to provide some space for a strong national government in a number of places:

1. The "necessary and proper" clause (sometimes called "the elastic clause" because of its ability to stretch to cover a lot of ground) of the Constitution (Article I, Section 8, clause 18): This says Congress shall have the necessary and proper authority to do what needs to be done.

2. The supremacy clause (Article VI, clause 2): The Constitution is established as the supreme law of the land.

3. The commerce clause (Article I, Section 8, clause 3): Only Congress has the ability to regulate interstate commerce.

4. The spending clause (Article I, Section 8, clause 1): Congress is expressly granted the ability to raise taxes and spend money.

Couple these features with the power of the presidency and the national government's greater ability to raise money, and you have a recipe for a strong national government. I don't think this is necessarily a bad thing. Others disagree. Then again, there's the 10th Amendment to the Constitution, and the last piece of the Bill of Rights: "The powers not delegated to the United States by the Constitution, nor prohibited by it to the States, are reserved to the States respectively, or to the people." That can be interpreted in any number of ways, and has been. Does it mean the federal government can only do things expressly described in the Constitution? Does it mean anything not addressed in the Constitution is up to the states? Does it create wiggl room for interpreting the Constitution, or take it away? Some people would tell you they are sure it means one thing or another, and others would simply disagree.

CHAPTER 5

The Declaration of Independence and the United States Constitution

The United States political culture resulted from the influence of English political culture and Western philosophical tradition. Since the United Colonies of America were English provinces, England has historically played an essential role in shaping American economics and culture. The ultimate political enforcer in Colonial English America was the British monarchy, which based its legitimacy on kings' divine rights. The English King was God's legitimate representative on Earth.

Since the independence period, the United States has developed a new political culture that still serves as inspiration for the rest of the world. At the time, there was no model to follow for the United States Founders. The process of writing the constitution required creativity, originality, and clarity. The Founders chose Thomas Jefferson to write the United States Declaration of Independence. The ideas of John Locke served as an inspiration to write the political document. Both legally and politically speaking, the national constitution was the founding document for the United States democracy.

5.1 The roots of the United States political culture

As a former colony, the nation was a political subject of the ruling country—England. America was economically dependent on England, and the United Colonies had cultural ties to it as well. The economic relationship between the mother country and its colonies was called *mercantilism*. England provided protection and settlement costs to the colonists. The colonies sent prime resources and cuts of the profits from their trade back to the mother country. The center of power denied colonists access to the lucrative markets in which England competed.

The ultimate political enforcer in Colonial English America was the British monarchy. England followed the *divine right of kings*, which had its roots in a political culture that understood the power to be vested in the king because he was God's legitimate representative on Earth. This situation put a significant burden on the colonists to produce a counternarrative to justify political independence that did not make them all sinners. As the American colonists began to consider themselves a separate cultural and political entity, the idea of struggling for independence started to look like a desirable and viable option for some American-born Englishmen.

More than anything, the Americans developed a new way of looking at the world during the independence days. The social contract theory was essential to the development of the United States as an independent country. This theory principally emerged and took shape from the writings of the British philosophers Thomas Hobbes and John Locke. In a *social contract*, power is to be held by all citizens, each of whom gives up some of their rights to the government in exchange for the right to use safely and securely the power citizens retained.

The recently-formed government based its legitimacy on the consent of those governed. If the government did not adequately protect and guarantee their remaining rights, subjects had the right to rebel and establish a new government. A government that does not secure the remaining rights of citizens lacks legitimacy.

British political philosopher Thomas Hobbes believed that free men had the right to subject themselves to a ruler who would protect them. The government was an all-powerful entity, and its subjects had no right to push back against its power. On the other hand, John Locke believed that the social contract was conditional upon rights' protection. Governed subjects could revoke the social contract if the government failed to safeguard their rights.

Of all the political thinkers who influenced American beliefs about government, the most relevant was assuredly John Locke, who wrote nearby in time that the founders of the United States were contemplating independence. The ideas of Locke were hugely popular in the United Colonies of America. When discussing the influences of the political philosophy of John Locke, one should start by analysing and focusing on the theory of natural law and rights. However, one should consider that the natural law concept existed long before Locke and was an integral principle of his philosophical theories. The natural law is a way to express universal moral truths that apply to all people. Universal moral law likely served as a preceding influence of the United States Constitution.

In many more than one pamphlet, the United States writers and thinkers cited Locke on natural rights and the social and governmental contract as well; they referred to Montesquieu and Delolme on the character of British freedom and the institutional prerequisites for its fulfilment; Voltaire on the evils and disasters of clerical oppression; Beccaria on the change of criminal law; Grotius, Pufendorf, Burlamaqui; and Vattel on the laws of nature and nations, and the standards of civil government. The pervasiveness of such citations is, on occasion, astonishing.[45]

The most significant early contrast was between natural and generally applicable laws and those conventional, which operated only in those

---

[45] Bailyn, Bernard. *The Ideological Origins of the American Revolution*, 1967. Massachusetts: Belknap Press.

places where specific particular customs existed. Simply put, this is a contrast between a universal moral right and a law created by society depending on culture and historical tradition. This distinction is known as one of the main differences between natural law and positive law.

Natural law also differs from divine law. Divine law is from the Christian tradition and customarily referred to those laws that God had directly revealed through visionary prophets and other enlightened writers. One can discover natural law by reason alone. Natural law applies to all people. On the contrary, one can get in touch with divine law only through God's special revelation, and it is only applicable to those whom the revelation God disclosed. For Locke, the biblical law did not apply to the modern human being[46].

5.2 The Declaration of Independence

The Founders chose Thomas Jefferson to write the *Declaration of Independence.* The ideas of John Locke served as an inspiration to write the document. Locke, born in 1632, is among the most influential political philosophers in history. In the *Two Treatises of Government*, Locke supported the claim that men are by nature free and equal against those that said that God had made all people naturally subject to a divinely-legitimate monarch. He argued that humans have natural rights, such as the right to life, liberty, and property.

The rights to life, liberty, and property are universal and natural. These rights have a foundation independent of the cultural and consuetudinary law built on any particular society's traditions. Locke stated that all men are naturally free and equal as part of the justification for understanding the legitimate political government that results from the social contract. This social contract is a condition in which people in the state of nature conditionally transfer some of their rights to the government,

---

[46] For an in-depth analysis of Locke's influence in United States independence, see Bailyn.

which subjects expect to provide stable and comfortable enjoyment of their lives, liberty, and property.

The Declaration of Independence is a political document about changing the rules about what makes power legitimate and who should reasonably hold it. The historical record represents the social contract between the government and the U.S. people. By relying on the social contract, the Declaration of Independence stated that Americans had *inalienable rights* that subjects could not give up to the government.

One should acknowledge that the American Constitution created the modern notion of citizens distinct from subjects. Even if related, both terms are not equivalent. The United States constitution writers laid blame on George III for breaking a political contract he barely understood. This incident was one of the main circumstances that legitimated the Americans' rebellion. It also attempted to convince the leaders of other colonial powers like Spain and France that they had nothing to worry about since supposedly they were not tyrants like George, King of Great Britain, and Ireland. Not every person in the new country was a citizen with full political rights. The task of creating a new government was not as easy as they had hoped, and it took more than one try to get things done right.

5.3 The United States Constitution

The constitution is the framework for the legal system of the United States. Depending upon the constitution's definition and since some Nation-States do not have a formal central constitution like the United States, one can argue that the United States Constitution is the oldest codified constitutional text still in use today. The United States Constitution is divided into Articles and Amendments. Congress Representatives have updated the American Constitution over the years, and courts continue to argue the text's applications. Both legally and politically speaking, the national constitution was the founding document for the United States democracy.

The Preamble of the United States Constitution—the document's famous first fifty-two words— introduces everything to follow in the Constitution's seven articles and twenty-seven amendments. It proclaims who is adopting this Constitution: "We the People of the United States." It describes why the country adopts the Constitution—the purposes behind the enactment of America's governing charter. Furthermore, it explains the principles adopted, as the United Constitution, a single authoritative written text, serves as the land's fundamental law.

While accurate, the word "preamble" does not quite capture the full importance of this provision. "Preamble" implies that these words are merely an opening rhetorical flourish or frill without meaningful effect. To be sure, "preamble" usefully conveys the idea that this provision does not itself confer or delineate powers of government or rights of citizens, outlined in the substantive articles and amendments that follow in the main body of the constitution's text.

5.4 The Articles of Confederation

Before the Civil War, the two leading and legislative power-affecting doctrines of American Constitutional Law were the Doctrine of Vested Rights and the Police Power Doctrine, both complementary to each other. The first one presumably flourished before the rise of the Jacksonian Democracy style in the United States. The Doctrine of the Vested Rights is the more fundamental doctrine[47].

The United States Constitution has a foundation in the Articles of Confederation. The founders' primary duty was to write a constitution or political rulebook that would determine who would have power, how that power would be limited, and how the new government functioned. The first constitution has been historically known as the *Articles of Confederation*. Because the states viewed themselves as sovereign, they

---

[47] Corwin, Edward. "The Basic Doctrine of American Constitutional Law." *Michigan Law Review*, vol. 12, no. 4, 1914, pp. 247–276. *JSTOR*, www.jstor.org/stable/1276027.

decided to limit their new constitution to a "firm league of friendship" amongst states rather than a complete union entity. This change was about the establishment of a *United States Confederation.* Economic troubles, drought, and crop failures meant that there were heavy demands for relief from state governments.

The Articles of Confederation provided new restrictions on the government's power. The national government was not allowed to take some measures under the Articles of Confederation, such as draft soldiers' power. Drafting soldiers allowed for a robust military force; whoever, not allowing a draft made it challenging to coordinate a response to a threat from a foreign power. The Articles of Confederation stopped citizens' taxation, making the Federal government dependent on the states for funds. The Articles could not regulate interstate commerce; consequently, it left the states to create their own markets, economic rules, and more. Furthermore, the Articles forbid establishing a central monetary system and having different currencies in each state.

The last draft of the Articles of Confederation, which framed the new country's government's basis, was acknowledged by Congress in November 1777 and submitted to the states for endorsement. It would not become the tradition that must be adhered to until every one of the thirteen states had endorsed it. Within two years, all except for Maryland had done so. Maryland contended that all domains west of the Appalachians, to which a few states had laid case, should instead be held by the public government as open land to help every state. When the remainder of these states, Virginia, surrendered its property claims in mid-1781, Maryland affirmed the Confederation Articles. Half a month later, the British capitulated. Americans aspired their new government to be a republic, wherein people, not a monarch or ruler, held power and chose agents to oversee as per law and order.

Many feared that a country as large as the United States would not be managed successfully as a republic. Those voices also stressed that even an administration of delegates elected by the people might become too powerful and overbearing. Subsequently, public administrators created a confederation as an entity in which independent, self-governing states form a union to act together in defense areas. Unfortunate of supplanting one abusive public government with another. Nonetheless, the Articles of Confederation's composers made collusion of sovereign states held together by a feeble focal government.[48]

The result of the problems with the Articles led to economic problems. When economic chaos arose, so did Shay's Rebellion. Shay's Rebellion was a march of angry farmers demanding debt relief in western Massachusetts. This rebellion drove some of the founders to meet in Annapolis in 1786 to discuss fixing the dysfunctional Articles. Later, some at the gathering in Annapolis decided the Articles were too broken to fix, and thus they decided to create a whole new Constitution instead.

5.5 The Constitutional Convention

The drafting of a new national constitution began with the Constitutional Convention of 1787. The most significant fracture came between two groups, the first known as the Federalists and the second as the Anti-Federalists. The Federalists were those who wanted a more robust national government. The prospect of a stronger government less threatened the Federalists because they mainly were representatives of large states who felt they could control national government power. Over time, they were known as the Federalists because they preferred to get rid of the Articles' confederal system, where the states ultimately held power and moved to a federal system, where power would be shared between states and national government.

There were multiple plans put forth at the Constitutional Convention as proposals for the new government. One plan put forward was a bicameral legislature by Virginia. The *Virginia Plan* was a comparatively strong but limited government whose signature institution would be a *bicameral legislature* (meaning it would have two chambers). The

---

[48] Corwin, 33-44.

representation in both chambers would be based on population and taxes paid. On the other hand, the Anti-Federalists were against a robust national government on principle and out of fear. They would have preferred to tweak the Articles to make them more valuable and practical. Mostly, representatives of smaller states feared a more robust government would roll over them, and the big states would always get their way. The *New Jersey Plan* wanted a slightly upgraded Articles of Confederation—a single chamber of the legislature where every state cast one vote, with a weak executive and a nonexistent court system, but some additional powers for the national government.

The solution to this political crisis was the agreements on compromises. The **Great Compromise** was "great" because it effectively worked to bring the two sides together. However, it was more remarkable for the Federalists than the Anti-Federalists since the outcome exceeded its initial expectations. The Federalists truly benefited from the negotiation results. The Compromise the two groups agreed on called for a bicameral legislature that split the difference between the two political sides. Parliamentary representation was based on the state's population in the House of Representatives. Every state received two members, regardless of population, in the Senate.

The result of the Great Compromise was the *Three-Fifths Compromise* indicates that, when determining representation, the population count would be made "by adding to the whole Number of Free persons ... three-fifths of all other persons." Both the Great Compromise and the Three-Fifths Compromise reduced the national government's popular control by countering it with state control and significantly empowering smaller, rural states.

The concerns of southern states to boost their power vis-a-vis the north had another lasting effect on the United States Constitution: we do not elect the United States president by direct popular vote. Instead, we have the Electoral College. In this settlement, the states had more power to choose the president. The number of electors a state gets in the Electoral College (that is, the number of votes that a state can cast for president) is determined by the total number of representatives that that state has in both houses. The South fought a direct popular presidential election because actual population totals would have determined the presidency in some cases.

5.6 Basic Constitutional Principles

The American founders had created a document that was path-breaking in its innovative approach to human governance. Several nations have throughout the years used the United States Constitution as an inspiration, but at the time, there was no model for the American founders to follow. The writers of the national constitution were original and have inspired other states throughout history. *James Madison* was the genius behind the United States Constitution. His fundamental idea was to design a system that takes human nature *as it is* (self-interested, greedy, and ambitious), not as you want it to be. James Madison wanted to create an internal mechanism based on the idea that human nature will produce fair laws and public policy because of it, not despite it.

Basic principles of the United States provided by the national constitution are to have separation of powers[49], checks and balances, and federalism. The United States Constitution gives the three branches of government their own powers, shared powers, and checked powers. In some countries, these functions are not separated (i.e., a *parliamentary system*).

Separation of powers is the government's division vertically into three branches: legislative, executive, and judicial. This power division gives each layer and branch independent status with some of its constitutional power.

The founders thought a presidential system would better protect against abuses of power. In the United States, we have a *presidential system*: the executive and the other two branches are constitutionally distinct.

---

[49] On the separation of powers in the United States constitution, see Corwin.

The three are given their own powers according to the United States Constitution. *Checks and balances* give each layer and branch just enough power over the others in its system that their jealousy will guard against the others' over-reach. Simply put, the *legislative branch* is the lawmaking component, the *executive branch* is the law-enforcing component, and the *judicial branch* is the law-interpreting component. *Federalism* divides the government horizontally into layers: national and state.

5.7 Constitutional Powers

The United States Constitution provides powers to the Federal government and the states. The constitutional provisions fostered federalism's development. Article I Section 8 (*enumerated powers*) spells out exactly what Congress (and hence the national government) is allowed to do, including coining money and managing interstate commerce.

The *necessary and proper clause* coming at the end of the enumerated powers indicates Congress can do anything "necessary and proper" to carry out its duties suitably. The United States constitution's necessary and proper clause defines the Congress's authority to exercise the necessary and proper powers it needs to carry out its designated functions. This power or clause of the United States Constitution also goes by a similar name, *the elastic clause,* because it stretches the national government's authority to include or imply anything written in the United States Constitution's text. In practice, this clause generally strengthens the national government at the expense of state power.

The *Tenth Amendment to the United States Constitution* indicates that any powers not explicitly given to the national government are reserved to the states. It ultimately depends on what the Court says, and the Court changes its mind repeatedly. Who gets the advantage? It is pretty much a tie; the balance of national state power again depends on judicial interpretation.

In Article VI of the Constitution, the *supremacy clause* states that the constitutional text itself and national laws made under it are the land's law. This clause found in the Constitution defines the national government's authority. The supremacy clause says that the national government's authority prevails over state or local government claims provided that power was given to the federal government. This idea found in the United States Constitution provides the federal government's implied powers, and when laws between States and Federal governments clash, the Federal Government's laws are supreme and take priority over the state's laws. Who gets the advantage? If national law clashes with state law, national law almost always wins if the federal government chooses to impose its will.

The founders were well aware of the tension between the states themselves as a threat to national stability. The United States Constitution's framers developed a formal way to balance federal vs. state rights. The *Constitution's full faith and credit clause* (Article IV, Section 1) says that the states have to respect the other states' legal proceedings and public acts. An example of the full faith and credit clause includes one's driver's license, which must be accepted across state lines as a valid form of identification. The *privileges and immunities clause* (Article IV, Section 2) indicates a state cannot deny a citizen of another state the rights its citizens enjoy.

The balance has changed over time, but the national government has often gained power at the states' expense. Battles over federalism are typically fought in the states, except for the Civil War. The history of federalism proves that national and state governments have periodically checked each other over time.

CHAPTER 6

Civil Liberties

6.1 Introduction to Civil Liberties

What is the difference between civil rights and civil liberties? It is the word *civil*—having to do with the non-political life of citizens—that gives the phrases *civil rights* and *civil liberties* specific and different meanings. In democracies and other non-authoritarian societies where, at least some political power is held by citizens, both civil liberties and civil rights are essential to operational societies. Civil liberties are individual rights that come from the *limitation of* government power. Civil rights *empower the government* to give us group rights. You could say civil liberties are about equal protection *from* the law and civil rights are about the equal protection *of* the laws.

So, what do civil liberties and civil rights actually mean in order to differentiate from one another? **Civil liberties** are the individual freedoms that limit government. These rights are guaranteed by the Bill of Rights and the text of the Constitution itself. Some others, like the right to privacy, come from Supreme Court decisions that have interpreted the Constitution. **Civil rights** are the freedom of groups to fully participate in the public life of a nation. These groups are defined by some particular characteristic—like race, gender, or sexual orientation—that is beyond their members' control. Rather than limiting government, the protection of civil rights often *empowers the government* to act.

6.2 Rights Equal Power

Giving citizenry rights empowers the people. Rights confer power on people and limitations on government. When a person has the ability to claim a right, it makes one a citizen, not a subject. The ability to deny rights gives citizens power over each other. The ability to use government to fight back against those who would deny their fellow citizens rights is also a form of power.

6.3 Where do our rights come from?

If we believe we have rights because the government, the Constitution, the Bill of Rights or any other amendments grant them to us, then those rights can also be taken away. These rights differ from **natural rights**, which are the inalienable rights conferred by "Nature and Nature's God" that no government can take away.

The rights of American citizens provided by the Constitution and the Bill of Rights are limited in two main ways. First, they become limited when they clash with other people's rights. Second, is when they conflict with collective societal values. Solving rights conflicts often involve compromise. These conflicts are resolved by different aspects of government such as Congress, the President and the bureaucracy, the courts, and the people.

6.4 The Bill of Rights

The Bill of Rights established the fundamental constitutional rights afforded to every American. These important rights are included in the Bill of Rights. These rights are:

- Amendment 1: Establishment clause, free exercise of religion, free speech, free press, right to assemble.

- Amendment 2: Right to bear arms necessary for a well-regulated militia.

- Amendment 3: You can't be forced to house soldiers during peace.

- Amendment 4: No unreasonable searches and seizures.

- Amendment 5: Grand jury indictment for capital crimes; no double jeopardy, self-incrimination, or deprivation of property without due process of law.

- Amendment 6: Right to a speedy trial and counsel.

- Amendment 7: Jury trials for civil cases where the value in controversy is over $20.

- Amendment 8: No cruel or unusual punishment or excessive bail.

- Amendment 9: The rights listed in the Constitution does not limit the possession of other rights.

- Amendment 10: All rights not given to the national government are reserved to the states.

The founders struggled with having a Bill of Rights. Alexander Hamilton argued in *Federalist* #84 that a Bill of Rights might be redundant, because the founders' intent was to create a government that was already powerless to do the things the Bill of Rights ruled out. All of the founders feared a powerful government; they just differed on ways to limit it. The Federalists thought they had created internal mechanisms—separation of powers, checks and balances—that would keep the government from over-reaching. The Anti-Federalists wanted to spell out restrictions on the government—limiting powers the Federalists didn't think the Constitution conferred.

The Bill of Rights limited the national government's power. On its face, the Bill of Rights applies to the national government and specifically to Congress. But most Americans don't interact with the federal government or commit federal crimes. States may have their own Bill of Rights within their own state constitutions, but states are not required to guarantee these rights and there are no regulations about what their state constitutions should cover.

The power of the states is checked or held accountable by the federal government. Americans are not helpless if a state denies them a basic right. **The Fourteenth Amendment** was originally drafted and intended to stop southern states from denying former slaves their citizenship rights after the Civil War. Using a process called **incorporation**, the Court was able to fold the national right into required state protections via the Fourteenth Amendment. Language in the Fourteenth Amendment can be interpreted to mean that no state can deny a citizen any of the rights the federal government guarantees. With incorporation, the Supreme Court expanded the national power at the expense of the state, changing the balance of federal power.

6.5 Civil Liberties—Understanding the First Amendment

The basic civil liberties of Americans include all the rights the founders felt were necessary to keep the states in check. The most important of those rights they packed into the First Amendment, because they wanted to indicate their primary importance. The reason that this amendment covers so many rights is that, for the founders, these were all fundamental to a fully functioning democracy.

The First Amendment prohibits Congress from establishing a religion or interfering with the exercise of religion, abridging the freedom of speech or the press, or interfering with the right of the people to assemble. These prohibitions have been made applicable to the states through the Fourteenth Amendment. The freedoms, however, are not absolute and encompass different boundaries that have been established by judicial interpretation.

6.6 Freedom of Religion.

Freedom of religion was important to the founders. The founders' main task was to write a constitution, or rulebook, that would determine how the new government was to function, who would have power, and how that power would be limited. The Articles of Confederation gave the foundational importance to the writing of the Bill of Rights because religious freedom was at the forefront of the founders' minds. Many of the original colonists had fled England to avoid an established church in the first place.

The First Amendment has two clauses that establish freedom of religion. The First Amendment provides "Congress shall make no law respecting an establishment of religion or prohibiting the free exercise thereof".

Establishment Clause

First, the **Establishment Clause** was designed to limit Congress and ensure that Congress shall make no law respecting an establishment of religion. The role of the state is to accommodate all religions. Unfortunately, this first amendment guarantee can be divisive. **Accommodationists** are people who want to support "all" religions equally. This is opposed to **separationists**: people who want a separation between church and state. Americans and, indeed, members of the Supreme Court, are divided on whether we need to keep church and state entirely separate, or whether it is okay to allow some state recognition and support for religion as long as it accommodates all religions. What is a constitutional issue—how far church and state can be intermingled—has become a cultural clash that it is almost impossible to solve to everyone's satisfaction.

The first step is to determine if the law has a religious preference. When determining if a law or government program violates the Establishment Clause and includes a preference for some religious sects over others, the law or program will be subject to a compelling interest analysis and ask if it is **narrowly tailored** to promote a **compelling interest**. In *Board of Education v. Grumet*, the Supreme Court struck down a state law that created a public school district whose boundaries were intentionally set to match the boundaries of a particular Jewish neighborhood.

Since the government had no other interest rather than one that was furthered by "religious favoritism", the Court held it failed to exercise governmental authority in a religiously neutral way.[50] Therefore, if there is a preference and the law is not crafted in a religiously neutral way, it will receive the compelling interest test.

Secondly, if there is no religious preference, and the compelling interest test is not used, then the law is subject to the Lemon Test. The **Lemon Test** was established in *Lemon v. Kurtzman* to provide a constitutional understanding on how much the government can establish a religion. The law or program will be valid under the Establishment Clause if it:

1. Has a **secular** purpose

2. Has a **primary effect** that neither **advances** nor **inhibits** religion; and

3. Does not produce excessive government **entanglement** with religion.[51]

"Secular", as opposed to sacred, means not having a religious, spiritual or temporal basis. If the government maintains a holiday-Christmas Times display that does not appear to endorse one religion and includes holiday decorations, such as a Christmas tree or a Santa Claus figure, the court will hold that the display has a **secular purpose** based on the history of government recognition of holidays.[52]

If the law **advances** or **inhibits** a particular religion or specific religious group, then that law will be invalid. But if a law favors or burdens a larger segment of society that happens to include religious groups, it will generally be upheld. For example, the IRS may provide deductions and other financial benefits to churches and other religious donations because the **primary effect** of the benefit does not only include religious

---

[50] *Board of Education v. Grumet*, 512 v. 687 (1994).

[51] *Lemon v. Kurtzman*, 403 U.S. 602 (1971).

[52] *County of Allegheny v. ACLU*, 492 U.S. 573 (1989).

organizations- but it also applies to all charitable organizations that happen to include religious groups.[53]

It is hard for the Court to decide what "excessive entanglement" means. **Excessive entanglement** can mean too much government involvement. There are times when government action can cross paths with private religions. It becomes excessive when government action crosses into religious action that they can run afoul of other people's actions or the state's obligation to exercise its police power to protect the health, well-being, and security of all citizens. For example, if a public school allows members of the public and private organizations to use school property when classes are not in session and a religious organization utilizes the space and the meetings are not run by school personnel, there is no excessive government entanglement.[54] The government was not a significant actor.

Free Exercise Clause

The freedom from an establishment of a religion afforded the free exercise of religion for the founders. Because the government cannot establish one or more religions means people have the freedom to practice any religion. The **Free Exercise Clause** states that Congress shall make no law… prohibiting the free exercise thereof.[55] The trouble with those words spelling out religious freedom protection is that they contain an inherent contradiction. Any effort to establish one of the founders' denominations as the official state religion would have doomed the new country from the start. When political differences are reinforced with religious differences, every conflict is infused with profound meaning and compromise is impossible. When a government can put the power of an Almighty behind its laws, it is very hard to resist it if it over-reaches.

[53] *Hernandez v. Commissioner of Internal Revenue*, 490 U.S. 680 (1989).
[54] *Good News Club v. Milford Central School*, 533 U.S. (2001).
[55] U.S. Const. Amend I.

The Free Exercise Clause prohibits the government from punishing, denying benefits to or imposing burdens on someone on the basis of the person's religious beliefs. For many years the Supreme Court had suggested that the government had to show it had a compelling reason to infringe on religious practice. But in 1990 it reversed course and put the burden of proof back on religious groups to show that the state regulation has violated the groups' rights. However, the test for such impermissible government action remains unclear as the Court has never found an interest that was so compelling that it would justify punishing or regulating a religious belief.

The Court has directed that the Free Exercise Clause prohibits the government from punishing conduct merely because it is religious or displays religious belief.[56] A law that is designed to suppress actions only because the actions are religiously motivated is not a neutral law and would be invalid. A city law that prohibits a precise type of animal slaughtering for a particular religion violates the Free Exercise clause because the law was not neutral and did not prohibit all animal slaughtering.[57]

But the states can prohibit or regulate conduct in general, and this is true even if the prohibition or regulation happens to interfere with a person's religious practices. The Free Exercise Clause does not require exemptions from criminal laws or other regulations. A law that regulates conduct of all persons can be applied to prohibit the conduct of a person despite the fact that his or her religious beliefs prevent him or her from complying with the law. For example, the prohibition against the use of peyote was permissible if it applied generally to all persons, even if individuals require use of peyote during religious ceremonies.[58]

---

[56] *Employment Division v. Smith.*
[57] *Church of the Lukumi v. Babalu Aye, Inc. v. Hialeah,* 508 U.S. 520 (1993).
[58] *Employment Division v. Smith.*

But what is a religious belief?

The Supreme Court has not defined or laid out elements for what constitutes a religious belief. However, it has made clear that religious beliefs do not require recognition of a supreme being[59] and need not arise from a traditional, or even an organized, religion.[60]

6.7 Why freedom of expression is a BIG deal

As important to the founders in limiting government as freedom from an established religion was **freedom of expression**. Freedom of expression includes speech, press, and **freedom of assembly**, the right to join together with other persons for expressive or political activity. While freedom of speech and press are mentioned in the First Amendment, freedom of association is not mentioned but is still protected by the First Amendment. The freedom of speech protects the free flow of ideas, a most important function in a democratic society. A regulation or law that tries to forbid speech of specific ideas (**content regulation**) is more likely to violate the free speech doctrine. It is usually unconstitutional for the government to prohibit speech based on its content. In *Brandenburg v. Ohio*, the Court held that the government could not prohibit political speech, or speech with political content, unless it is linked to immediate lawless behavior[61]. However, **conduct regulation**, which is content-neutral and regulates how the speech is conducted, is more likely permitted (*i.e.*, law prohibiting billboards for purposes of traffic safety).

Speech and communication, and its conduct from which it is expressed, can take many forms and, if that conduct is intended to express an idea, can still be protected under the First Amendment much like content speech. In *Masterpiece Cakeshop v. Colorado Civil Rights*

---

[59] *Torcaso v. Watkins*, 367 U.S. 488 (1961).
[60] *Frazee v. Illinois Department of Employment Security*, 489 U.S. 829 (1989).
[61] *Brandenburg v. Ohio*, 395 U.S. 444 (1969)

Commission, a cake shop owner refused to sell a wedding cake to a same sex couple, claiming, in part, requiring him to create the cake would violate his First Amendment right to free speech by compelling him to exercise his artistic talents to express a message with which he disagreed. The Court did not rule on the speech claim but agreed with the Court of Appeals holding that preparing a wedding cake is not a form of protected speech or would force the cake shop owner to adhere to and express an ideological point of view. In their concurring opinion, Justices Kagen and Breyer, note and insinuate that cake making is certainly a conduct for which speech is expressed, which is generally permitted. However, the Justices noted that "the Court has recognized a wide array of conduct that can qualify as expressive, including nude dancing, wearing a military uniform and conducting a silent sit-in" and cake making also be a type of protected speech conduct if it intends to express an idea. Here the Justices suggest that conduct, like making a cake, can be protected speech if the cake maker uses his artistic talent of cake making as an expression of value, or opinion. [62]

Freedom of expression is important predominantly for the right to criticize the government. Denying free speech sets a dangerous precedent—if we can stop our opponents from speaking out today, they might stop us from speaking out tomorrow. So, if free speech is so important, why do we ever limit it?

The Supreme Court has at various times ruled that speech (and symbolic speech) can be limited. As indicated above, very few restrictions on the content of speech are tolerated. The Court allows them only to prevent grave injury. The following is a list of the reasons for which the Court has allowed content-based restrictions on speech:

- For purposes of national security during war (**sedition**)
- Because it is **obscene**

---

[62] *Masterpiece Cakeshop v. Colorado Civil Rights Commission*, 138 S. Ct. 1719 (2018).

- Speech that is inherently likely to incite immediate physical retaliation (**fighting words**)
- Because it maliciously damages a reputation (**libel** when printed; **slander** when spoken)

To determine what is unprotected speech, the Court has come up with a series of tests, many of which have introduced even more ambiguity. The **clear and present danger test** was meant to distinguish speech that was immediately harmful from that posed only a remote threat.[63] The **imminent lawless action test** protected speech unless it was directed to producing or inciting imminent lawless action and is likely to produce or incite such action.[64] The ***Miller* test** defines standards for obscenity and asks whether the work lacks "serious literary, artistic, political, or scientific value".[65] The **prior restraint test** prohibits censoring and refusing to allow the publication of something, even though it very well might fail one of its tests after publication. The Supreme Court has been fairly steady on its refusal to engage in prior restraint.[66] Only a national emergency could justify such censorship.

6.8 Electronic communication makes it vastly more complicated.

In addition to the wide variety of types of speech discussed above, electronic communication can also be a type of speech. The question as to whether media companies can limit access to the internet is evolving. The role of **net neutrality** is the way the Internet works now on the principle that service providers cannot speed up or slow down access for customers or make decisions about the content they see or the apps they download. The Supreme Court is constantly, and likely indefinitely,

---

[63] *Scheneck v. United States*, 249 U.S. 47 (1919).
[64] *Brandenberg v. Ohio*, 395 U.S. 444 (1969).
[65] *Miller v. California*, 413 U.S. 15 (1973).
[66] *Near v. Minnesota*, 283 U.S. 697 (1931)

interpreting the Free Speech Clause to keep up with new types of speech created through new technology.

6.9 Civil Liberties—Understanding Due Process Rights

What are due process rights? **Due process rights** are the rights that give Americans some protections against being railroaded into jail by the police and the courts, especially for political purposes. The founders devote half the Bill of Rights to this subject to protect the citizens from a police state. A chief fear of the founders was a government so strong that its leaders could use the police power and the judicial system for political purposes. These protections provide that the government shall not take a person's life, liberty, or property without due process of law. Due process contemplates fair procedures, which at least require at least an opportunity to present objections to the proposed action to a fair, neutral decision maker, like a judge. There are two separate clauses protecting due process: (1) The Due Process Clause in the Fifth Amendment (applies to the federal government) and (2) The Due Process Clause in the Fourteenth Amendment (applies to state and local governments).

6.10 What do the due process rights include?

Article I provides that Congress cannot suspend habeas corpus, pass a bill of attainder, and pass an ex post facto law. Congress cannot suspend a person's right to be brought before a judge. The writ of **habeas corpus** is the right from unlawful imprisonment and includes the right to be brought before a judge and informed of the charges and evidence against you. The due process rights of people cannot be violated by acts of Congress unduly targeting them by passing a bill of attainer. A **bill of attainder** is a law directed at an individual or group that accuses and convicts them without a trial. The due process of people is so important that Congress was precluded from making laws to incriminate people for actions previously committed. An **ex post facto law** is a law that makes a criminal act (not civil regulation, such as denial of a professional license) illegal that was innocent when done, or "after the fact", hereby not allowing an accused to make an informed decision about the legality of his or her actions before he or she acts.[67] The right to be brought before a judge, informed of the law and charges and receiving a trial, ensures a due or appropriate judicial process before a conviction.

Due process rights include civil liberties. The **exclusionary rule** prohibits evidence from being introduced at a criminal trial if it was obtained by violating your civil liberties protected under the Constitution. The main purpose of the exclusionary rule is to deter the government, usually the police, from violating a person's civil liberties and constitutional rights. If the government cannot use evidence obtained in violation of a person's rights, it will be less likely to infringe on the person's rights.

The right to self-protection in a police arrest is guaranteed under the Fifth Amendment which provides that no person "shall be compelled to be a witness against himself…".[68] This has been interpreted to establish a guarantee against compelled incrimination. *Miranda* **rights** come from the case that established that you have the right to be told that you possess these rights and guarantees.[69] Miranda rights are a set of warnings that must be given to an accused person that is in custody prior to any police interrogation. In order for the accused statement's to be later admissible in court, the accused must be clearly informed that: (1) he or she has the right to remain silent, (2) anything he or she says can be used against him in court, (3) he or she has the right to an attorney, and (4) if he or she cannot afford an attorney, one will be appointed.

While the above are some examples, additional civil rights and liberties include a right to be told why you are being arrested, a right to not

---

[67] U.S. Const. Art. I §9 prohibits the federal government and U.S. Const. Art. I §10 prohibits the states from passing ex post facto laws.

[68] U.S. Const. Amend. V.

[69] *Miranda v. Arizona*, 384 U.S. 436 (1966).

be tried twice for the same crime, a right to an attorney and the right to resist questioning.

6.11 Civil Liberties—Understanding the Right to Privacy

What is the right to privacy? While one can argue that the founders created a limited government and never intended it to be powerful enough to infringe on the private lives of Americans, none of them thought it a serious enough threat to put it into the document itself. The right to privacy is a judicial creation of the Supreme Court in the 1965 case of *Griswold v. Connecticut.*[70] In this case the Court declared that the Constitution does guarantee a "zone of privacy" within a "penumbra" of existing fundamental constitutional guarantees and amendments. Since there was no actual right to privacy mentioned in the Constitution or any of the amendments, the justices "found" such a right to be implied in the Bill of Rights. These specific rights for privacy emanated from:

- The First Amendment protection of one's beliefs and speech
- The Fourth Amendment protection against unreasonable searches and seizures
- The Fifth Amendment protection against self-incrimination
- The Ninth Amendment's promise that one's rights weren't limited to the ones enumerated in the document

The Supreme Court extended this right to privacy marriage, sexual relations, abortion, childrearing and LGTBQ rights in later decisions. The right to privacy has become controversial because, through constant interpretation of the Constitution, the Court creates new rights not explicit in the Constitution. The disagreement arises because the precedent set in *Griswold* was the basis for the landmark, and most

---

[70] *Griswold v. Connecticut*, 381 U.S. 479 (1965).

controversial, decision in *Roe v. Wade*, which held the right to privacy includes the right to abortion with some limitations.[71] Although contraception may not be all that controversial when considered today (unless we are talking about the provision of health care), abortion still definitely is decades after the *Roe* decision.

The conflict over the right to privacy brings us back to Hamilton's *Federalist #84*. Underlying this controversy is an interesting constitutional issue: whether the Constitution should be read literally as the founders wrote it or whether it can be read flexibly in the light of contemporary circumstances. The first position is exactly the argument that Hamilton feared would be made if a Bill of Rights were to be attached to the Constitution. The right to privacy has become a target of those who argue that position.

The method in which the court systems interpret the Constitution can be either strict constructionists or judicial interpretivists. **Strict constructionists** are scholars and judges who believe that the Constitution should be read just as it was written. **Judicial interpretivists** are those who believe that the founders could not have anticipated all the changes that make the world today different from theirs and, therefore, that judges should read the Constitution as the founders would write it in light of modern-day experience. Strict constructionists generally interpret the Constitution to limit rights to privacy, while judicial interpretivists recognize the evolving right to privacy as implied in the Constitution.

The method in which a justice interprets the Constitution determines how rights are created from the constitution. The political significance of this argument today can give people new civil rights and liberties or take them away. Since individual interpretations of the Constitution have such clear policy implications, Supreme Court confirmation hearings have often become battlegrounds as well. Reproductive rights are not the only ones that fall under the right to privacy. Supporters of LGBTQ rights tried to use the right to privacy to fight laws

---

[71] *Roe v. Wade, 410 U.S. 113 (1973).*

that criminalized homosexual behavior but were initially unsuccessful. Slowly, the Court recognized the LGBT community has some protections under the right to privacy by holding unmarried couples (largely LGBTQ couples since same sex marriage was illegal at the time) had the same right to obtain contraception as married couples.[72] The movement has had setbacks in 1986 when the Court held that the Constitutional guarantees don't prohibit states from criminalizing sex between people of the same sex. In *Bowers v. Hardwick*, the Court held that the right of privacy recognized in cases such as *Griswold* and *Roe* does not prevent the criminalization of homosexual conduct between consenting adults. [73] The opinion of the Supreme Court pendulum swung again in 2003 and reversed their prior decision and held that the due process clause gave people "the full right to engage in private conduct without government intervention…[and there is] no legitimate state interest which can justify its intrusion into the individual's personal and private life."[74]

A landmark decision in 2015 held that the fundamental right to marry under the right to privacy is guaranteed to same-sex couples in *Obergefell v. Hodges*.[75] While the law is slowly moving in the direction to eventually provide full equal protection for the LGTBQ community, it is likely that real change will be incremental, and the movement has a long way to go.

Recently, the Supreme Court overturned Roe v. Wade. ***Dobbs v. Jackson Women's Health Organization, 597 U.S. ___ (2022)*** Supreme Court case that reversed *Roe v. Wade* and *Planned Parenthood of Southeastern Pennsylvania v. Casey*, the decisions that originally asserted the fundamental right to an abortion prior to the viability of the fetus. *Dobbs v. Jackson* states that the Constitution does not confer a right to abortion;

---

[72] *Eisenstadt v. Baird*, 405 U.S. 438 (1972).
[73] *Bowers v. Hardwick*, 478 U.S. 186 (1986).
[74] *Lawrence v. Texas*, 539 U.S. 558 (2003).
[75] *Obergefell v. Hodges*, 576 U.S. 644 (2015)

and the authority to regulate abortion is "returned to the people and their elected representatives."

The overturning of Roe v. Wade last summer dramatically changed the landscape for people seeking reproductive care. It has impacted other aspects of American privacy as well. Since the Dobbs decision, concerns about data privacy have grown. Research has shown that mainstream period tracking apps have faulty or weak security. A person's browser history, search history, location and private messages can be used by law enforcement or private citizens to pursue people who are suspected of having or aiding an abortion. There are cases in which American prosecutors have used text messages and online research as evidence against women facing criminal charges related to the end of their pregnancies. In Nebraska, a woman was charged with helping her teenage daughter end her pregnancy at about 24 weeks after investigators uncovered Facebook messages in which the two discussed using medication to induce an abortion. The landscape of privacy is changing.

CHAPTER 7

Civil Rights in America

Chapter summary

Not all people have always had equality under the law in the United States of America. The dilemma of equal protection is vital to ensure that some people in America do not have more rights afforded them than others. Discrimination occurs when the government treats its citizens differently and usually takes the form of denying a benefit or imposing a burden or penalty on a group of persons simply because of a societal dislike for that social class. The deal is to know what kinds of discrimination are permitted and what kinds are not.

Slavery abolitionists and women's rights, and African American civil rights movements set a precedent in American political history. Three civil rights amendments to the United States Constitution, the Fifteenth, Nineteenth, and Twenty-Sixth— prevent both the states and the federal government from abridging citizens' right to vote based on race, sex, and age. Their tactics to engage people around spreading their ideas and their tricks to influence public opinion and the policymaking process still serve as inspiration these days. The rights gained have significantly improved the quality of life for many in America, especially for minorities. Boycotting and desegregation practices are still prevalent among human rights activists.

7.1 Introduction to Civil Rights in America

Civil rights are constitutionally supported, which guarantees that government officials will treat citizens equally and base their decisions on merit rather than race, gender, or other personal characteristics. In the United States of America, it is unlawful for a school or university to discriminate against a student based on its identity and background. In the 1960s and 1970s, many states still had separate schools where only students of a certain race or gender could study and afford a career. Over time, the courts ruled that these policies violated students' civil rights who could not be admitted because of those discriminatory rules.

Although the United States Constitution, as written in 1787, did not formally include a *Bill of Rights*, the idea was proposed and discussed. United States Constitution framers decided to dismiss the bill during the final week of the Constitutional Convention. They dismissed it because there were more important issues to address since the union was still weak and national unrest was still likely to happen. Besides, they perceived that they already had appropriately covered rights concerns in the American Constitution's main body.

The United States' founding principles are liberty, equality, and justice. Throughout its history as an independent country, not all its subjects have enjoyed equal access to rights and opportunities, nor have they been considered citizens by law. Discrimination can take many forms, from *segregation to forced mass sterilization policies*, based on sex, income, race, ethnicity or country of origin, religion, sexual orientation, or physical or mental abilities. Federally-funded sterilization programs took place in 32 states continuously through the 20th century in America; for around 70 years, California led the country in the number of sterilization procedures performed on men and women. For much of United States history, most of its people have been deprived of civil and fundamental rights, and sometimes of citizenship itself.

The struggle for equality and civil rights for all continues today since many subjects still encounter prejudice, violence, injustice, and negative stereotypes that lead to exclusion, discrimination, and marginalization.

7.2 Constitutional Source

The Equal Protection Clause of the Fourteenth Amendment only applies to the states and provides that "[no state shall] deny any person within its jurisdiction the equal protection of the laws".[76] There is no equivalent counterpart in the United States Constitution applying to the federal government. Therefore, the language of the Fourteenth Amendment is limited to state action.

Nevertheless, the Supreme Court has held that the federal government's grossly unreasonable discrimination violates the *Due Process Clause of the Fifth Amendment*, where the language applies to the federal government. Thus, there are two equal protection guarantees for each state and federal government. While the protections stem from different constitutional sources, the Court applies the same standards in interpreting those protections and determining appropriate discrimination.

When the Court tries to answer what is permitted governmental discrimination, it applies three different standards based on the classification of persons involved: (1) *suspect classifications or fundamental rights*, (2) *quasi-suspect classification*, and (3) any other classification of persons.

7.3 Discrimination based on Suspect Classifications

The Supreme Court has held that specific kinds of government actions that discriminate against individuals are inherently suspect and, therefore, must automatically be subject to the strictest judicial scrutiny. This stipulation means the government must have a valid reason to discriminate and has the burden of proof, or the party must prove that their actions are constitutional. The Court determined that there are generally four suspect classifications of people: race, religion, national origin, and alienage. However, this is not a complete list, and as the law develops, the current classifications could be modified, and they may later add more classifications.

---

[76] For more information, see the Constitution of the United States, Amend. XVI, Sec. 1.

Suppose a law or governmental action discriminates against persons that belong to a suspect classification. In that case, the Court will review the law under the most rigorous review called strict scrutiny. Strict scrutiny means asking if the law is necessary to achieve a compelling state interest. If strict scrutiny is applied, the law or government action will be struck down unless the government proves and demonstrates to the Court the crucial or necessary reason for the discriminatory action to accomplish a vital or compelling governmental interest or result.

Instances whereby the government classifies or uses an individual's race and national origin when applying the law, have been closely reviewed by the Court over the last century. During World War II, Franklin Roosevelt issued an executive order requiring people of Japanese descent, two-thirds of whom were citizens, to be relocated and placed in internment camps, where they stayed until the order was suspended in 1944. The order was challenged on equal protection grounds and reached the Supreme Court in 1944. In *Korematsu v. United States*, the Supreme Court decided that laws that treat people differently because of race are highly suspicious, making race a suspect classification.[77] In the majority opinion, Former Associate Justice of the Supreme Court of the United States Hugo Black declared "all legal restrictions which curtail the civil rights of a single group are immediately suspect. That is not to say that all such restrictions are unconstitutional; it is to say that courts must subject them to the most rigid scrutiny. Pressing public necessity may sometimes justify the existence of such restrictions; racial antagonism never can".

Since the government action, the executive order has used individual's race and national origin; the Court had to apply *strict scrutiny* when asking if the action was constitutional. In Korematsu, it was the only clear racial discrimination case upheld despite applying strict scrutiny.

---

[77] See Kenney, Karen L, and Friedman, Richard D. *Korematsu V. the United States: World War II Japanese-American Internment Camps*. Minneapolis: ABDO Pub, 2013. Print..

The Court found placing the Japanese Americans in the camps was necessary to achieve *national security's compelling interest*. The Court held there was a compelling state purpose in national security. However, this holding was vital because it set a precedent and legal standard of review that legislators have used to evaluate laws that had discriminated against based on race and national origin.

Becoming a suspect class sounds like a good thing since it means that laws that discriminate against one's group get the strictest level of scrutiny. Nevertheless, it has proven to be a double-edged sword for racial groups because it tends to strike down laws that discriminate against one and laws that discriminate in one's favor. The efforts that groups have had to gain higher levels of scrutiny applied to the laws that treat them differently have been grueling. Moreover, even when the outcome is successful and discriminatory laws get annulled, only de jure discrimination formally is ended, while de facto discrimination may still be prevalent.

In United States constitutional law, when a court finds that a law infringes a fundamental right, it will also apply the strict scrutiny standard to hold it until the government can demonstrate that the law or regulation is necessary to achieve a *compelling state interest*. The United States Constitution protects certain fundamental constitutional rights and civil liberties.[78] If rights are denied to everyone, it is a substantive due process problem. If they are denied to some individuals but not to others, it is an equal protection problem. In either case, the standard of strict scrutiny will be applied.

Various privacy rights, including marriage, sexual relations, abortion, and childrearing, are fundamental rights. Thus, regulations affecting these rights are reviewed under the strict scrutiny standard and upheld only if necessary to protect a compelling interest.

---

[78] Even if lawyers and political scientists use to make a distinction between civil liberties and civil rights, they have interpreted the United States Constitution to protect both.

7.4 Discrimination based on Quasi-Suspect Classification

Laws that discriminate according to gender do not get the same level of scrutiny applied to race and other suspect classifications. *Quasi-suspect classifications* are based on gender and legitimacy (such as legitimate and illegitimate children), and representatives review them with a less rigorous analysis. When analyzing government action based on quasi-suspect classifications, the Court will apply the intermediate standard and strike down the law or government action unless it is substantially related to a significant government interest. As with strict scrutiny, *intermediate scrutiny* also places the burden of proof on the government.

First, when a law creates a gender classification, intermediate scrutiny will apply. As stated in *United States v. Virginia*, "parties who seek to defend gender-based government action must demonstrate an exceedingly persuasive justification for that action." (Ginsburg and Supreme Court Of The United States). *The important governmental interest* used to justify discrimination based on gender must be genuine, meaning it has to be reliable and cannot be overly broad or generalized. When, in *United States v. Virginia*, a state military school's policy of admitting only men was challenged, the state attempted to justify it, claiming that it offers a diversity of *educational approaches*. Also, that females would not be able to meet the male-only military school's physical requirements.

The Supreme Court found these arguments unconvincing. There was no evidence that that the single-sex school was established or maintained with a view of fostering diversity of educational opportunities, and there was some evidence that some women could meet the school's physical requirements. The state's argument of a vital governmental interest was not genuine and had no evidence to prove their claims were valid.

Intermediate scrutiny is not as hard to overcome as strict scrutiny. Therefore, there are more examples of where the Court has upheld classification or discrimination based on gender. A state law that excluded normal pregnancy and childbirth from state disability benefits was upheld that the law did not create a classification based on gender. The program's purpose was to create classifications based on the risk of disability, and normal pregnancies did not create such a risk.[79]

The Court has also reviewed discrimination against men. Laws punishing males but not females for statutory rape were upheld because the Court found the classification to be substantially related to the vital interest of preventing minors' pregnancy.[80] While other laws that preferred males over females to act as an administrator of an estate[81] or only authorize wives to be eligible to receive alimony[82] were struck down because there was no substantial relationship to a significant government interest.

7.5 Discrimination based on Other Groups' Classifications

All other classifications are reviewed under the rational basis standard and will be upheld unless they bear no rational relationship to any conceivable legitimate government interest. Nevertheless, if the government has no interest in discriminating against a group of persons other than a societal fear or dislike of them, the classification will not meet the standard. The understanding is that for any class of persons that is not a suspect or quasi-suspect class defined by the Court, then the rational basis standard will apply.

The Court has held that several classifications are not suspect. Age is not a suspect class. Thus, the government action based on age will be

---

[79] For more information, see Stewart, Potter, and Supreme Court Of The United States. *U.S. Reports: Geduldig v. Aiello, 417 U.S. 484. 1973.* Periodical. Library of Congress, www.loc.gov/item/usrep417484/.

[80] See Rehnquist, William H, and Supreme Court Of The United States. *U.S. Reports: Michael M. v. Sonoma County Superior Court, 450 U.S. 464. 1980.* Periodical. Retrieved from the Library of Congress, www.loc.gov/item/usrep450464/.

[81] See Supreme Court Of The United States. U.S. Reports: Reed v. Reed, 404 U.S. 71. 1971. Periodical. Retrieved from the Library of Congress, www.loc.gov/item/usrep404071/.

[82] See Brennan, William J., Jr, and Supreme Court Of The United States. *U.S. Reports: Orr v. Orr, 440 U.S. 268. 1978.* Periodical. Library of Congress, www.loc.gov/item/usrep440268/.

upheld if there is a conceivable rational basis for the classification. Laws that force police officers to retire at age 50, even though physically fit as a young officer, or judges to retire at age 70 do not violate the *Equal Protection Clause*. Mental disabilities are also not suspect classifications. The Court struck down a zoning ordinance that prohibited a group of mentally disabled persons from sharing a residential home because the only reason to deny them the benefit was their mental condition. The government has no legitimate interest in prohibiting mentally disabled persons from living together.[83]

Utterly because a law or governmental action results in discrimination is not sufficient to trigger strict or intermediate scrutiny or the rational basis test, the government's law or action must be intentional. The intent is shown in three different ways: (1) *facial discrimination*, (2) *discriminatory application*, or (3) *discriminatory motive*. Once the Court has determined that there was an intent to discriminate, the Court will then apply and look at the law through one of the strict standards of review.

Facial discrimination is when a law includes classifications that make evident social distinctions based on race and gender on its "face" or within its terms. In *Strauder v. West Virginia*, the Supreme Court considered a law that provided that only white males can serve as jurors[84]. In such cases, the Court can then apply the appropriate standard of review for racial and gender classifications. Another indicator of facial discrimination is *de jure discrimination*, which is discrimination by laws. De jure segregation, or legalized segregation of Black and White people, was present in almost every aspect of life in the South during the Jim Crow era: from public transportation to cemeteries, from prisons to health care, from residences

---

[83] See White, Byron Raymond, and Supreme Court Of The United States. *U.S. Reports: Cleburne v. Cleburne Living Center, 473 U.S. 432. 1984.* Periodical. Library of Congress, www.loc.gov/item/usrep473432/.

[84] See Strong, William, and Supreme Court Of The United States. U.S. Reports: Strauder v. West Virginia, 100 U.S. 303. 1879. Periodical. Library of Congress, www.loc.gov/item/usrep100303.

to libraries. Under segregation laws that, on their face, created racial classifications, Black and White people were to be separated, purportedly to minimize violence. De jure segregation, or "Jim Crow," lasted from the 1880s to 1964. *Jim Crow laws* were efficient in perpetuating the idea of "white superiority" and "black inferiority."

In contrast, *de facto discrimination* results from life circumstances, habits, customs, or socioeconomic status. De facto segregation is the direct manifestation of de jure segregation. While the Court eventually held laws that segregated races were unconstitutional, it could not change its people's hearts and minds. If people did not want to be in the presence of another ethnicity or race, they could certainly make this a reality. So, de jure segregation was implemented by law, de facto segregation, shared understandings, and personal choice.

Second, *discriminatory application* applies when a law appears neutral and fair on its face but is applied differently to different groups of people and cultures. If the persons challenging the governmental action can prove that the government officials applying the law had a discriminatory purpose, representatives will likely annul the law. In *Yick Wo v. Hopkins*, a law prohibited people from operating a laundry mat in wooden buildings but gave local governmental officials discretion to grant exceptions[85]. At that time in history, the laundry mats in that area were owned almost exclusively by people of Chinese descent. The governmental officials ended up only granting the exceptions to non-Asian laundromat owners. The law had a discriminatory application based on the suspect classification of race and national origin and was annulled.

Sometimes, a law or government action will appear neutral and fair on its face and its application but will have a discriminatory impact on a particular class of persons. Such law will be found to involve a prohibited classification (and be subject to the level of scrutiny appropriate to that

---

[85] For more information and insights, see Matthews, Stanley, and Supreme Court Of The United States. *U.S. Reports: Yick Wo v. Hopkins, 118 U.S. 356. 1885.* Periodical. Library of Congress, www.loc.gov/item/usrep118356.

classification) only if a court finds that the law-making body enacted the law for a discriminatory purpose. It can be challenging to prove that the government had a discriminatory purpose when passing a law. In *McCleskey v. Kemp*, the statistics and historical facts showing that black defendants in capital cases are much more likely to receive the death penalty than white defendants in similar cases. However, the statistical evidence was not enough to prove that the state had a discriminatory motive or purpose when convicting the black defendants. Moreover, the convictions, the governmental action were upheld. It takes more than statistical evidence to prove a discriminatory purpose.

It is important to remember that the Equal Protection and Due Process Clauses only prohibit state or government action. Furthermore, while private actors are not subject to the *Equal Protection Clause*, they may be subject to other laws preventing discrimination. For example, the federal Age Discrimination in *Employment Act* prohibits age discrimination for people who are age 40 or older. Similar laws prohibit workplace discrimination based on disability, race and national origin, genetic information, pregnancy, religion, and sex. These laws were passed by Congress and enforced by the *Equal Employment Opportunity Commission*.

7.6 The Case of Race

It is essential to understand the origins of discrimination to understand the journey and development of civil rights. Why do some people call slavery America's original sin? The narratives that white slave-owners used to justify slavery created an image of an inferior race that required white mastery. These tales established a set of stereotypes of African Americans that continue to haunt the nation. Researchers have evidenced stereotypes' lingering effects in the relatively recent cases and development of law discussed above. While slavery has not been prevalent in the United States for over a century, racial stereotypes are still prevalent today.

As slavery persisted in the country's beginnings, the landmark decision in *Dred Scott v. Sandford*[86], which held African Americans were not citizens and could not be free, increased tensions between the North and South and helped incite the anti-slavery movement. The Supreme Court came up with the principle of separate but equal. This decision created a two-class system in America. The Civil War did not settle the issue of slavery in the United States. The American Civil War (1861–1865) was fought mainly over slavery, and even the conclusion of that event did not put the issue to rest. Immediately following the war and the passage of the *Thirteenth Amendment* of the United States Constitution banning slavery, white southerners tried to seize back the power they had lost, bypassing state and local laws.

The laws passed after the Civil War limited the rights of African Americans. The arena of national legislative politics was closed to African Americans after the North turned to its own affairs following the Civil War Amendments' passage. Black codes were known as state and local laws that denied freed blacks the right to vote, go to school, and own property. The era of Jim Crow laws began. To shut down the black codes, the Northern-dominated Congress passed the Fourteenth and Fifteenth Amendments that granted citizenship and the right to vote to African Americans. *Jim Crow laws* were passed by white southerners that tried to re-create the power relations of slavery by running around the amendments designed to give blacks citizenship rights. These were forms of de jure discrimination that created a segregated society.

While the Civil War attempted and failed to remedy the societal damage of slavery, Congress and the Supreme Court were also slow with their efforts. Decades after the Civil War, in *Plessy v. Ferguson*[87], the Supreme

---

[86] See Taney, Roger Brooke, and Supreme Court Of The United States. *U.S. Reports: Dred Scott v. Sandford, 60 U.S. 19 How. 393. 1856.* Periodical. Retrieved from the Library of Congress, www.loc.gov/item/usrep060393a/.

[87] See Supreme Court Of The United States. *U.S. Reports: Plessy v. Ferguson, 163 U.S. 537. 1895.* Periodical. Retrieved from the Library of Congress, www.loc.gov/item/usrep163537/.

Court still did not provide equal treatment of all citizens and came up with the principle of separate but equal use of public facilities by different races and put the seal of constitutional approval on segregation. This established a two-class system in America.

In the 1930s, the NAACP began to use a law school-centered strategy to undermine Plessy slowly. The separate but equal view held a standard that separate facilities were legal if they were equal. Of course, this was not equal at all. This circumstance gestured that the courts would not be a profitable arena for blacks to fight in either. In 1910, African Americans who refused to accept the Jim Crow second-class citizenship organized the National Association for the Advancement of Colored People.

The NAACP's calculation was that to most Americans, law schools would be a less threatening area for desegregation than primary education, but one where the justices of the Supreme Court were particularly well suited to find arguments against segregation to be persuasive. In Brown v. Board of Education, the Court finally reversed its prior ruling, holding that segregation itself was unequal and the separate but equal doctrine that had prevailed in the legal community for more than half a century was unconstitutional.[88]

Even after the Brown decision, the right to equality was fought with boycotts to address systematic discrimination. One year after the Brown decision, when Rosa Parks refused to vacate her bus seat for a white man in Montgomery, Alabama and launched the bus system boycott, African Americans realized that their purchasing power could be a considerable political weapon[89]. This circumstance was to be followed by the quick realization that television's new technology could bring their plight out of isolation in the South to the whole country's attention.

---

[88] See Warren, Earl, and Supreme Court Of The United States. *U.S. Reports: Brown v. Board of Education, 347 U.S. 483. 1953.* Periodical. Library of Congress, <www.loc.gov/item/usrep347483/>.
[89] See Krutz, Glen S. *American Government 2e.*, 2019. Internet resource. especially chapter 5, for an in-depth analysis on how boycotts were used to address systematic discrimination in the United States.

The battle for equality was also fought with public opinion. The civil rights movement was fought in the arenas of public opinion and, finally, in Congress. In 1964 and 1965, civil rights legislation, initiated by President John Kennedy and then pushed through Congress by President Lyndon Johnson after Kennedy's assassination, removed most of the legal barriers to integration. Southern Congress members staged a filibuster to prevent a vote on the Senate's legislation, voting against their party's president. Most notably, the Civil Rights Act of 1964 prohibited segregation in public places based on race, religion, or national origin. It also created the Equal Employment Opportunity Commission that enforces laws that prohibit discrimination in the workplace. The civil rights movement was the combination of all these strategies used to alleviate African Americans' plight.

Did the civil rights movement eradicate de facto discrimination as well as de jure? One irony of all the legislative changes was that it ended the de jure discrimination in the South but pointed out the shortcomings of legal change as a method to redress de facto segregation in the North. Segregation in the North arose from long-term economic patterns and demographic changes that left African Americans in the city centers and succeeding waves of newly assimilated white immigrants in the suburbs. De facto discrimination cannot be remedied by fixing laws. It requires an effort to fix the outcomes, which strikes many Americans as fundamentally unfair. Despite the hard-won changes in laws, demeaning racial narratives were still woven into the American story and still determined how African Americans were treated and fared in rules and institutions based on white privilege.

Does the United States still have a race problem? Racial discrimination endures as one of American politics' defining issues, especially as demographic change forces whites to grapple with sharing minority status with other racial groups. Systemic racism is built into the American system to give whites preference and stacks the deck against people of color. The battle for equal rights does not end with African Americans. People of color who have had to fight for equal treatment by the law also include Native Americans, Latinos, and Asians. The assimilation of

European immigrants has traditionally been about their ability to fit in; the assimilation of people of color has depended on the willingness of the white population to give up racist narratives to accept them.

The government has a compelling interest in remedying past discrimination against a racial or ethnic minority. Thus, if a court finds that a governmental agency has engaged in racial discrimination, it may exercise affirmative action, a race-conscious remedy to help end the discrimination and ease the effects. A remedy of this type is permissible under the *Equal Protection Clause* because it is narrowly tailored to further the compelling interest to eliminate discrimination. For example, when it has been proven that a public employer engaged in persistent racial discrimination, a court may order relief that establishes a goal for hiring or promoting minority persons to eliminate the effects of the past discrimination.

7.7 The Case of Gender

The women's rights movement began in Seneca Falls in 1848. Sexism, like racism, is pervasive, often unrecognized, and has deep cultural roots. The women's rights movement is commonly dated from the Seneca Falls (NY) Convention of 1848, where the first woman's rights convention was held. The widely accepted narrative that kept wealthy white women out of public life was that they were too good and pure for the rough and tumbled corruption of public life. As with the racial equality movement, the women's suffrage movement was also gradual and spanned several decades.

Women fought for equality across all levels of government. On the western frontier, women worked side by side with men to carve a life out of the wilderness. The state-level effort promised more but slower success for women's rights. By 1912, women could vote in states that accounted for 74 electoral votes for the presidency. The *Nineteenth Amendment (1920)* gave women the right to vote. More equal rights would have required the passage of the *Equal Rights Amendment*. It was never ratified by the states but still discussed in current political platforms.

Modern legislation has called for equality for women. The *Lilly Ledbetter Fair Pay Act of 2009* requires equal pay for equal work. Women often make less money than men for the same work. The glass ceiling is the concept that women are still a minority in places where power is wielded. *Cultural attitudes* toward women are changing (e.g., the #MeToo movement) and will continue to change.

7.8 Sexual Orientation and Gender Identity

Unlike race and gender, the movement for equal protection for LGBTQ (lesbian, gay, bisexual, transgender, and queer or questioning) is still in its beginnings. It has only gained momentum in the last couple of decades. The movement seeks to accomplish what the race and gender movements have only recently achieved- guarantees for federal and state civil rights and protections against discrimination.

The Court addressed the first step in considering LGBTQ rights in *One, Inc. v. Olsen*, which primarily expanded the right of free speech by establishing that material published for a gay audience was not inherently obscene.[90] The movement had had setbacks in 1986 when the Court held that the *14th Amendment's Due Process guarantee* does not prohibit states from criminalizing sex between people of the same sex. The opinion of the Supreme Court pendulum swung again in 2003 and reversed their prior decision and held that the due process clause gave people "the full right to engage in private conduct without government intervention… [and there is] no legitimate state interest which can justify its intrusion into the individual's personal and private life". (Kennedy and Supreme Court of The United States, Lawrence et. al. Texas)

A landmark decision in 2015 held that the fundamental right to marry under the right to privacy is guaranteed to same-sex couples in *Obergefell v. Hodges*. While the law is slowly moving toward providing complete equal protection for the LGBTQ community eventually, real change will likely be incremental. The movement still has a long way to go.

---

[90] See Supreme Court Of The United States. *U.S. Reports: One, Incorporated, v. Olesen, 355 U.S. 371. 1957.* Periodical. Library of Congress, www.loc.gov/item/usrep355371/.

CHAPTER 8

The Legislative Branch

Chapter summary

To successfully prevent the national government, or any group within it, from becoming exceedingly powerful, the United States Constitution divided the government into three branches with different powers and attributions. Congress can pass laws, but its power to do so can be checked by the United States president, who can veto potential legislation so that it ultimately cannot become a law.

Most of Congress's work activities and work take place in *l*egislative committees. The House of Representatives has 20 permanent committees. The Senate has 21, and there are four joint committees with members from both chambers. These congressional committees have purview over specific issues, and they identify potential issues that could be subject to legislative review. Some areas in which these committees jurisdiction include agriculture, foreign affairs, budgets, and finance. House members from states with significant sectoral interests, such as agriculture, will likely seek these specific committees' positions.

To sit in the United States Congress, almost every member has to run for election and beat their opponent. The Seventeenth Amendment outlines how representatives should fill a vacancy caused by death, resignation, or removal from office should.

8.1 Introduction – What is the Legislative Branch?

The *legislative branch* is one of the three branches of the United States government as outlined by the Constitution. The legislative comprises the two chambers of Congress, the House, and the Senate. The legislative government branch produces the laws, declares war, and regulates taxes, among other duties.

One hundred elected representatives, two from each state, compose the *United States Senate*. It is the Senate's upper chamber and has more powers than the House, such as the power to impeach the United States President and confirm Cabinet positions, Supreme Court Justices, and other positions. Since it has more specific powers and has fewer members than the House, politicians have a more sought-after position. Citizens elect *Senators* to six-year terms with elections staggered, so approximately 1/3 of the Senate is up for election every even-numbered year.

The *House of Representatives* is the lower chamber of Congress, and it has 435 elected members. Unlike the Senate, the House is divided proportionally based on the population size of each state. The seven states with the lowest population have only one representative, while the most populous state, California, has 53 representatives in the House. The House also has powers that are unique to it, including impeaching federal officers and electing a United States President in the event of an Electoral College tie. A *Representative* serves a shorter term than a Senator, only two years, and is up for election every even-numbered year.

8.2 How the Constitution Established Congress

The Constitution outlines the role of Congress in Article I. Article I, Section I, states:

> "All legislative Powers herein granted shall be vested in a Congress of the United States, which shall consist of a Senate and House of Representatives."

One of the key design elements from the Founding Fathers was making Congress bicameral. A *bicameral legislature* is a legislative body that has two chambers. When discussing the government's structure under the United States Constitution, the delegates from Virginia called for a bicameral legislature consisting of two Houses. Delegates from small states objected to the Virginia Plan, which ultimately prevailed.

Another proposal, the New Jersey Plan, called instead for a unicameral legislature with one House, in which each state would have one vote. Consequently, smaller states would have the same power in the national legislature as larger states. Notwithstanding, the larger states argued that they should be allotted more legislators to represent their interests because they had a more significant population. (Corwin, 48)

The two chambers of Congress in the United States were created with different characteristics to represent different interests to protect any region or state from getting too much power. Each state has equal representation in the Senate, while in the House, states with a higher population have more seats and thus more voting power. The House of Representatives has developed a more robust and structured leadership than the Senate. Because its members serve two-year terms, they regularly answer their constituency's demands when running for election or reelection. Even House members of the same party in the same state will occasionally disagree on different issues because of their specific districts' particular interests. The House can be highly partisan at times. In contrast, members of the Senate are furthest from the demands and scrutiny of their constituents. Because of their longer six-year terms, they will likely see every House member face their constituents multiple times before they have to seek reelection.

The foundation of Congress and the Constitution's contents resulted from the bitter battle between Federalist and Anti-Federalist factions. The Federalists supported a strong federal government, while the Anti-Federalists wanted more power in the states' hands. In the Constitution's passage, the Federalists ultimately prevailed, but Congress's structure was a source of compromise. While not all Anti-Federalists agreed between the House's proportional representation and the Senate's equal representation, they also created state legislatures to compromise with Anti-Federalists.

Another compromise to Anti-Federalists was who elected members of the Senate. While the voting public elected members of the House, state legislatures initially elected their state's senators. This setting gave the state legislatures more power over federal policy. State legislatures elected senators until the Seventeenth Amendment's ratification in 1913, which changed senators' election to a popular vote by voters in the state.

The Senate and the House were made with two different structures so that they would represent different constituencies. Each member of government has a *constituency*, the individuals and groups whose interests the elected official represents. Senators represent their whole state when they go to Congress, and until 1913 they were closely tied to political interests in their state's legislature. Each House member represents a district in their state. For example, California has 53 distinct districts. Under this original design, representatives were supposed to represent the people and their opinions, while senators were representatives of their state and legislature.

The two chambers of Congress also have different qualification requirements and restrictions. A senator has to be at least 30 years old, a United States citizen for at least nine years, and be a resident of the state they are running to represent. A representative only has to be 25 years old, be a United States citizen for seven years, and live in the state they politically represent.

8.3 How Congress Does Its Job

To adequately perform the duties given to Congress by the Constitution, the legislative body's structure has various leadership roles. Throughout United States history, the division of power for congressional leadership positions has evolved. Partisanship, narrow margins between the two parties, and the rise in leadership positions' power have marked and shaped modern congressional politics. The Speaker of the House and the Senate majority leader, the majority party's congressional leaders, have all-powerful tools at their disposal to conveniently punish party members who defect on a particular vote.

Most of Congress's work activities and work take place in *legislative committees*. The House of Representatives has 20 permanent committees. The Senate has 21, and there are four joint committees with members from both chambers. These congressional committees have purview over specific issues, and they identify potential issues that could be subject to legislative review. Some areas in which these committees jurisdiction's include agriculture, foreign affairs, budgets, and finance.

Initially, Senate committee membership was determined either by a vote by the full Senate or appointments by the committee's presiding officer. In 1846, the Senate changed its rules on committee appointments in order to streamline the process. Today, each party's leadership determines Senate committee membership and submissions to the floor for approval. Similarly, in the House, Democratic and Republican leadership determine which representatives to submit for committee membership approval. This situation gives each party's leadership significant power to keep incoming and incumbent Congress members in line with the respective party's vision.

In Congress, four main types of committees perform different roles and specialize in specific public policy areas. *Standing committees* are permanent as laid out in the House and Senate rules that have specific legislative jurisdiction. In this type of committee, members review and recommend legislative measures and monitor government agencies relevant to their jurisdiction. The Senate has 16 standing committees with 67 subcommittees, and the House has 20 standing committees with 97 subcommittees.

Select or special committees are established for a limited time, often to conduct investigations or research. If an emerging issue does not fall under a standing committee's purview or crosses multiple committees' jurisdiction, a select committee will be set up. While they put these committees in place for a limited time, they can renew them by their respective chambers, and sometimes they become permanent standing committees.

Conference committees are used to reconcile bills passed in both the House and the Senate. The conference committees are appointed on an ad hoc basis when a bill passes the House and Senate in various forms. Congress members sometimes skip these committees in the interest of expediency, in which one of the chambers relents to the other.

Lastly, *joint committees* are composed of members of both the House and the Senate. Joint committees are permanent and mainly perform housekeeping duties or conduct studies rather than doing legislative work. Leadership on these committees alternates between the Senate and the House.

The most influential role in the Senate is the *Speaker of the House*. This position was established in Article 1 Section II of the Constitution, but the office's power has grown significantly in the modern era. The Speaker is the House's presiding officer, the lower chamber of Congress's administrative head, and the majority party's head in the House. The Constitution does not call for the Speaker to have a partisan role, but the role has developed significantly over the years. The Speaker of the House is also third in line for the presidency.

The leader of the majority party in the Senate is known as the *Senate Majority Leader*. Unlike the Speaker of the House, the United States Constitution does not set this position. They are the majority party's head in the Senate and derive their power from their party and various Senate precedents. While the Senate Majority Leader does not enjoy as much formal power as the House's Speaker, they serve as the chief spokesperson for their party in the Senate. The leader of the party with fewer members in the Senate is known as the Senate Minority Leader. The Constitution established the Vice President as President of the United States Senate.

8.4 Congress's Role in the System of Checks and Balances

The Founding Fathers established the federal government as a system of checks and balances so no single branch of government, person, or political interest would become too powerful. The framers of the Constitution created such a system to satisfy the concerns of those who feared an overly strong central government. In this vein, Congress plays a crucial role and has some power over the executive and judicial branch, and vice versa.

Congress has three key ways to check the executive branch, and they give the legislative branch power to balance the President's power. The first and most important is *congressional oversight*. This provision refers to Congress's powers to oversee the executive branch and numerous federal agencies. Congress can review and keep an eye on various federal programs, administrative activities, and policies. The power to create an investigative committee, hold legislative hearings, and set budgets also fall under this category. The Constitution does not explicitly state that Congress has these powers; instead, these powers have been built up over time under the principle of implied powers.

One of the most visible powers of Congress in the modern presidency has been the power of impeachment. Congress has the sole power to impeach a government official and remove them from office. The House has the power to impeach government officials. The Senate can take up the House's impeachment, hold a trial, and vote in the Senate to convict and remove the impeached official from office. The Constitution explicitly gives Congress the power to impeach federal officials, and it also gives the legislative branch the power to bar impeached and convicted officials from running for office.

The House has passed articles of impeachment 21 times, three times against a sitting president. Presidents Andrew Johnson, Bill Clinton, and Donald Trump have all been impeached by the House, and the Senate later acquitted all. President Richard Nixon resigned in 1974 rather than face certain impeachment and a likely conviction in the Senate after the

Watergate scandal. President Donald Trump is the only federal official to be impeached twice, and he was acquitted both times.

The final important check Congress has on the executive branch is advice and consent, the Senate's role of confirming presidential appointments, including Supreme Court appointments, Cabinet officials, and ambassadors. The Constitution only grants this power to the Senate and not the House, and it is outlined in Article II Section 2 Clause 2. Initially, the Founding Fathers disagreed about the Senate's role in advising the President on nominations. In modern American politics, this power mostly plays out in high-profile congressional hearings with a majority of senators needed to approve appointments. A two-thirds majority of the Senate is also required to approve international treaties signed by the President.

Not only does Congress check and balance the power of the executive branch, but they also have powers to do the same with the judicial branch. Some of these powers are also within the above powers to check the executive, such as approving or denying judicial appointments and impeach and remove federal judges from office.

One of the leading powers that Congress has to check the judicial branch's power is to amend the Constitution. As the highest court in the land, the Supreme Court takes cases and gives rulings based on the justice's interpretation of the legislation or executive order constitutionality. As the federal courts use the Constitution as the basis for their legal rulings, the ability to amend the Constitution through the legislative process is one of Congress's most important powers.

Congress also has significant organizational power over the judicial branch. The United States Constitution grants Congress the power to determine how many Supreme Court Justices sit on the court and establish inferior courts. The Constitution only required the Supreme Court, but Congress has established a vast and powerful judicial branch with many inferior federal courts. Congress established the district courts system in the Judiciary Act of 1789. Today, there are 94 district courts in the country. Congress also established the 13 courts of appeals.

Furthermore, Congress can also pass laws that circumvent the courts' rulings. While one has traditionally assumed that the Supreme Court has the final say on applying the law regarding new legislation, congressional overrides have become more common in the modern era. William Eskridge Jr. and Matthew Christiansen found that congressional overrides grew dramatically between 1967 and 1990. While they have decreased after the Clinton impeachment, they remain a relevant tool for Congress to override the judicial branch.[91] Former Supreme Court Justice Ruth Bader Ginsburg asked Congress to override the Supreme Court's ruling in 2013 and said, "Congress has, in the recent past, intervened to correct this Court's wayward interpretations of Title VII."[92]

While Congress has significant power to check the executive and judicial branches, these two branches also have been granted the ability to check and balance the legislative branch. The President's most important check on Congress is the power to veto legislation, thus directing the legislative agenda. However, this power is not ultimate, and Congress can reject a presidential veto by a two-thirds vote. The judicial branch primarily checks Congress's power through judicial review. One of the Supreme Court's primary roles is to review the legality of legislation passed by Congress.

8.5 How Congress Makes the Law

How does Congress go about performing its most important duty, making laws through passing legislation? Both the Senate and House are constrained by the Constitution and norms that have been built up over

---

[91] Eskridge and Christiansen state that, before 1975, the United States Congress regularly overrode Supreme Court decisions interpreting federal statutes, but this mostly was an occasional phenomenon. The big turning point in United States history of statutory overrides was the 94th Congress (1975-1976), where the post-Watergate representatives overrode twenty Supreme Court decisions. Amid political polarization, the 1990s was the golden age of overrides. Eskridge Jr., William N., and Matthew R. Christiansen. "Congressional Overrides of Supreme Court Statutory Interpretation Decisions, 1967-2011." *Texas Law Review*, vol. 92, 2014, doi:https://digitalcommons.law.yale.edu/cgi/viewcontent.cgi?article=5895&context=fss_papers.

[92] For more information, *see* Supreme Court. Vance v. Ball State University. 24 June 2013.

time. Political interests may influence Congress members, who also have different commitments to their state or district's particular interests. Specifically, in the House, where representatives face reelection every two years, Congress members are constrained by electability concerns. With all this said, Congress is the place all new federal legislation has to go through, and it performs an essential role in American democracy.

Congress members are often drafting and working on bills for years before they reach the floor of Congress, and many bills go through a long and arduous process before they become the law of the land. Bills do not necessarily originate from Congress members, as political interest groups, think tanks, policy groups, and more pitch ideas to congresspeople regularly. Whether a member of Congress presents himself with a bill or ideates and finetunes the whole piece of legislation, the next step for a bill is to be introduced in either Congress's chamber.

The bill's *sponsor* is the representative or Senator who first brings the bill to Congress. In addition to the bill's primary sponsor, other senators and representatives who sign on supporting the legislation in this early phase are cosponsors.

Next, the bill is sent to a relevant committee or multiple committees if the bill spans multiple jurisdictions. The committee then assigns the bill to a subcommittee, where representatives kill most legislation. Here the senators or representatives on the committee discuss and hold hearings on the bill and either decide to kill the bill through inaction or make amendments to the bill and send it to the floor for a chamber-wide vote.

If the bill makes it to a vote in the House or Senate for a debate and vote, a simple majority supporting it will send it to the other chamber for approval. The two chambers have some minor differences in how a bill comes out of committee and debating on the floor. In the House, the House Committee on Rules decides for approval before representatives can debate it on the House floor. A bill in the Senate will be put to open debate, but it can be subject to a *filibuster*.

Unlike in the House, which got rid of the filibuster in 1842, the Senate filibuster allows a senator as much as they want to slow down a bill's passage and take floor time away from it. The practice is a Senate rule and not in the Constitution, and it has become increasingly used in the modern era. The longest filibuster by a single senator was Strom Thurmond's unsuccessful 24 hour and 18-minute attempt to stop the 1957 Civil Rights Act. Thurmond also participated in a 60-day filibuster by multiple senators attempting to stop the 1964 Civil Rights Act. The only way to stop a filibuster is by *cloture*, a vote which requires 60 senators.

Once sent to the other chamber, it faces a similar cycle where relevant committees hold hearings on the bill and make potential amendments before approving it or killing the bill. A bill can pass one chamber of Congress but be voted down or killed through inaction, and both chambers have to agree on the final version of the bill. Once both the House and the Senate approve a bill, they send it to the President for signature and approval. A president can either sign the bill, approve it, make it law, or veto it. United States presidents have historically used the line-item veto and signed statements to influence the laws they will sign. While a presidential veto will often kill the legislation, Congress can override a veto if two-thirds of each chamber votes to override the President.

While this is the standard procedure for a bill to become a law, there are multiple ways that congressional leadership or a congressperson can bypass committee hearings to fast-track legislation through various congressional rules not outlined in the Constitution. If a Congress member asks for unanimous consent to put a bill on the agenda and nobody votes against it, a bill can bypass committees. The Senate Majority Leader can also use Senate Rule XIV to bypass committee hearings.[93]

---

[93] On pieces of noncontroversial legislation, Senate leaders and representatives might use one of two informal processes called clearance and hotlining to determine the feasibility of expeditious or immediate consideration of a measure. The process of passing noncontroversial measures may include bypassing a Senate committee or truncating committee action, even though a committee might well have played a key role in the development of the measure sought to be passed or in the measure's clearance. For more information, *see* Koempel, Michael L. "Bypassing Senate Committees: Rule XIV and Unanimous Consent." *Congressional Research Service*, fas.org/sgp/crs/misc/RS22299.pdf.

There are also ways for the Senate to bypass the traditional rules around the filibuster by using *reconciliation*. While bills in the Senate require a 60-vote supermajority to avoid a filibuster, the Senate can use reconciliation to pass legislation by a simple majority on bills related to spending, revenue, and the federal debt limit. The Senate can do this three times a calendar year, one per subject.

Another modern development in Congress is *omnibus legislation*; unrelated legislation packaged together for a single vote. Due to their large size and scope of multiple subjects, many congresspeople do not have enough time to read and understand the bill. In modern politics, this creates what is known as "pork," unrelated and sometimes controversial spending that gets attached to bills that will quickly pass. For example, many criticized elements within the various stimulus package deals during the coronavirus pandemic as senators filled omnibus bills with unrelated spending.

8.6 How Congress is Challenged and How Congresspeople Represent Voters

Modern Congress is shaped and constrained by the Constitution, the precedence set over hundreds of years, and present-day political realities.

First, in that list, the Constitution contains the foundation for Congress, both its powers and limitations. The founding fathers shaped the legislative branch's structure after the Constitution's predecessor, the Articles of Confederation, left the then unicameral legislature with some shortcomings. As it lacked power and was challenging to have all the relevant members meet with an impending war with Britain looming, the Founding Fathers saw it necessary to change Congress while submitting it to a system of checks and balances.

While the Constitution set the Congress foundations, the political body has gone through many changes since its inception. As the country has expanded, so has Congress, making the balance of power between big and small states all the more delicate to balance. The country's demographics have changed immensely since the Constitution called for proportional representation in the House of Representatives; one should before calculate by counting each slave as three-fifths of a person for population counts.

This situation leads to the modern political constraints that Congress has. The body is supposed to represent everyone in the country. With diverging political interests and growing corporate power, Congress members are beholden to a wide variety of political groups.

As a rule of thumb, Congress has to answer three constituencies: the voters who elected them, the nation, and their party. In Congress, the people who elect congresspeople all reside in the same state. These politicians are supposed to focus on the *representation* of this group mainly. This political representation means a congressperson has to look out for the constituents' interests in their state or district. Each state is divided into *congressional districts* by their state legislatures. Each member of the House of Representatives represents one of these congressional districts.

In modern politics, congresspeople attempt to represent their constituents in several ways. The first form is *policy representation*, the passing policy that will benefit the people's interests in their constituency. A particular policy proposal may be prevalent in a congressperson's constituency, and voting for its passage is a form of political representation. Secondly, members of Congress often represent their district or constituency by *allocative representation*. These conditions work by a congressperson securing funds for allocating to their district or state that will materially benefit their voters. In section 11.5, "pork" is mentioned, and this is one of the most prominent forms of allocative representation. This obligation also works through *earmarks*, providing taxpayer dollars to projects related to a specific district. Congresspeople also represent their constituents by doing *casework* and solving problems faced by people living in their district and through *symbolic representation*, representing the district and its people at public events.

Congress also passes legislation that impacts the nation as a whole. By the process of *national lawmaking*, Congress passes legislation meant to benefit the entire country. However, it is often perceived as real contractions between the national interest and a congressperson's district or state's interests. Nationally popular legislation can be hamstrung by individual congress people's decision to vote against the popular will in favor of constituents in their district. The tension between national and local interests is inherent in Congress's structure. In case a congressperson does not represent their constituents' interests, they enjoy an *incumbency advantage*. The sitting congressperson is more likely to be elected under these conditions.

Senators and representatives are also beholden to their political parties. Many United States Founding Fathers opposed political parties at the outset of the nation, and President George Washington did not belong to a party. The Constitution does not mention political parties at all. In the Federalist Papers, Founding Fathers James Madison and Alexander Hamilton wrote about the dangers they perceived in political parties. Nevertheless, the pipedream of non-partisan politics quickly dissipated, and parties formed on Federalist and Anti-Federalist lines. While the American political party system has been through multiple iterations, a two-party system has reigned after Washington's presidency.

While the Founding Fathers were concerned about political parties, Congress was established without considering the implications of a two-party partisan system. Throughout the history of Congress and the United States, there have been ebbs and flows in *partisanship*. If a politician is notably partisan, they will fall in line with the direction of his party. If political parties differ on significant, key issues, *political polarization* leads to high levels of partisanship. They perceived that the public's increasing polarization levels were also prevalent within the political parties and Congress. In *hyper-partisanship times*, party members stick strictly to their party line, leading to a *gridlock* in the legislative branch. If there is a divided legislative branch, where each party controls one chamber, and parties have high partisanship and polarization levels, legislators can pass very scarce meaningful legislation through Congress.

The Pew Research Center found in 2014 that Democrat and Republican voters had become significantly more polarized in previous decades.[94] Beginning in the 1980s and escalating since then, the Democratic and Republican parties began to polarize in Congress. The moderate members in each party started diminished, while more ideologically motivated candidates began to win election to the House and later the Senate. Consequently, the Democrats in Congress generally turned more liberal, and the Republicans became more conservative than before. The moderates from each party, who had earlier been able to work together, were politically edged out. It became more likely that the party opposite the President in Congress might be more willing to question his initiatives, whereas, in the past, it was uncommon for the opposition party to publicly stand against the United States president in foreign policy affairs.

If the legislative branch is divided or the President is from a different party than both chambers, Congress often has to rely more on *bipartisanship* to pass legislation. The two parties often work together to craft legislation and compromise on issues. However, bipartisanship does not solve all the tension and constraints within Congress. Local versus national interests still would play a significant role. All in all, the different levels of representation and how Congress is organized play crucial constraints on Congress's ability to pass sweeping legislation.

8.7 Elections

To sit in Congress, almost every member has to run for election and beat his opponent. The Seventeenth Amendment outlines how representatives should fill a vacancy caused by death, resignation, or removal from office should. In the House, a special election always has to be held when a vacancy occurs. However, the Constitution leaves vacancies in the Senate to state legislatures, so some states' governors are required to appoint someone to fill a Senate vacancy rather than hold a special election.

---

[94] *See* Pew Research Center, for an insightful analysis of this trend. Republicans and Democrats seem to be more divided along ideological lines, and partisan antipathy is deeper and more extensive than at any point in the last two decades. Political Polarization in the American Public. Pew Research Center, 12 June 2014, www.pewresearch.org/politics/2014/06/12/political-polarization-in-the-american-public/

Other than the difference when a vacancy occurs, Senate and House elections also have other distinctions. Senate elections are more straightforward as every state receives two senators, and these borders do not change. Every six years, a senate seat is up for election, so a sitting senator or a challenger has plenty of time to prepare for an election. In the House, they regularly redraw districts to reflect demographic changes as each district has to have about the same number of residents living in the area. Representatives are also up for reelection every two years, so they often have to campaign and raise money more regularly.

One of the most critical determinants of House elections is how districts are drawn and redrawn. The districts are drawn based on pre-set rules and political lines. Districts are drawn based on United States Census results held every ten years, mandated by Article I, Section 2, of the United States Constitution. The Constitution sets out that Congress members will use this data every ten years to finalize *congressional apportionment*, dividing up to the now 435 seats in the House.

The number of representatives may fluctuate based on state population. For the 2016 and 2020 presidential elections, there were 538 electors in the Electoral College, and a majority of 270 electoral votes were needed to win the presidency. Once the President of the Senate has read the electoral votes during a special joint session of Congress in January, the presidential candidate who received the majority of electoral votes is officially named President of the United States.

While the Census might seem apolitical, it often becomes a politicized and controversial topic. If someone does not return their census form, he will not be counted. Republicans have long attempted to exclude undocumented immigrants from the Census,[95] and President Donald Trump

---

[95] One should also consider that, weeks before the 1980 census formally began, the Federation for American Immigration Reform launched its campaign to exclude unauthorized immigrants from population counts, *See* Lo Wang, Hansi. "Immigration Hard-Liner Files Reveal 40-Year Bid Behind Trump's Census Obsession." *National Public Radio*, 15 Feb. 2021, www.npr.org/2021/02/15/967783477/immigration-hard-liner-files-reveal-40-year-bid-behind-trumps-census-obsession.

pushed hard to include a citizenship question on the 2020 Census. The Democratic Party has pushed statistical estimation to represent better who lives in each district, including undocumented immigrants, which would theoretically benefit the Democrats. If a state increases its population relative to other states, it will increase its share of seats in the House and political power.

There are other manners in which the two parties attempt to tip the congressional district system in their favor. *Redistricting* is one of the most politicized ways that the House's make-up is determined, which is the process of redrawing congressional district lines based on the Census results so that all districts remain about equal in population. Every ten years, the state legislature has the final say on how they will redraw districts, and in the end, the majority party in the state legislature has the most significant say. This provision makes state legislatures quite influential in determining the look of Congress. These districts are subject to *gerrymandering*, a highly politicized process that redistricts the congressional lines to benefit one party over another. This situation leads to bizarre congressional districts drawn to include voting populations that the majority party in the state legislature believes will benefit their party. The name gerrymandering originates from Massachusetts Governor Elbridge Gerry, who redrew a district in 1812 to resemble a salamander.

Historically, *gerrymandering* has been used in the United States to change districts' racial composition to marginalize racial minorities. This process of racial gerrymandering was made illegal in the Voting Rights Act of 1965. However, the Supreme Court had to intervene in several cases in the 1990s to overturn *redistricting* and drawing on racial lines. Now districts are often redrawn to benefit one party, known as partisan gerrymandering. Some have argued that this is an extension of racial gerrymandering and still marginalizes racial minorities and other groups. The Supreme Court has ruled that this type of gerrymandering is a political question with a 5-4 ruling on a conservative-liberal line.

8.8 Does Congress Look Like and Represent America?

While anyone over a certain age and a United States citizen can run for Congress, there are high barriers to running and winning a successful campaign. In 2016, the average winning Senate campaign spent $10.4 million, and the average winning House campaign spent $1.3 million.[96] While this money often does not come from the candidate's wealth, it often means a politician has to appeal to monied interests, including either the Republican or Democratic Party, to have political success. Although about 40% of Americans identify as political independents[97], there is very little room for citizens who do not want to run in either party to succeed at the national level.

Outside of money spent on a political campaign, other factors determine who runs and wins Congress seats. As mentioned in section 11.6, incumbents have typically enjoyed an advantage electorally. Thus *open seats* without an incumbent are much more desirable. Congress elections also often are impacted by presidential elections to be held in the same year. Suppose a Republican wins the presidency by a large margin. In that case, Republicans running for the Senate and House may enjoy the *coattail effect*, which boosts their chances of winning thanks to a solid presidential campaign from the candidate in their party. After two years in office, the President's party quite frequently will be subject to a *midterm loss* and see their seats in Congress diminished.

And how about the representation of the American electorate? Does Congress look like the voters who elect them? Throughout history, Congress and the American government have had shallow *descriptive representation* levels, how much the legislature looks like the population.

---

[96] For more information on current spending by campaigns in the United States, *see* Kim, Soo Rin. "The Price of Winning Just Got Higher, Especially in the Senate." *OpenSecrets*, 9 Nov. 2016, www.opensecrets.org/news/2016/11/the-price-of-winning-just-got-higher-especially-in-the-senate/.

[97] Significantly more U.S. adults continued to identify as political independents (42%) in 2018 than as either Democrats (30%) or Republicans (26%). *See* Jones, Jeffrey M. "Americans Continue to Embrace Political Independence." *Gallup*, 7 Jan. 2019, news.gallup.com/poll/245801/americans-continue-embrace-political-independence.aspx.

While this representation has increased since the times in which only white land-owning males in government, Congress does not have a high descriptive representation level. The 117th Congress is the most racially and ethnically diverse in history, but it is still 77% white[98], which is a percentage significantly higher than that of the general population (60% white). Furthermore, only a handful of congresspeople are not college graduates, despite only 22.5% of Americans above 25 finishing four years of college.[99] Congress is also significantly wealthier than the general population, and only 3% of congresspeople are immigrants despite the United States having the highest immigrant population in the world at 47 million people.

[98] Among today's United States senators and representatives, the overwhelming majority of racial and ethnic minority members are Democrats (83%), while 17% are Republicans. See Schaeffer, Katherine. "Racial, Ethnic Diversity Increases Yet Again with the 117th Congress." Pew Research Center, 28 Jan. 2021, www.pewresearch.org/fact-tank/2021/01/28/racial-ethnic-diversity-increases-yet-again-with-the-117th-congress/. .

[99] See the official release of the US Census for more information Bureau, US Census. "U.S. Census Bureau Releases New Educational Attainment Data." The United States Census Bureau, 30 Mar. 2020, www.census.gov/newsroom/press-releases/2020/educational-attainment.html#:~:text=In%202019%2C%20high%20school%20was,from%2029.9%25%20to%20 36.0%25

CHAPTER 9

The Executive Branch

9.1 Introduction to the Executive Branch

What is an executive, anyway? By definition, the **Executive** is one who has the power to carry out plans, strategies or laws. In some countries around the world, the chief executive is a prime minister. The United States does not have a prime minister, and instead the United States chief executive is a **president**. The executive branch is led by the President who is the leader of the entire federal bureaucracy system. The **Federal bureaucracy** is the vast network of departments, agencies, boards, and commissions that constitute the Federal government. In the United States, these agencies include the FBI, CIA, EPA, and so forth. The president is only the head of the federal bureaucracy and not the legislative branch of government, unlike a prime minister who typically has more control over legislation. The executive branch in the United States is tasked with carrying out and enforcing the law as stipulated in the Constitution. In addition to the President, the Vice President and the Cabinet are tasked with aiding the President.

9.2 The Job of the American President

The American President has specific job descriptions and powers and authority that are granted to the office. The key elements of the President's job description are codified in the Constitution and have been granted to the office through Congress and the Courts. The United States Constitution originally limited the power of the Executive Branch, but throughout the history of the American presidency, the power of the President has been significantly expanded. Yet still, the Constitution gives the president less power than many other chief executives around the world. One of the president's most important powers is executive privilege. **Executive privilege** allows the president to keep certain documents that concern the executive branch or national security confidential.

According to the Constitution, the president must meet certain requirements and conditions in order to serve. The Constitution also lists several restrictions upon the office. The President of the United States must be:

- At least 35 years old
- A natural-born citizen of the United States
- A United States resident for at least 14 years
- Chosen by the Electoral College to serve a four-year term
- Succeeded in the event of death or incapacity by the vice president, elected at the same time
- Removed from office only for "high crimes and misdemeanors" by the House and the Senate
- Unable to receive "emoluments" (that is, profit beyond their normal salary) from the country or any of the states

The job of the American president has been significantly modified through the years despite the formal powers granted by the Constitution remaining the same. Several amendments have modified presidential power and each of these amendments to the constitution have addressed changes in society.

The different amendments of the constitution have contributed to defining the roles of the Presidency. The most important amendments to the office of the president have been the Twelfth, Twentieth, Twenty-Second, and Twenty-Fifth Amendments.

When the Twelfth Amendment was passed, it limited and changed how the President and Vice President were elected by the Electoral College. During the first years of our nation, the two candidates who received the most votes in the Electoral College would serve as President and Vice-President. The Twelfth Amendment states that the President and Vice President would be voted in distinct ballots rather than the second-place in the Electoral College presidential election being selected as the Vice President. The change was made to limit the chance of a President and Vice President being elected from different parties. Additionally, under this amendment, the President and Vice President are not allowed to be residents in the same state. In 2000, the Twelfth Amendment became a point of contention in the election of President Bush and Vice President Cheney. Bush was the Governor of Texas and Cheney had lived in Texas for five years while maintaining a residence in Wyoming[100].

The Twentieth Amendment set the official start and end date for a term in office for the President, Vice President, Senate, and House of Representatives. After the amendment, the President and Vice President's term begins and ends on January 20 at noon. Newly elected Senators and Representatives begin their term on January 3, which gives the incoming Congress the power to break a deadlock in the event of a tie in the Electoral College, rather than the outgoing Congress. This section of the amendment served to limit the "lame duck" session, or the time in between presidential terms. It also set out that the vice president takes over if the president dies before taking the oath.

In an effort to limit the power of a popular politician, Congress approved the Twenty-Second Amendment to create term-limits for the President. The amendment was a direct response to President Franklin Delano Roosevelt who served four terms and enjoyed high levels of

---

[100] Maravilla, Christopher Scott. "That Dog Don't Hunt: The Twelfth Amendment after Jones v. Bush." *Pace Law Review*, vol. 23, no. 1, 2002, pp. 214–270.

popularity leading the country out of the Great Depression and through World War II. The Twenty-Second Amendment implemented a two-term limit for any president. Roosevelt is the only American president to serve more than two terms after President George Washington established a two-term norm as the first President of the country.

The impeachment process to remove the President or Vice President from office is mostly laid out in Articles I and II of the Constitution. But, the Twenty-Fifth Amendment created a mechanism for the president to be removed without impeachment. The vice president and a majority of the cabinet or the Congress can remove a president if they determine the president is unable to perform their job. Near the tail end of President Donald Trump's first term in office, several Democratic Representatives called on Vice President Mike Pence to invoke the Twenty-Fifth Amendment to remove Trump from office[101]. The amendment also outlines presidential succession stating "In case of the removal of the President from office or of his death or resignation, the Vice President shall become President."

9.3 The Presidential Job.

The Presidential Succession Act of 1947 delineates additional detail on who does the president's job when he cannot, and it fundamentally changed the Presidential Succession Act of 1886. In the wake of President Roosevelt's death in office in 1945, his successor President Harry Truman sought to change the line of presidential succession. Under this act, the Speaker of the House and the president pro tempore of the Senate were made third and fourth in line for the Presidency, respectively, after the Vice President. The new act changed succession and moved members of the President's cabinet further down the line of succession, thus not allowing a President to appoint their own line of succession.

---

[101] Cicilline, David N. *Cicilline, Lieu Lead Judiciary Committee Dems Urging Pence to Invoke 25th Amendment.* cicilline.house.gov/press-release/cicilline-lieu-lead-judiciary-committee-dems-urging-pence-invoke-25th-amendment.

In order to govern and lead the country, the president relies on their **cabinet,** an advisory group to the President composed primarily of the heads of the major departments of the federal bureaucracy and the vice president. Each cabinet member carries out elements of the President's agenda. The President's cabinet has 23 members including the vice president, 15 department heads including the Attorney General, Secretaries of State, Treasury, and Defense, and seven other cabinet level members. The Cabinet does not possess any collective executive power, and they have to be submitted to the Senate for approval by a simple majority. While the Cabinet-level positions need to be approved by the Senate, the president can remove Cabinet members at their discretion.

So as no single entity or branch gets too much power, the executive branch exists in a system of checks and balances, and the role of the executive is to make sure that Congress and the Judicial Branch do not usurp more power over other branches of government. In theory, the president has been given just enough legislative and judicial power to hold the other branches in check. While the system is built on checks and balances, the president is the leader of the county and serves as both the head of state and head of government.

In countries with two separate heads of state and government, the **head of state** is a largely ceremonial, apolitical role that rallies the country together. This can be done through the moral or historical influence of the office. The **head of government** is a partisan role, as in the United States, the President serves as the head of the president's political party. Each president utilizes this role differently. A president's talents might suit them better for one or the other of these tasks, for example President George Washington is considered by many to be a great statesman. America, unlike some other countries, has one person, the President, do both jobs.

The Constitution gives the president a limited number of powers, and they are all in Article II, but it grants the president three main executive powers. The president is the chief executive, the commander in chief, and the chief foreign policy maker. As the **Chief executive**, the president is head bureaucrat, making sure the laws are enforced. One of the president's most important powers in this role is **appointment power**. The President has the power to nominate ambassadors to foreign countries, public Ministers, Supreme Court Judges, and various other bureaucrats. As a check on the President's power, some of these nominations have to be approved by the Senate, for example Supreme Court Justices.

The president also serves in the position of commander in chief. In the United States, the **commander in chief** is the civilian head of the armed forces of the United States. The President's exact powers within this role have been hotly contested throughout American history. The President is the commander in chief, but they are not legally allowed to declare war on another country without the approval of Congress. So, the President cannot unilaterally declare war, but if Congress approves a war resolution, the President is considered the head of the operation.

The president is also the **chief foreign policy maker**. As the chief foreign policy maker, the president negotiates treaties with the approval of two-thirds of the Senate. The president also receives ambassadors and represents the United States on the global stage. While Article II of the Constitution grants the president only the limited power to receive foreign ambassadors, this clause is cited to justify the president's powerful and much broader role in foreign affairs.

The president also has a unique power afforded to the office to issue executive agreements. An **executive agreement** is an agreement issued by the president with other countries that enter the countries into binding international obligations. These executive agreements describe how the president will abide by an agreement and can terminate with a new president. An executive agreement is not a treaty, and it is often implemented to circumvent other country's laws regarding the signing of a treaty.

While the president's main responsibilities are related to the office's executive power, the president also has powers of legislative authority. These legislative powers are part of the checks and balances built into the American system. Every year, the president offers **the State of the Union address**. The Constitution says that the president will regularly inform Congress of the state of the union and recommend the measures he considers useful or necessary. While it is not constitutionally required to be a speech, President Woodrow Wilson began the tradition in 193 of addressing Congress and the American people in an annual address.

One of the President's most well-known powers over legislation is the veto. The **Presidential veto** in the Constitution gives the president the option of refusing to sign a bill that Congress has passed. This is a power given to the executive branch in line with the model of checks and balances. There are two types of veto, a direct veto when the President formally sends back the bill with objections, and a pocket veto where the President simply allows the 10-day review period to elapse, leaving the space for the President's signature blank. While the presidential veto is powerful, it can be overridden by Congress. Two-thirds of the Senate and House are required to overturn a presidential veto. Only 4% of all presidential vetoes have been overturned.

Congress has the legislative power to write and pass laws, but when a president wants to create policy that is not passed as law, the president can issue an executive order. An **executive order** is what presidents can issue to fill in details and enforce the laws passed by Congress. These powers direct the federal bureaucracy to act in a particular way. Executive orders can be overturned by the Judicial branch if they are found to be unconstitutional. Executive orders can also be cancelled or revoked by the President, so when a new President is elected, they often review the executive orders of their predecessor. While executive orders are not mentioned in the Constitution, they have become an integral part of a president's power. Before 1900, executive orders were informal and often not made public, nonetheless nearly every president has made some kind of declaration that can be considered an executive order. Modern presidents have issued many more executive orders than their predecessors. Three presidents, Theodore Roosevelt, Calvin Coolidge, and Franklin Delano Roosevelt, issued over 1,000 executive orders during their time in office. More recent presidents have often issued several hundred executive orders.

The president has strong powers of judicial appointment. With **appointment power**, the president can appoint judges, with the advice and consent of the Senate, to the entire federal judiciary. Some of the judicial posts that the president can appoint include the solicitor general, Supreme Court justices, courts of appeals judges, and district court judges. **The solicitor general** is the legal officer who argues cases before the Supreme Court when the United States is a party to that case, as it often is. The president also has removal power. While not in the Constitution, the Supreme Court has ruled in several cases that the president has the sole power to remove some federal appointees. The most important case was *Myers v. United States* in 1926 in which the Supreme Court ruled the president has sole removal authority of federal appointees, except for federal judge appointments.[102]

The president also has the power of the pardon. **The pardon power** of the president means the president can pardon those accused or convicted of federal crimes. The Constitution grants the president the power to pardon. In recent years, many presidents have issued pardons near the end of their terms, and these pardons have caused a great deal of controversy.

9.4 How the American Presidency has changed

The job of the president has become more involved as America itself has become larger and more complex. Citizens' expectations of the presidency have grown over time, but the job's formal powers outlined in Article II of the Constitution have not. The Twenty-Second Amendment is the only constitutional change to affect presidential powers, and it limited them by imposing term limits. The founders envisioned a presidency with limited powers; however, many Presidents have expanded the office's informal powers and the formal powers have

---

[102] Supreme Court of the United States. *Myers v. United States.* Oyez, www.oyez.org/cases/1900-1940/272us52.

been broadly interpreted to increase presidential power. And through this process, the presidency has shifted from a traditional presidency to a modern presidency. The **traditional presidency** was a presidency consistent with the founders' intentions of a president with the limited powers set out by the constitution as the groundwork for the powers of the president. There are 19 powers given to the national government from the constitution, and these powers are known as **delegated powers**. The delegated powers are the explicit forms of power given by the constitution to the federal government. In Article I, Section 8, the itemization of powers to the United States Congress includes functions such as commerce, taxation, and declaration of war. In Article II, Section II, the president is delegated powers including those noted previously (Commander in Chief powers, pardon powers, treaty-making powers, etc.).

The presidency also has inherent powers that have built up over time. **Inherent powers** are powers that were not explicitly laid out but rather were implied in their constitutional duty to take care that the laws be faithfully executed. The inherent powers are given to the federal government so that they can operate the federal bureaucracy systems and government according to new laws that have been passed. Examples of inherent powers given to the federal government include the federal government's oversight of food production and the environment in the form of the FDA and the EPA. The government can use their powers to revise warnings and lists to the American citizens regarding food poisoning health matters and environmental impact issues. There are other certain powers not given to the federal government that were thus reserved for the states by the Tenth Amendment.

These powers not explicitly given to the presidency in the constitution are therefore retained for the individual states. These **reserved Powers** are powers listed in the Tenth amendment to the constitution, and it says that the states retained government authority not explicitly granted to the national government. Some of these reserved state powers include public education, public health, commerce within the state, organizing state elections, prisons and police, other issues regarding arrests and incarcerations, highway and road maintenance, and many more. When the constitution allows for powers to be shared between the national and state governments, these powers are known as **concurrent powers.** A concurrent power is known as the power shared by the national government and the state government such as taxation, and the minimum wage.

The executive branch changed significantly and became much more powerful with President Franklin Delano Roosevelt's New Deal. The limited vision of the executive changed with the stock market crash of 1929 and subsequent economic collapse known as the Great Depression. President Roosevelt's New Deal created a variety of jobs programs and turned the government into a much larger employer to help people out of the Great Depression and build the country's infrastructure. The **wide-reaching** social program built infrastructure, public works, and art, created social insurance programs like Social Security to ensure that a safety net existed for the elderly, disabled, and orphaned, and it reformed the financial system to prevent another repeat depression in the future. The New Deal also signaled the birth of the **modern presidency**, and with this the modern presidency grew the role of the president as compared to the traditional presidency.

After the growth of the modern presidency with FDR, the government grew at all levels. Though presidential candidates started promising to do more and more, the formal powers of the office as outlined in the Constitution stayed the same. The presidency had to find ways to expand its power and influence through more informal channels. It did this through the **power to persuade** and convince Congress to support the executive office plans. This could be done by going directly to the people, known as **going public.** The president's increasing capacity to talk to citizens through the media made this method particularly successful. FDR began having "fireside chats" to talk to the American people informally and discuss the state of the nation.

9.5 Presidents, Popularity, and Congress

To be effective, presidents need to have some level of popularity with the public. This is a minimum requirement to be elected; but it may not be sufficient to make a successful presidency. What factors make a president popular? The president often suffers from steadily declining popularity after an initial peak when they take office. Almost all presidents go through a period called the Honeymoon period. This **Honeymoon period** is the first 100 days of a presidency, when the press is likely to be most kind and the majority of the public is giving the new president the benefit of the doubt. Not all presidents do enjoy a honeymoon. Factors like the state of the economy and external events like wars and natural disasters can influence how popular a president is.

A president's popularity is often split between political parties, with the president enjoying the most popularity within their own party. Due to the **polarization** within American politics, the president's approval is often tied in with how popular their political party is at the moment. This limits how the president can cooperate effectively with Congress, and it can help or hinder how real legislative change occurs because these changes require congressional cooperation. If there is a majority in at least one house that is different from the president's party, then the current government is known as a **divided government** and the power of the president can be significantly hindered. In many divided governments, Congress chooses not to work with the president or the president's legislative liaison. The **congressional liaison** is a presidential appointee whose chief job is to coordinate with Congress on behalf of the president to find points of potential agreement and create a legislative agenda.

CHAPTER 10

The Judicial Branch

10.1 Introduction to the Judiciary

The judiciary is an integral part of checks and balances between different branches of government. Alexander Hamilton wrote an essay advocating for the ratification of the United States Constitution called the Federalist Paper No. 78. Here, Hamilton described what the newly created judicial branch would look like and that the judiciary would be the weakest and thus the "least dangerous branch" of government. Through time, the power of the judiciary has changed. The **judiciary** is the branch of government that interprets and applies the law and solves disputes involving citizens and other government actors.

The courts have changed in their capacity to influence both branches of government. The judiciary has become an enormously powerful branch through *the power of the pen*. The Constitution does not explicitly state that the Supreme Court may determine the constitutionality of an act of the other branches of government. However, judicial review of other branches of the federal government was established in *Marbury v. Madison* when the Court claimed this power for itself.[103] The Court held that American courts have the power to strike

---

[103] *Marbury v. Madison*, 5 United States 137 (1803).

down laws, statutes, and some government actions that they find to violate the Constitution of the United States. *Marbury v. Madison* gave the Supreme Court (itself) the ultimate power of deciding what the Constitution means.

10.2 A Kinds of Laws

The United States is a democracy. In a democracy, laws rule. The **rule of law** is a system in which laws are known in advance, they apply the same way to everyone, and if we feel they have been applied unjustly we can appeal to a higher authority. The laws we notice most limit our behavior and stop us from acting on impulses that are damaging to other people. Laws make collective life possible and even comfortable.

There are different types of laws in the United States judicial system. There are substantive laws, and these laws govern how members of a society are to behave. **Substantive laws** are a body of rules that define what we can or cannot do. When determining what a person cannot do, thereby limiting their freedom, **criminal laws** are a form of substantive law that prohibit behavior that makes collective living difficult or impossible. Engaging in a prohibited behavior is considered a crime and subject to a legal punishment. A **crime** is an action that breaks criminal law. When regulating interactions between people or organizations, it is a civil law. **Civil laws** are laws that regulate interactions between individuals or other private parties, such as a corporation. When an action between individuals causes harm against another person it is a **tort,** which is an action that violates a civil law.

Substantive laws are contrasted with procedural law, which is the set of procedures for making, administering, and enforcing substantive law. **Procedural laws** define how the laws are used, applied, and enforced. Court procedures were founded from the United States Constitution's Fifth and Fourteenth Amendment's guarantee of due process which both state no one shall be "deprived of life liberty or property without due process of law"[104]. Due process requires the government to abide by fair procedures before depriving a person of life, liberty or property.

10.2B Forms of Law

What form do laws take? Laws originate from different places and different entities have authority to create them. The form of laws and how they are interpreted are important to the judicial system. **Constitutional laws** are established by federal and state constitutions. This body of laws establishes the legal infrastructure of our governments. Constitutions set the framework for the court systems, determine how the three branches of federal government relate to each other and shape the relationship between the federal and state governments. More notably, constitutional law determines how the game of politics is played. Much of constitutional law has grown from federal and state supreme court rulings interpreting their respective constitutions. Constitutional law, and most other court rulings, create **case law or common law** that can be binding precedent. **Precedents** are a series of court rulings of similar issues and facts. These rulings create an authority for courts to apply the same law to future cases that have similar issues or facts.

Unlike case law that was developed by court rulings, **statutory laws** are laws that are made by legislatures. Statutory law is written law passed by a legislative body of local, state or federal government and codified in statute- which means law that is arranged and numbered into a systematic code. **Administrative law** is the body of law that governs the activities of administrative agencies of government. Executive level governmental agency action can include rule making, adjudication, or the enforcement of a specific regulatory agenda. Administrative law is considered a branch of public law. Examples of federal administrative law is the regulation of civil aviation, planes and pilots to protect public safety through the Federal Aviation Administration.

---

[104] United States Const. Amend. X and XIV.

Finally, **executive orders** are rules that also have the full force and effect of law and are issued by the executive branch, such as the President of the United States or the Governor of a state. They are issued based on authority granted to the President or Governor in their respective constitutions and must be consistent with that authority.

10.3 The American Legal System

Legal systems around the world are different. The American legal systems are heavily influenced by political culture. The United States system in particular can be adversarial and is litigious in nature.

The United States system is adversarial in nature. The **adversarial system** or adversary system is a legal system used in the common law countries where two advocates represent their parties' case or position before an impartial person or group of people, usually a judge or jury, who attempt to determine the truth and pass judgment accordingly. An adversarial system is a system that is primarily concerned that the legal process will be fair, and result in a just judgment. This type of system is different from an inquisitorial system. An **inquisitorial system** is a legal system in which the court, or a part of the court, is actively involved in investigating the facts of the case. This is distinct from an adversarial system, in which the role of the court is primarily that of an impartial referee between the prosecution and the defense. An inquisitorial system is a system in which the truth is the goal and if it requires that the judge leave his or her neutral perch to ask questions and investigate, so be it.

The United States legal system is a **litigious system**. Litigation refers to the process of resolving disputes by filing or answering a complaint through the public court system. A litigious system is a system in which citizens prefer to settle their differences in court.[AM1] As discussed above, if the issue of the case is one of criminal law, the two parties will be the state and the defendant where the state is charging the defendant for violating a criminal law. If the issue of the case is based on civil law, the two parties will be private individuals alleging harm was caused to one or both parties.

10.4 The Criminal Justice System

The criminal justice system focuses on justice. Through the process of **adjudication,** the truth can be discovered, and justice served by providing a formal judgment in a disputed matter. If there has been a mistake in the trial, an **appeal** can be filed, which is a process brought by a petitioner if that party believes there has been a procedural error or that the judge has applied the law incorrectly.

A right given in criminal trials in the United States is a right to a jury trial. The right to a jury trial in criminal cases is found in both Article III[105] and the Sixth Amendment[106]of the Constitution. If you are accused of a serious offence that carries a potential sentence of more than six months' imprisonment, you are guaranteed a trial by a jury of your peers[5][107]. Jury duty is a collective action problem—we all want to share in the outcome, but many of us try to get out of providing the effort that makes that outcome possible.

10.5 Equality and the Criminal Justice System

One of the hallmarks of American political culture is that everyone should be treated the same. But the procedural value that everyone be treated the same is often not the way things actually work in America. The equality for all people, regardless of race, gender and class has not always existed. Even though the Constitution established the **equal protection clause** which provided in part that "[no state shall] deny any person within its jurisdiction the equal protection of the laws,"[108] the judiciary did not originally interpret this to mean equal protection for black Americans.

---

[105] United States Const. Art. III, § 2 provides "The trial of all Crimes, except in Cases of Impeachment, shall be by Jury".

[106] United States Const. Amend. XI provides "In all criminal prosecutions, the accused shall enjoy the right to a speedy and public trial, by an impartial jury."

[107] *United States v. Nachtigal,* 507 United States 1 (1993).

[108] United States Const. Amend. XIV, § 1

From its beginnings, the United States has had what amounts to separate criminal justice systems for black and white Americans. America has had stronger punishments for those of color. An example of this was the case of Emmett Till. Till, a 14-year-old boy, was caught and lynched in Mississippi in 1955 for allegedly offending a white woman who later admitted she lied. The white men who killed Till were acquitted by a white jury.

The role that justice has served white and African Americans has developed inconsistently since the inception of the nation. There are dual narratives about who are the "good guys." African Americans and whites have developed very different narratives about the role the criminal justice system plays in their lives.

Racial profiling has prevented African Americans from receiving equal access to justice. **Racial profiling** is a violation of civil rights in which police target people because they fit the mental image of what a criminal looks like. Obviously, it is not possible to have a stereotype based on race, gender, or class of a person and profile them as a police target. This difference in application of the law is racism. Racism isn't just what you say, it is also an acceptance of different rules of treatment according to race built into the norms of the system. In the criminal justice system, the issue is *equal treatment*. In the civil justice system, the issue is *equal access*.

10.6 The Constitution, Congress, and the Dual Court System

The founders wanted to avoid having a national court system and chose to root the court system under the foundation of Federalism. Because the question of whether there would be a national court system with jurisdiction over the states was such a hot-button issue, the authors of the Constitution tended to gloss over it.

Article I Courts

Only the actions of Article III courts are the subject of this chapter, but it is important to note there are two types of federal courts. Article I courts are created by Congress in order to implement its various legislative powers. For example, the United States Tax Court has jurisdiction over federal income tax subject matters. Judges of such Article I courts do not have a life tenure or protection from salary decreases. Article I courts are sometimes vested with administrative as well as judicial functions, and the congressional power to create such "hybrid" courts has been sustained by the Supreme Court.[109]

Article III Courts

Article III of the United States Constitution states that the "judicial Power of the United States, shall be vested in one supreme Court, and in such inferior Courts as the Congress may from time to time ordain and establish."[110] What this means is that the Constitution provides for one Supreme Court and lower courts established by Congress as necessary. Although Congress has the complete power to set the jurisdictional limits of the federal courts, it is still bound by the standards of judicial power set forth in Article III as to subject matter, parties, and the requirement of "case or controversy" (discussed later). Therefore, Congress cannot require the federal courts to perform nonjudicial functions.

What are lower courts? Most court systems have an entry-level court to which you first bring your case or in which you are first tried before a jury. If you lose this entry level court case, you have a **right to appeal,** which is to ask a higher or appeals court to ensure that everything was handled properly and to review the process.

Federal Judges

The Article III constitutional section also authorizes Congress to appoint Judges of federal courts for life terms. This means these judges can only be removed through a vote of impeachment, so they hold their jobs as

---

[109] *Glidden v. Zdanok*, 370 United States 530 (1962).
[110] United States Const. Art. III, § 1.

long as they behave themselves. In order to be a judge in the federal court system, the Constitution requires judges to be appointed according to certain procedures but sets forth no specific required qualifications to serve as a judge. There are no age, citizenship or other requirements. The Constitution specifies only that the judges shall be appointed by the president, with the advice and consent of the Senate. The judiciary is the only unelected branch of the government.

In order to protect federal judges from political interference or pressures, they receive a salary that cannot be reduced during their lifetime terms. The Constitution gives federal judges this protection so that they can make fair and trustworthy decisions on cases without worrying their decision will be publicly or politically unpopular. Judges can, however, be removed from office only if impeached and convicted by the House of Representatives and the Senate, a process that has resulted in only 15 impeachments and eight convictions in more than 200 years.

Federal Court System

The federal court system is three-tiered. First, the lowest level of the federal judiciary hierarchy consists of 94 federal district courts. Each state has at least one **federal district court** located within its borders while the largest states have four. Federal district courts will hear the case first because district courts have **original jurisdiction**. At this level, the court will consider and rule on all the facts of the case during a trial. Each federal district court has a United States attorney that are government attorneys that represent the United States in criminal and civil cases. United States attorneys are appointed by the president and approved or affirmed by the Senate for four-year terms.

Next, once a case is decided by the federal district courts, it can be appealed and heard by the federal **Courts of Appeals**. These courts are arranged into 12 circuits. These circuits are large super districts that encompass several of the district court territories. Each circuit has its own Court of Appeals. The 12th circuit covers just Washington, D.C., and hears all appeals involving government agencies. Cases are heard in the circuit that includes the district court where the case was heard originally. The sole function of these courts is to hear appeals from the lower federal district courts if the losing party believes the law was applied incorrectly and to review the legal reasoning behind the decisions reached there. This is referred to as **appellate jurisdiction.** These courts do not hold trials and generally do not consider the facts of the case. The decisions in the courts of appeals are made by a rotating panel of three judges who sit to hear the case. The judges rotate in order to provide a decision-making body that is as unbiased as possible. Having all the judges present (*en banc*) gives a decision more legitimacy and sends a message that the decision was made carefully.

The third and highest tier of the federal court system is the United States Supreme Court and is discussed below.

The judicial ideology is important for the courts because it can sway important legal concepts in the public policy of the United States, such as abortion rights. Judicial ideology varies by the president that nominates a justice. These days an increasingly important qualification for the job of federal judge is the ideological or policy positions of the appointee. The Senate confirmation process has become more rancorous. The nomination process has been more important to conservatives than to liberals.

State Court System

State court systems are different from federal court systems. Each state establishes their own state courts through state law or their constitution. Therefore, the structures of state court systems vary from state to state. Each state has a tiered system that has a highest court for appeals, which is often, but not always, called a state supreme court. State courts have jurisdiction over state law subject matter and interpret their respective state law and constitutions.

State courts judges are chosen differently than the federal court judges and, again, the procedures are established by state laws. State judges are chosen through three different methods: Appointment by the governor, election by the state legislature, and election by the state population as a whole. The state election of judges can be controversial. Critics argue that judicial elections can create a conflict of interest because few people are able to cast educated votes in judicial elections. There is a further problem that the political nature of elections and campaigning may influence judges' rulings.

10.7 The Supreme Court

The Supreme Court is the highest court of the land. In the United States Judiciary, the top player is the Supreme Court. The founders wanted the Supreme Court to be above politics. The President is not seen going to the Supreme Court and the Supreme Court Justices are not seen visiting the president in order to keep a perceived bias from occurring. The Supreme Court is still a POLITICAL institution. The very reasons that the founders could not be frank about their plans for the Court in the Constitution shows just how politically volatile the whole institution was. As discussed above, the primary job is to determine if laws are permitted under the United States Constitution and provide judicial review of those laws.

The political nature of the Supreme Court can influence laws, freedoms, and civil rights for all Americans for generations. The Supreme Court is political in three respects: (1) How justices are chosen, (2) How the justices make decisions, and (3) The impact of those decisions on all the rest of us.

It is very difficult to get on the Supreme Court. The president appoints Supreme Court justices, and the Senate approves or affirms the nomination of the president. The president and the Senate consider the merit and demographics of the nominee, but mostly the appointing entities are fixated on ideology. Supreme Court justices have always been attorneys, had extensive careers in the legal field and have overwhelmingly been white males. In 1967, Justice Thurgood Marshall became the first African American Supreme Court Justice. And shortly thereafter in 1981, Sandra Day O'Connor became the first woman appointed.

The type of justice appointed to the Supreme Court can either be someone who is a judicial interpretivist or a strict constructionist. A **Judicial interpretivist** is one who believes that the founders could not have anticipated all the changes that make the world today different from theirs and, therefore, that judges should read the Constitution as the founders would write it in light of modern-day experience. A **strict constructionist** is a scholar and judge who believes that the Constitution should be read just as it was written. This is a political hot-button issue now because, until Justice Antonin Scalia's death in 2016, there was a 5-4 majority who were sufficiently committed to interpretivism that they supported the right to privacy and the case that was based on *Griswold*, *Roe v. Wade* (1973).

10.8 Federal Court Jurisdiction

Jurisdiction is the authority of the court to hear the case. The federal courts have jurisdiction over all cases involving a federal question, or **subject matter jurisdiction,** that seeks to answer a question based on federal law or the United States Constitution. Any subject matter involving the federal government or foreign governments would also be within the jurisdiction of federal courts. Federal courts also have **diversity jurisdiction** where the disputes are between two parties that are from different states. Additionally, courts have diversity jurisdiction to resolve disputes between two different state governments. If Tennessee and Arkansas are disputing rights to Mississippi, the case would be heard in federal court.

Even if a federal court has subject matter or diversity jurisdiction, it still might refuse to hear a case. Whether the court will hear the case (*i.e.,* whether the case is justiciable) depends on whether a **case or controversy** is involved, and whether the other elements of jurisdiction are met. Article III, Section 2 of the United States Constitution also requires federal courts to decide questions that arise out of actual disputes or real cases and controversies.[111] Therefore, federal courts cannot issue advisory opinions in cases involving challenges to governmental legislation or policy whose enforcement is neither actual nor threatened. Although, some state supreme courts do have the judicial power to issue advisory opinions.

A party to a case is generally not entitled to review of a law before it is enforced. Therefore, a federal court will not hear a case that is not **ripe** (case is brought too early). This means the party must have been harmed or there is an immediate threat of harm. A federal court will also not hear a case that has become **moot** (case is brought too late). A "real, live controversy" must exist "at all stages of review", not merely when the complaint is filed.[112]

A person who brings a case to federal court must also have **standing** and show he or she has a concrete stake in the outcome of the controversy. This means the party bringing the action must show an actual injury or harm done and a causal connection between the injury and the conduct complained of (*i.e.,* the injury is traceable to the challenged conduct of the defendant and not another third party). Generally, people do not have standing to challenge the way the government spends tax dollars simply because the person bringing the action is a taxpayer, because their interest is too remote, and the person has not suffered an injury-in-fact.

10.9 The politics of making a decision

Getting a case to the Supreme Court may seem very political and, because the decisions of the Supreme Court affect every American and the Court hears a small majority of the applications it receives, it can be difficult to get your case before the Court. In fact, the Court accepts 100-150 of the 7,000 cases that it is asked to review each year.[113] If four of the nine

---

[111] United States Const. Art. III, § 2.

[112] *De Funis v. Odegaard,* 416 United States 312 (1974).

[113] https://www.uscourts.gov/about-federal-courts.

justices agree to hear the case, then the case will be heard. The court can decide to hear a case or not and is generally under no obligation to approve or deny an application to hear the case.

There are a couple ways that the parties can get their cases heard before the Supreme Court. If a party is not satisfied with a lower court decision and wants to get before the Supreme Court, the party can ask the court for review or certiorari. In law, certiorari is a court process to seek judicial review of a decision of a lower court or government agency. Certiorari comes from the name of an English prerogative writ, issued by a superior court to direct that the record of the lower court be sent to the superior court for review. **Writs of certiorari** are pleas from a party who lost in a lower court who believes there is a procedural or legal problem with the previous verdict. Most cases come before the Supreme Court through writs of certiorari.

When a party who is not a party to a lawsuit would like to influence the court to hear a case, the party may write an amicus curiae brief, **Amicus curiae briefs,** also known as "friend of the court" briefs, are submitted by concerned groups. They are someone who is not a party to a case who assists a court by offering information, expertise, or insight that has a bearing on the issues in the case. The decision on whether to consider an amicus brief lies within the discretion of the court. The phrase amicus curiae is legal Latin.

When a case goes before the Supreme Court that involves the United States and not two private parties, it is led under the **solicitor general,** who is a lawyer of the federal government and supervises the litigation.

Once the Court decides to hear the case, the parties submit written arguments with a **brief**, which is a summary of the argument and states the reasons the Court should rule in their favor. Next, the lawyers for each party will present **oral arguments** before the Court where the justices are able to ask questions. Often, the justices have already reviewed the briefs before the oral arguments and can express how he or she is leaning when asking questions. The justices then meet in private **conference** to discuss the case and make their decisions.

If a case is to be won by any party, it must receive **majority opinion** of the court, which is the opinion of at least five Supreme Court justices. Usually, one justice is tasked with drafting the majority opinion that represents the views of the other justices. The opinion will state the decision, the reasoning for the decision and sets a precedent for lower courts to follow. Sometimes the Supreme Court will issue **concurring opinions,** which are written by justices who agree with the majority opinion but for different or extra reasons. A **dissenting opinion** is written by justices who disagree with the opinion and want to be on the record even though the dissenting opinion is not considered binding precedent that lower courts are required to follow.

10.10 Important Supreme Court Decisions

Some important Supreme Court decisions over the past 200+ years have provided integral interpretations of the rights guaranteed, although not always explicitly, under the United States Constitution. The judiciary is tasked with interpreting exactly what this means and providing judicial review of laws that may violate these rights. Therefore, whenever the government seeks to regulate these rights or freedoms, the Court will weigh the importance of the right against the interest or policies sought to be served by the governmental regulation.

As discussed above, an important issue decided by the Court was that the Court should be the ultimate decider of what is constitutional in the United States federal government and the states. *Marbury v. Madison*[114] was a landmark United States Supreme Court case that established the principle of judicial review in the United States, meaning that American courts have the power to strike down laws, statutes, and some government actions that they find to violate the Constitution of the United States.

---

[114] *Marbury v. Madison*, 5 United States 137 (1803).

While the Constitution separates governmental powers among the branches of government, the United States Supreme Court interpreted and specified that the separation of powers doctrine specifically prohibits the legislature from interfering with the courts' final judgments in *Plaut v. Spendthrift Farm, Inc.*[115] In this case, the legislature, through Congress, passed a law to provide a special motion for reinstating the cases dismissed as time-barred by Supreme Court rulings. The Court held the law providing for the reinstatement of dismissed cases violated the separation of powers doctrine- the legislature can't tell the judiciary what to do.

The Constitution also established the **equal protection clause** which provided in part that "[no state shall] deny any person within its jurisdiction the equal protection of the laws."[116] In 1896, the Supreme Court first dissected the meaning of the equal protection clause in *Plessy v. Ferguson*.[117] The Court reviewed a Louisiana law . railroads in the state to provide separate cars for white and African American passengers and upheld the constitutionality of the state-mandated racial segregation law for all public facilities as long as the segregated facilities were equal in quality, a doctrine that came to be known as "separate but equal". It took the United States sixty more years to reverse this decision and undo the damage done with the "separate but equal doctrine". *Brown v. Board of Education*[118] was a landmark decision of the United States Supreme Court in which the Court ruled that state laws establishing racial segregation in public schools are unconstitutional, even if the segregated schools are otherwise equal in quality.

The Court also declared that the Constitution required equal protection for women when it held that a state law that discriminated against women was unconstitutional in *Reed v. Reed.*[119]

---

[115] *Plaut v. Spendthrift Farm, Inc.*, 514 United States 211 (1995).

[116] United States Const. Amend. XIV, § 1.

[117] *Plessy v. Ferguson*, 163 United States 537 (1896).

[118] *Brown v. Board of Education*, 347 United States 483 (1954).

[119] *Reed v. Reed*, 404 United States 71 (1971).

Certain fundamental rights are protected under the Constitution. Various **privacy rights,** including marriage, sexual relations, abortion and childrearing, are fundamental rights. Modern rights to privacy guaranteed under the Constitution have been clarified by the Supreme Court. In *Griswold v. Connecticut*, the Supreme Court established a "marital zone of privacy" and the fundamental right of a marital relationship protects couples right to buy and use contraceptives without government restrictions.[120] The Supreme Court has also held in *Roe v. Wade* that the right of privacy includes the right of a woman to have an abortion under certain circumstances without undue influence from the state.[121]

Another fundamental right is the **freedom of speech** which provides that "Congress shall make no law ...abridging the freedom of speech."[122] The freedom of speech protects the free flow of ideas, a most important function in a democratic society. A regulation or law that tries to forbid speech of specific ideas (**content regulation**) is more likely to violate the free speech doctrine. It is usually unconstitutional for the government to prohibit speech based on its content. In *Brandenburg v. Ohio*, the Court held that the government could not prohibit political speech, or speech with political content, unless it is linked to immediate lawless behavior.[123] However, **conduct regulation**, which is content-neutral and regulates how the speech is conducted, is more likely permitted (*i.e.,* law prohibiting billboards for purposes of traffic safety).

While the Constitution remains largely unchanged and is the most important consideration when deciding a case and applying the facts to the law, the Court has recognized the law needs to be flexible and adapt to changing times. The Court has, and will continue to, overrule outdated precedents.

---

[120] *Griswold v. Connecticut*, 381 United States 479 (1965).
[121] *Roe v. Wade*, 410 United States 113 (1973).
[122] United States Const. Amend. I.
[123] *Brandenburg v. Ohio*, 395 United States 444 (1969).

CHAPTER 11

Public opinion, campaigns, and elections

Chapter Summary

The media can influence the governmental implementation of public policies and the development of public opinion. Policymakers pay attention to both preferences and trends among the public. Preferences are not static and may not remain the same over time. Political involvement relies on how strongly people feel about current political issues. Public opinion polls track and affect election campaigns, the Electoral College and strategic campaign considerations, and the ultimate poll—choosing a president at the ballot box.

Opinions start to develop during childhood, and beliefs subjects acquire early in life are unlikely to change much as they age. The socialization process leaves citizens with attitudes and beliefs that create a personal ideology depending on attitudes and beliefs and prioritizing each belief over the others. To run a successful campaign requires understanding the nature of public opinion and its effects during elections. Campaign managers want to know how citizens will vote and persuade them. Candidates and elected public officials use polls' results to decide their future legislative votes, campaign messages, or propaganda.

11.1 Introduction to public opinion, campaigns, and elections

Why does it matter what the American public thinks about political issues? In a federal constitutional democratic republic such as the United States, the national government, headed by the president, shares powers with the Congress and the judiciary as mandated by the Constitution. The federal government also shares some powers with state and local governments, again as prescribed in the Constitution. The American people elect their governmental representatives to serve their interests and influence the policymaking process.

Political office-seekers often use *public opinion polls* to determine voters' preferences on various issues, so they can tailor their campaign messages to secure the possible votes hopefully ascend to public office. They seek to persuade citizens during the *campaign*.

Public opinion is what the people may think on any given topic, especially on political issues for our purposes. In our representative democracy, there are two ways of determining what people may be thinking; first, by taking a headcount through polling, second, by asking them to vote in elections.

Polling public opinion is very different from "going to the polls" in actual elections. First, in a public opinion poll, for the sake of accuracy, those taking the poll sample respondents to create a group as representative of the voting public as possible during periods leading up to the actual casting of ballots. In elections, however, the voters take the lead and select whom they wish to lead their country, states, and localities.

Second, timing is a crucial element in polling. Researchers can conduct polls whenever an educational institution, marketing company, or media outlet has the time, money, and inclination to conduct them. Elections are different, as they are held on scheduled dates.

Third, polls are not binding on anyone, and one can pay them attention or choose to ignore them while elections are final. Still, public opinion polling and elections are essentially two ways of doing the same thing, finding out what people think at a specific point in time.

11.2 The quality of public opinion

Opinions start to develop during childhood, and beliefs subjects acquire early in life are unlikely to change much as they age.[124] The socialization process leaves citizens with attitudes and beliefs that create a personal ideology depending on attitudes and beliefs and prioritizing each belief over the others. To run a successful campaign requires understanding the nature of public opinion and its effects during elections.[125] Ideally, all citizens would be well informed about government, rules, and relevant political actors. They would also be tolerant of ideas other than their own and willing to compromise to further the collective interest, and happy to participate at various political levels and engage in civic activities. Subjects should receive their news from diverse sources to get in touch with different viewpoints and perspectives.

Most Americans do not always receive their news from high-quality sources, and while they may be theoretically tolerant, they are often less so in practice. Increasingly, some groups have come to view political compromise as a fundamental betrayal of their values. Additionally, United States elections tend to have meager voter turnout rates compared with other democratic countries. All of which leads people to a fundamental question about their government: Whose views should count?

One of the ideals of democracy is *tolerance*, which means that some people who vote in elections may not necessarily be the ones one would prefer. Some voters may even be pursuing a path of *rational ignorance*, that is, choosing not to be informed about politics because the payoff from participating feels too remote or the difference they make seems to be insignificant.

Still, the country may be delivered from an ill-informed populace by specific shortcuts that can lead people toward rationality. Many citizens suffer from a phenomenon known as *online processing*, which is about ending the day with one's head full of opinions picked up on the fly with

---

[124] *See* Krutz, Glen S. *American Government 2e.*, 2019. Internet resource. Accessed 9 Mar. 2021. Lau, Tim. Brennan Center for Justice, https://www.brennancenter.org/our-work/research-reports/citizens-united-explained, *Citizens United Explained*, accessed 19 March 2021.

[125] On the manufacturing of public opinion, see McNair.

no clear idea of how one arrived at them. While people often have good reasons for holding their views, sometimes they process them too quickly and with insufficient information. People probably are not as ignorant as they sound. Moreover, they may find that others around can offer them clues as to the nature of things.

The *two-step flow of information* is a psychological process by which *opinion followers* look to opinion leaders for understanding and cues on how to vote[126]. Opinion followers are the vast majority of citizens. In contrast, *opinion leaders* usually prepare themselves through study and research to be well informed and subsequently get involved in civic activities. Journalists often interview them on TV news and talk shows. Some subjects who receive some higher education may become opinion leaders themselves, providing cues and guidance to family members, friends, and members of groups to which one belongs.

Political parties and interest groups may provide subjects with a form of comprehension similar to the two-step flow, except that the opinion leader is not an individual but a group. Still, one should bear in mind that these shortcuts are not foolproof. There is no guarantee that these shortcuts will lead to decision-making that is, in fact, informed and smart.

11.3 How to know what Americans think?

The science of public opinion polling has come a long way. According to The Gallup Organization, a Washington, D.C.-based analytics company founded in 1935, polls can accurately "tell what proportion of a population has a specific viewpoint."[127]

---

[126] See Zaller, especially chapter 9, to better understand two-sided and two-step information flows. Zaller, John. *The Nature and Origins of Mass Opinion.* Cambridge University Press, 2011.

[127] Even if polls tell one what proportion of the population has specific viewpoints and shares certain ideas, their purpose is not to change one's mindset. Social researchers are the ones who explain why people believe as they do and what to do about that. For more information, *see* Nielsen, Eric. What Is Public Opinion Polling and Why Is It Important?, *Gallup World Poll*, http://media.gallup.com/muslimwestfacts/pdf/pollingandhowtouseitr1dreveng.pdf, accessed 15 March 2021.

The modern science of public opinion polling is quite complex. Although statisticians have determined that a random sample of only 1,000 to 2,000 people can be very representative of a state or the country as a whole, modern polling consists of numerous methodologies, techniques, and considerations. Done correctly, this can be a fairly accurate gauge of what people are thinking. Scientific survey research involves random sampling of a population, and some fancy math to extrapolate those results to the public at large. A random sample means that everyone in the target population has an equal chance of being chosen. Survey research firms generate random lists of telephone numbers of voters in a state, district or even an entire country.

What you should look for in reports about survey research is:

1. a specified margin of error (you don't get one without doing the fancy math), and

2. the sample size. The margin of error is a way of judging how confident we are that the results of the survey are in range of what the entire population thinks. If this information is included in the survey, you have some assurance that it's a scientific survey, and not, say, one taken by a congressman by mass-mailing his district.

Legislators and members of Congress infrequently survey people back home, usually by doing a mass mailing to all the registered voters in the district. The problem with those sorts of surveys is that they are not random samples, but self-selecting samples. The only people who respond to such surveys are those with really strong feelings about an issue, and what we know about them is that there tend to be fewer of them than the mass of folks in the middle.

A *random sample* is a representative subset of a larger population in which everyone has an equal chance of being chosen, and no one group is over-represented. *Sample bias*, however, is when one part of the population has been accorded disproportionate weight. One of the most challenging parts of polling these days is persuading people who may be busy or distracted to offer their responses to questions. A *nonresponse bias* may occur in polls if a particular group is less likely to respond than another. To compensate for any sampling bias, polling companies may use a statistical process called *weighting*. Some groups are given more weight to make the results more accurately reflect what the wider public is thinking. Still, in the end, it is an inexact science, and no poll will be perfect.

One way of narrowing the sample is by taking *likely voter polls*, that is, by questioning people who are the most likely to vote in a forthcoming election. In this effort, pollsters may use *likely voter screens*, which are methods that attempt to weed out nonvoters. Furthermore, no matter what techniques pollsters use, polls' accuracy will always be problems, generally called *sampling errors*. Polls may also be skewed by house effects or how a pollster's results favor Democrats or Republicans. Thus, in light of all this, one finds that all polls will vary at least slightly. Sometimes, in an attempt by media outlets to arrive at more accurate results, methods may be used that pull together the results of several polls in what one calls *polling aggregators*.

Polling came into its own when enough Americans owned telephones to make spot digit dialing an effective way to draw a random sample. *Random digit dialing* was how pollsters could randomly sample Americans by calling them on their landlines. Different kinds of national polls measure where Americans stand on particular issues that are released periodically by major media organizations. *Tracking polls* show data movements over periods to detect changes in support for people or issues. They can be particularly helpful to those running for political office, enabling them to see how they are doing than their opponents.

Researchers take *exit polls* as people leave their places of voting immediately after casting their ballots. The raw data are sometimes leaked early, before the polls close, creating false expectations of who might win or even influence the eventual results. *Fake polls* are sometimes released to manipulate results, but they tell nothing about the real world. The upshot is that polls, in general, are notably informative if researchers conduct them scientifically, but any individual poll can suffer from sampling errors.

11.4 How do subjects form their opinions?

What elements may combine to shape one's political views when gathering and processing information? For one, a transfer of political attitudes, narratives, and beliefs from one generation to another, called *political socialization*, probably contributes to one's outlook. It helps create a stable, loyal citizenry who buys into the system's foundational values by bringing people together around shared values. Some of the socialization agents are families, schools, religious institutions, peer groups, and the media. *Patriotism*, or shared loyalty to one's country and its institutions, is also a potent socialization agent.

Still, some agents may socialize citizens to break into separate groups. Socialization works through a set of interests and values that tend to divide people according to ideologies. *Party identification*, or which political party one identifies with, is probably the most significant influence on one's opinions and votes. Party identification is not a randomly assigned feature to subjects. Data can reveal to researchers critical information concerning this vital component of political socialization.

Race and ethnicity play significant roles in determining party affiliations. Over time, the Republican Party has become whiter, and one sees that African Americans are far more likely to be Democrats, at about a ten-to-one ratio. So are Latinos and Asian Americans, both at two-to-one. There is also a clear *gender gap* in that women are more likely to be Democrats than are men, who are more likely to be Republicans. This situation is even more evident in the case of millennials than in previous generations. *Religion* may also play a role in party affiliation. White evangelical Protestants are much more likely to be Republicans, while Roman Catholics split along ethnic lines, and religiously unaffiliated people are predominantly Democrats. *Education* factors into party alliances, with more-educated voters moving in recent years toward the Democrats. The *location* has become another determinant factor nowadays, with Democrats tending to cluster in urban and, increasingly, suburban areas. Republicans, on the other hand, tend to live in outer suburban and rural areas.

The generations into which people of varying ages may fall also seem to influence how they vote. All the trends one has discussed here become increasingly more robust as the voter pool gets younger over time. Democrats are what journalist and data analyst Ron Brownstein[128] calls the *coalition of the ascendant*—that is, of the racial and ethnic groups getting more prominent and more visible. Republicans are becoming smaller and aging out, what Brownstein calls the *coalition of restoration*—a group composed of older, blue-collar, evangelical rural whites who want to "restore" the last century's social order. Brownstein's research suggests that without a change in the current trends, the parties' gulf will only widen when post-millennials begin to come of age in the next few years.

People may identify with a party initially because it takes policy positions that they agree with, but eventually, the party can become a kind of information shorthand for them. As Americans become more polarized, adopting "*Us vs. Them*" attitudes, voters are becoming less likely to leave their party's comfort zone to vote with the other.

If partisanship is remarkably important in shaping voters' opinions, do natural and practical concerns even matter? Well, some voters will not consider voting for a candidate who does not share their views on one issue that they consider to be fundamental, regardless of party. One refers to them as *single-issue voters*. A growing segment of voters, perhaps as much as thirty percent, eschew any party affiliations. Researchers call them *independent voters* or swing voters. The upshot is that whether one chooses to act on party cues or other socialization influences may depend on whether a particular candidate can motivate people to vote.

---

[128] *See* Brownstein, Ronald and National Journal. "The Clinton Conundrum." *The Atlantic*, 17 April 2015, www.theatlantic.com/politics/archive/2015/04/the-clinton-conundrum/431949.

11.5 The ultimate poll is voting in elections

The United States has one of the lowest voter participation rates among industrialized democratic nations. *Voter turnout* is the percentage of eligible voters who cast ballots, and efforts to legally limit who can vote are known as *regulating the electorate*. These efforts to determine who is allowed to vote, which reached a peak in the decades following the United States Civil War, are still alive and well, even resurging in recent years.

The voters who reliably tend to vote are older, whiter, wealthier, and more educated Americans. Younger voters, newer voters, people of color, single moms, and people lower on the socioeconomic scale are less likely to vote, and if they do, they are more likely to vote for the Democrats.

The voters who reliably tend to vote are older, whiter, wealthier, and more educated Americans. Younger voters, newer voters, people of color, single moms, and people lower on the socioeconomic scale are less likely to vote, and if they do, they are more likely to vote for the Democrats. Republicans reportedly want to make voting less open, and Democrats want to make it simpler for everyone. Republicans have expressed their concerns about voter fraud, specifically people who are not legal voters casting votes, so they want to tighten regulations.

The political stakes in regulating the electorate are high. The continuing battles about regulating the electorate are a political struggle over which party will have the advantage. Since about 2010, Republicans have found it easier to regulate folks out of the electorate than to reach out to groups that tend to vote against them.

The political stakes in regulating the electorate are high. The continuing battles about regulating the electorate are a political struggle over which party will have the advantage. Since about 2010, Republicans have found it easier to regulate folks out of the electorate than to reach out to groups that tend to vote against them.

So, if Americans stopped regulating the electorate, would the United States voter turnout rates increase? Studies show that voter turnout rates would probably increase if Americans decided to reduce the legal barriers to voting. Studies also show that voter fraud is not the problem that Republicans claim it is. Still, one would not achieve 100 percent turnout rates in the United States, as some potential voters have many personal reasons for not voting. They do not have time in their busy schedules to inform themselves enough to care about their voting issues. According to their mindset, their votes will not make a difference, and thus, they do not feel engaged or connected with American society. These citizens perceive there are no meaningful offers to choose from, or it may seem to them that all the available choices are corrupt.

Sometimes their parties do not engage in *voter mobilization*; they fail to make an effort to get out the votes of people who would support them. Encouraging party members to go to the polls can also be referred to as *get-out-the-vote (GOTV)* efforts. As one has seen above, this is a burden that tends to weigh more heavily on Democrats.

What difference does it make if people do not vote? People's decisions not to vote or their failure to exercise their rights affect the Democrats more than the Republicans, and not voting can reduce an elected government's legitimacy. An endorsement from the voters to govern is called an *electoral mandate*. The upshot is that voting is of great importance so that policymakers, politicians, and researchers account for everyone's policy preferences, and people can feel invested in their government's actions.

11.6 Presidential elections

The ones that usually attract the most attention are the *general elections* held every four years. On the ballot are the president, every member of the House of Representatives, one-third of the Senate, various state and local offices, and any petition initiatives that may make the ballot in some states.

What are the requirements to run for president? Which are the steps to follow? There are three critical steps in the election process:

The first step usually takes place behind the scenes. The *invisible primary* is when candidates test the waters to see if they can obtain support and promises of big money without launching a viable campaign.

The second step is about *getting the nomination*. *Party primaries* are held, statewide elections among members of the same party, or in some states, *party caucuses*, which are meetings where party members may debate the merits of the various candidates, and delegates can then decide for whom they wish to stand. The earlier state contests attract many candidates and media attention, so naturally, everyone wants to be among them. However, New Hampshire and Iowa have made it their business to remain first in line. *Frontloading* is a process by which states try to move their primaries or caucuses to earlier dates, which may not be suitable for democracy. Only the most fervent party activists are paying attention to politics that early in the season. During the primary season, the goal is to be the front runner and hold on to that position through the final contest. The *front runner* is the leader of the pack, as seen in the polls.

Candidates attempt to grab and keep the *momentum* by winning debates and maintaining an advantage in the early contests. If, for some reason, one does not perform as well as one has set up the media to expect, one may look like a loser, which can diminish the momentum during the campaign.

The third step is about rallying the party in the *national nominating conventions*, which are party conventions held near the end of summer or early in the autumn before the election, offering a chance to bring the party together behind a political candidacy. Conventions are party mending, strengthening, and rallying events that the media does not have serious interest in covering. The upshot is that most voters will not be paying close attention until the summer ends in the election year.

11.7 The general election and the Electoral College

The general election campaigns open on Labor Day, even though it may feel like they have been going on forever by then. The campaigns keep their eyes on the ultimate prize--more valuable even than the popular vote! When it comes to presidential elections, the final prize is the *Electoral College*, a body of electors from each state who votes for the president. When a citizen votes for a presidential candidate, one is doing it for a delegate (or an elector) to the Electoral College. He will ultimately go on to vote for one's candidate on behalf of the state.

The Electoral College's inner workings may appear mysterious to the average citizen, established in the United States Constitution in 1787 as a compromise between electing a president by a vote in Congress or a popular vote in an election. State distribution indicates electoral votes. Each state has a certain number of electors equal to their total number of Congress members, including two senators. Except for two, Maine and Nebraska, all states cast all their votes to their state's plurality winner. Any state can change its method of how to allocate its votes. The critical point is that different allocation methods may produce different winners and losers.

The Electoral College has a significant impact on candidates' campaign strategies. Some states have much higher elector payoffs than others, and some states are not really in contention.

There are 538 total electoral votes, and a candidate has to get at least 270 to win. So he or she has to win enough states to get to 270. This changes how candidates pursue their campaigns, because all of them are smart enough to realize that a state such as Texas likely will vote Republican, while California will vote Democrat. The election then tends to come down to "swing states"— states that can go either way depending on the year. Candidates thus concentrate their efforts on those states, while not completely neglecting the others. On the other hand, the states with only three electoral votes don't get as much attention.

The political coloring book with which candidates concern themselves is red, blue, and purple. While these colors do not have any significance in and of themselves, they are a media convention that has become a tradition. Those states that are not reliably Democratic blue or Republican red, even though they may trend one way or the other in a given election, are called swing states.

These "purple" political entities have become the battlegrounds in which elections are ultimately contested. There are also swing voters who do not reliably vote for either party and must be vigorously courted by aspiring officeholders' campaigns because they often display a resistance toward traditional candidates. Independents become independents because one is repelled by the current political system--by the self-dealing and arrogance of politicians and political parties.

Winning campaigns are usually notable for having competent teams behind them. These days, campaigns are professional organizations. Generally, the campaign with the most money, expertise, and best data-gathering operation will be able to out-strategize and out-perform those that may be less adept. Also, increasingly necessary to gain access to the winner's circle is a solid and memorable message. Most swing voters will want to know what a candidate stands for before casting ballots for them. Thus, citizens expect candidates to clearly explain why they are running for office and towards which goals and objectives. They may also search for *wedge issues*, political disputes that they can use as levers to divide an opponent's voting coalition.

Furthermore, because paid advertising is incredibly costly for any campaign, one of the campaign's first goals is to maximize free coverage by staging events and making appearances that the media will cover. Still, for candidates, a good commercial that goes viral and is seen multiple times on cable news and the internet without paying for it is a great thing. *Negative advertising*, or criticizing the opponent, even without mentioning the advertising candidate's name, runs the risk of turning people off and restraining them from coming out to vote. Still, if the issue over which a candidate goes negative connects with the voters, it may prove to be an effective strategy. *Issue advocacy ads* help a candidate by promoting his or her issues or criticizing the opponent's stances.

One absolute certainty is that advertising requires money, and money is a resource to which candidates devote a great deal of their time chasing. Campaign finance law limits how much hard money an individual can donate (currently $2,900 per election).[129] *Hard money* is those funds donated directly to a candidate, *while soft money* is that they give to parties and other groups that can spend it on a candidate's behalf. Wealthy individuals spend *dark money* without having to identify themselves. *Citizens United v. Federal Election Commission* (2010) was a Supreme Court decision that tilted the financial playing field of elections toward corporations, outside groups, and wealthy donors by allowing them to spend without limit and without identifying themselves.[130]

The court's 5-4 majority opinion held that limiting "independent political spending" violated the right to free speech. In doing so, it overturned election spending restrictions that dated back more than a century. The court ruled that there was no threat of corruption if the spending was not coordinated with a candidate's campaign. The upshot of all this is that elections are big business, and all of the citizens are stakeholders in them and in their results, which will significantly affect our lives.

---

[129] The Federal Election Commission clearly states the contribution limits, *see* Contribution limits, https://www.fec.gov/help-candidates-and-committees/candidate-taking-receipts/contribution-limits/, Federal Election Commission, accessed 19 March 2021.

[130] Dark money is usually election-related spending where the source is disclosed or secret. Citizens United contributed to a major jump in this type of spending, which often comes from nonprofits that are not required to reveal their donors. See Tim Lau and Brennan Center for Justice for more details.

CHAPTER 12

Bureaucracy

12.1. What Is Bureaucracy and Why Do We Need It?

Bureaucracy comes from the French *bureaucratie* – from *bureau* (office) and *cratie* (power) – and it originally indicated the group of officials who, divided into various hierarchical levels, carry out the functions of the public administration in the state. In this broad sense, bureaucracy is a hierarchical structure that operates following precise rules. At the same time, bureaucracy has been widely considered as being the most efficient form of organization achieved so far - at least at the level of the ideal model - since it is a functional structure for the management of large quantities of work. Hence, this term does not only define political management, but any set of officials of a body, who in some way conduct the management of this organization (Albrow 1970; 16-30).[131]

Drawing from these features, there have been several definitions of bureaucracy in the literature, of which the most famous is Max Weber's definition of **bureaucracy** as: "an organization where tasks are divided among technical specialists who devote their full working capacity to the organization and whose activities are coordinated by rational rules,

---

[131] Albrow M. (1970), *Bureaucracy*, Macmillan International Higher Education, New York.

hierarchy and written documents".[132] According to Weber, bureaucracy was an improvement compared to previous societal forms of political management and it was necessary to resolve many political issues in current societies. Whereas in ancient democracies, such as the Athenian one, small dimensions of the republic and a conception of political involvement based on liberty as self-government required the whole citizenry to take part in the political management of the community, current societies are too complex and large to grant equal direct political participation to each citizen. For this reason, current political systems have shifted towards representative forms of government, which means that citizens elect ruling elites which are afterwards in charge of the political decisions of the country (Manin 1997; 67-80).[133]

Representative systems yet encompass certain problematic features from a democratic point of view, since elections are simultaneously aristocratic and democratic. On the one hand, elections are aristocratic because they do not produce similarity between rulers and ruled, rather the opposite. Elections tend to create aristocracies, since they select candidates that prove to have the politically relevant qualities and that are deemed superior by the dominant values in the culture. Yet, on the other hand, elections are also democratic: even if there is inequality regarding who can be selected, citizens possess an equal power in deciding who is worth assuming a certain position (Manin 1997; 156-160).

This dual character is reflected by bureaucracy, since this mechanism can be good at some things - making decisions quickly and consistently and maximizing expertise - but at the same time it can also be easily corrupted because of the lack of transparency and democratic accountability. For this reason, bureaucracy has been a central topic of study in

---

[132] Weber, M. (1978). Bureaucracy. In Economy and society: An outline of interpretive sociology. Trans. and ed. G. Roth and C. Wittich. Berkeley: University of California Press.

[133] Manin B. (1997), *The Principles of Representative Government*, Cambridge University Press, Cambridge.

political science over the last centuries. That is, political literature has tried to explain why certain public policy decisions are preferred over others and how relevant officials in the government use these policies to protect or promote their own agency's special interests against other bodies. To understand this debate better, it is first essential to consider how bureaucratic theory has developed over time and how it has been connected to the development of modern society.

12.2. The Framework and History

Bureaucracy is a result of both an economic and political development of our societies. On the one side, the development and enlargement of capitalist industries required economic companies not only to employ more employees, but also more technical and managerial personnel within the industry to deal with the increased managerial requirements of these businesses. On the other side, the expansion of the State into new areas of welfare provision and economic regulation, and the emergence of a mass political party required the expansion of a bureaucratic administration. In this regard, bureaucratization has become a universal feature of modern society and because of its indispensability, any modern organization must rely on some form of bureaucratic management to carry out its tasks. In Weber's words (1968; 223)[134]: "the choice is only between bureaucracy and dilettantism in the field of administration".

Bureaucratization was thus the management response to the development of the territorial state and the capitalist economy, whose administrative needs could not be met by traditional means employed by previous societies. In this regard, the wave of democratization that has occurred in western societies over the last centuries has played a significant part in fostering bureaucracy's importance. Democracy has

---

[134] Weber M. (1968), *Economy and Society. An Outline of Interpretative Sociology*, Bedminister Press, New York.

levelled traditional status differences by requiring a system operating on the basis of impartiality between citizens and by offering opportunities for bureaucratic careers that are linked to education and merit rather than family status only.

However, democracy did not foster bureaucratic development by itself, since this latter has always been intertwined with another process typical of modern societies, namely the process of **rationalization**. This latter can be defined as the historical drive towards a world in which "one can, in principle, master all things by calculation" (Weber 1946 [1919]; 139).[135] As for bureaucracy, rationalization processes can be found in many different spheres of society. In the economy, modern capitalism depends on a calculable process of production structured on division of labor, centralization of production control and other processes that enhance the calculability of the production process. For what concerns the legislative and administrative sphere, precise rules, an autonomous judiciary and a professional bureaucracy enhance the predictability in the sociopolitical environment, thus making it easy to govern a large mass society.

This process of rationalization has become so intertwined with modern society that it has influenced the people's values and identity. It is in this regard that Weber maintained that modern organizations require a "person of vocation", namely a rational personality type connected to the protestant ethic (Weber 1946; 140-141). Hence, according to Weber, the interplay between rationalization and bureaucracy structured modern rational western civilization in three main regards.[136]

First, rational action presupposes *knowledge* of the ideational and material circumstances structuring the action. To act rationally is to act conscious of the consequences of the action and it thus requires a means-ends relationships in order to maximize the outcome of the action with

[135] Weber M. (1919), "Science as a Vocation", in Gerth. H.H., and Wright Mills C. (1946), *From Max Weber: Essays in Sociology*, Oxford: Oxford University Press.
[136] Brubaker R. (1992), *The Limits of Rationality*, London: Routledge.

the least expenditure of resources. Weber called this process 'intellectual-ization', whereby modern knowledge replaces old metaphysics based on superstitions and irrational thoughts. Second, rational processes must be *impersonal and objective*. For example, workers in industrial capitalism are reduced to sheer numbers and non-economic considerations are not relevant to their judgment. In the same way, rules obey formal codes and apply equally to all the citizenry. Third, *control* is essential, since techno-logical and scientific development have offered societies the chance to impose their mastery not only over nature, but also over human beings' social life. It is in this regard then that a rational and disciplinary ethos has increasingly penetrated into every aspect of social life.

Finally, bureaucracy and rationalization are also connected because the latter is essential in giving bureaucracy a different source of legiti-macy than traditional powers. That is, while traditional societies relied on societal custom and habit to legitimize their power, modern societ-ies achieved this legitimation simply by adhering to precisely defined rules, such as following the conduct of office, governing the criteria for appointment and the scope of authority (Albrow 1970; 84.91). In a nut-shell, bureaucracy imposed itself as an indispensable system of adminis-tration rooted in the requirements of the modern world, since it allowed governments to coordinate action over a large area, to ensure continuity of operation, to acquire a monopoly of expertise and to guarantee an internal social cohesion and morale.

However, the development of bureaucracy did not lead to positive consequences only, since it also paved the way to political debates con-cerning its efficiency and negative consequences. One of the first debates arose regarding the **patronage system,** namely the political system where the appointment or hiring of a person to a government post is decided on the basis of partisan loyalty. By means of this system, elected offi-cials had the opportunity to use their power to reward the people who helped them win and maintain office. Originally, proponents of patron-age sustained that it promoted direct accountability of those who were selected and it also diminished elitism in politics by allowing commoners to occupy important roles.[137]

Political patronage has a long history in the United States, since it was already included in the Article 2 of the constitution. In this article, it is specified that the President has powers of appointment to choose a large number of U.S. officials, such as ambassadors, agency heads, military office and other high-ranking members of government. This power is yet not absolute, since the Senate has confirmation powers to check this selection. Nonetheless, this practice has often been a powerful political tool for the President. For this reason, appointments became so widespread that they formed a '**spoils system**', namely a political organization where the political party which won the elections gives high-ranking civil service jobs to its supporters, both as a reward for working toward victory and a way to make sure that they continue working for the party after the victory.[138]

This process is different from a merit system in which offices are assigned independently of political affiliation and according to impartial procedures meant to award candidates on the basis of some measure of merit. This difference created problems at the end of the 19th century, when 'spoils system' became too widespread, especially at local level, thus giving political leaders the opportunity to dominate local government and politics by building a community of supporters whose main aim was to maintain power from one election to another. Hence, patronage encompasses also several deficiencies that may erode public confidence in this system, since it can favor corruption and it can create a system where those appointed are unlikely to speak freely and to criticize their bosses on whom their job depends.[139]

---

[137] Pollock, J.K. (1937), "The cost of the patronage system.", *The Annals of the American Academy of Political and Social Science*, 189 (1), 29-34.

[138] Folke, O., Hirano S., and Snyder Jr J.M. (2011), "Patronage and elections in US states.", *American Political Science Review*, 105 (3), 567-585.

[139] Friedrich C.J. (1937), "The rise and decline of the spoils tradition.", *The Annals of the American Academy of Political and Social Science*, 189 (1), 10-16.

For this reason, at the end of the 19th century, the Pendleton Act of 1883 shifted the appointment process to a merit-based system, in which recruitment was made by means of competitive exams meant to assess competence rather than partisan affiliation. In this way, **neutral competence** became the primary selection method and rulers used it to deliver the message that in an ideal bureaucratic structure power is hierarchical and rule based. That is, a well-functioning bureaucratic system must appoint individuals according to their expertise and it must promote bureaucrats on the basis of merit, not personal affiliations. In this way, a neutral bureaucratic organization can make decisions better and more quickly than a patronage system and even than a democracy based on a self-government ideal.

The percentage of civil service employees recruited according to a neutral competence principle has steadily increased over the years in any society, and in the United State it reached more than 90% after both the Civil Service Reform Act signed by President Jimmy Carter in 1978 and the amendments enacted by the Supreme Court over the years to limit the externalities of partisan patronage (Ingraham & Ban 1984).[140] Nowadays, political patronage is less prevalent than in the past, since presidents now appoint less than 1% of all federal positions. Yet, this does not mean that patronage has lost all its relevance, since strategic appointments are still an important political means used by presidents to reward their supporters and to create a working relationship with members of congress.

In sum, the historical development of bureaucracy describes that this form of organization has become an essential feature for the management of complex modern societies. However, at the same time, bureaucracy transfers political power from the citizenry to technical officers, so the former may question the latter's power and they could request increased accountability and transparency in return for the transfer of power. That

---

[140] Ingraham, P. W. and Ban C. (1984), *Legislating Bureaucratic Change: Civil Service Reform Act of 1978*, SUNY Press, New York.

is, citizens want to have some form of control over the elites ruling government and other institutions and corporations. Above all, citizens want to know how governments are using the people's money, especially concerning taxpayer funds.

One way of posing such control is to make bureaucrats accountable by requiring them to follow rules designed to treat people fairly, to refrain from politics on the job, and to fill out paperwork. However, these requests may also lead to unforeseen externalities, such as **the Red Tape issue**, which defines an excessive regulation or conformity to formal rules that is considered redundant and hinders action or other decision-making processes. This issue draws its name from the case in the 16th century when Henry VIII besieged Pope Clement VII with a significant amount of petitions for the annulment of his marriage to Catherine of Aragon. The pile of documents was rolled and stacked in original condition, each one sealed and bound with the obligatory red tape, as was the custom. Hence, the name red tape issue to describe an excessive amount of procedures to follow.[141]

The problem is thus that in order to respond to the people's request for accountability, civic service employees may be asked to fill out unnecessary paperwork, to obtain unnecessary licenses, to have multiple people or committees approve a decision and finally, to follow various minor rules that unavoidably slow down the whole bureaucratic process. In short, "red tape" indicates the governmental problem for which any official routine or procedure marked by excessive complexity results in delay or inaction. Therefore, governments must find a way to balance their need to get things done and to satisfy the people's need for transparency and accountability. To resolve this problem, the US government divided the federal bureaucracy in three branches: legislative, executive and judiciary.

---

[141] Bozeman, B. (1993), "A theory of government "Red tape", *Journal of public administration research and theory*, 3.3, 273-304.

12.3. Bureaucracy in the United States

The legislative branch drafts proposed laws, confirms or rejects presidential nominations for heads of federal agencies, federal judges and the Supreme Court, it has the authority to declare war and finally, it also disposes of substantial investigative powers. American citizens have the right to vote for Senators and Representatives through free, confidential ballots. This branch includes a *Congress* composed of two parts: The Senate and the House of Representatives. In order to pass legislation and send it to the President for the signature, both these bodies must pass the same bill by majority vote (Little & Ogle 2006; 25-31).[142]

The Senate includes two elected senators per state for a total of 100 Senators, with the Vice-President serving as President of the Senate. These latter are in charge for a period of six years and their terms are staggered so that about 1/3 of the Senate is up for reelection every two years, even though there is no limit to the number of terms an individual can serve. Overall, the Senate is meant to confirm President's appointments that require consent, to provide advice on treaties' ratification, to impeach cases for federal officials and it has also to approve appointments to the Vice Presidency and any treaty that involves foreign trade.[143]

The House of Representatives has several powers, such as initiating revenue bills, impeaching federal officials, and electing the President in the case of an Electoral College tie. This institution includes 435 elected Representatives, which are divided among the 50 states in proportion to their total population. There are additional 6 non-voting delegates who represent the District of Columbia, Puerto Rico and the territories. The presiding officer of the chamber is the speaker of the House and it is elected by other representatives. These elected officials serve a two-year term, and there is no limit to the number of terms an individual can serve.

---

[142] Little, T. H., Ogle D. B. (2006), *The legislative branch of state government: people, process, and politics*, ABC-CLIO, California.
[143] The White House Government, "The Legislative Branch", retrieved at: https://www.whitehouse.gov/about-the-white-house/our-government/the-legislative-branch/

The legislative branch encompasses also special agencies and offices that provide support services to Congress, the list of which includes agencies such as the Architect of the Capitol, the Congressional Budget Office, the Congressional Research Service, the Copyright Office, the Government Accountability Office, the Government Publishing Office, the House Office of Inspector General, the House Office of the Clerk, the Joint Congressional Committee on Inaugural Ceremonies, the Library of Congress, the Medicaid and CHIP Payment and Access Commission, the Medicare Payment Advisory Commission, the Office of Compliance, the Open World Leadership Center, the Stennis Center for Public Service, the U.S. Botanic Garden, the U.S. Capitol Police and the U.S. Capitol Visitor Center.

Second, the **executive branch** carries out and enforces laws. Executive power is vested in the President of the United States, namely the individual in charge of leading the country. He or she is the head of state, leader of the federal government, and Commander in Chief of the United States armed forces. The president serves a four-year term and can be elected no more than two times. During his or her mandate, the president is responsible for implementing the laws written by Congress, while it is responsibility of the Cabinet and of independent federal agencies to take care of the day-to-day enforcement and administration of federal laws. These bureaucracies do so by providing regulations and restrictions on businesses and individuals, like limitations on allowable air pollution from factories, or the requirements that cars have airbags, or making sure that people do not have unfettered access to certain classes of drugs or overstay their visas.[144]

The president is supported by the Vice-president and when the former is unable to serve, the latter becomes president. The vice president can be elected and can serve an unlimited number of four-year terms as vice president, even under a different president. Vice-President is part of

---

[144] The White House Government, "The Executive Branch", retrieved at: https://www.whitehouse.gov/about-the-white-house/our-government/the-executive-branch/.

The Cabinet together with other advisors such as the heads of executive departments and other high ranking government officials. These advisors are nominated by the President and must be approved by a simple majority of the Senate.

Much of the work in the executive branch is thus done by executive departments, independent agencies and other boards, commissions, and committees. The most important executive department is 'The Executive Office of the Presidency' which was born in the New Deal expansion of federal power and that is aimed at coordinating the bureaucracy. The Executive Office of the Presidency (EOP) is home to agencies that the president appoints to help him manage the large range of issues that the White House has to deal with on a daily basis. This office – composed by different bodies such as the office of the President, the National Security Council, the Office of the United States Trade Representatives, etc. - is in charge of communicating the president's message and deals with the federal budget, security, and other high priorities.[145]

The office of the president cooperates with the **Executive Departments**, namely the 15 main agencies of the federal government that cover essential government functions or policy areas where clientele groups have been effective at lobbying for representation at the executive level, such as the U.S. department of Defense, Commerce, Justice, Labor and so on. The heads of these 15 agencies – also called "secretaries", except for the head of the Justice Department, who is called the "attorney general" are also members of the president's cabinet. These 15 main agencies are divided in Executive Sub-agencies and Bureaus, namely smaller sub-agencies aimed at supporting specialized work within their parent executive department agencies.

Finally, there are also independent agencies that are not represented in the cabinet and are not part of the Executive Office of the president, but which are structured similarly to other executive bodies with

[145] Branches of the U.S. Government, USA Government, retrieved at: https://www.usa.gov/branches-of-government.

a presidential appointee at the top (some of whom can be fired by the president, and some of whom cannot). These bodies deal with government operations and issues concerning the economy and regulatory oversight. In case there are areas that do not fall under these agencies (historic preservations, endangered species, Nuclear waste, etc.), Congress or the President can establish Boards, Commissions and Committees to manage these specific tasks. Even though they are not officially part of the executive branch, these bodies are also quasi-official agencies, namely organizations that are required by federal statute to release certain information about their programs and activities in the Federal Register, the daily journal of government activities.[146]

Overall then, the executive branch consists of several agencies as the president's cabinet, the departments under the responsibility of the cabinet members and all the agencies, boards, and commissions that put the laws of Congress into action. Moreover, these bodies also include everyone serving in the U.S. military and public corporations like the U.S. Post Office. Overall then, the Federal bureaucracy performs different central functions like diplomacy, defense, and internal affairs. Yet, these branches also perform 'minor' tasks such as responding to clientele groups of veterans, farmers, teachers, or other groups who feel that they have particular concerns.

Third, **the Judicial Branch** interprets the meaning of laws, applies laws to individual cases, and decides if laws violate the Constitution. It is composed of the Supreme Court and other federal courts. The former is the highest court in the United States, whose nine Justices – a Chief Justice and eight Associate Justices - are nominated by the president and must be approved by the Senate. To decide a case. there must be a minimum or quorum of six Justices, while if there is an even number of Justices and a case results in a tie, the lower court's decision stands. These

---

[146] Cohen, J. E. (1988), *The politics of the US cabinet: Representation in the executive branch, 1789-1984*. University of Pittsburgh Press, Pennsylvania.

Justices' service is not fixed term, since they serve until their death, retirement, or removal in exceptional circumstances.[147]

Together with the Supreme Court, the Constitution gives Congress the authority to establish other federal courts to handle cases that involve federal laws including tax and bankruptcy, lawsuits involving U.S. and state governments or the Constitution, and more. Other federal judicial agencies and programs support the courts and research judicial policy. The appointments for these federal judgeships follow the same basic process as the one for the appointment of Supreme Court Justices.

First, the President nominates a person to fill a vacant judgeship, then the Senate Judiciary Committee holds a hearing on the nominee and votes on whether to forward the nomination to the full Senate. If the nomination moves forward, the Senate can debate the nomination. Debate must end before the Senate can vote on whether to confirm the nominee. A Senator will request unanimous consent to end the debate, but any Senator can refuse. Without unanimous consent, the Senate must pass a cloture motion to end the debate. It takes a simple majority of votes - 51 if all 100 Senators vote - to pass cloture and end debate about a federal judicial nominee. Once the debate ends, the Senate votes on confirmation. The nominee for Supreme Court or any other federal judgeship needs a simple majority of votes - 51 if all 100 Senators vote - to be confirmed.

Therefore, these three sides of government are bureaucracies that perform essential tasks for the management of the United States, since they provide administration, rule-making which is filling in all the technical details in the laws Congress passes so that they can be enforced, and bureaucratic discretion when the bureaucracy exercises legislative power delegated to it by congressional law through judgment.

---

[147] The White House. "The Judiciary Branch", retrieved at: https://www.whitehouse.gov/about-the-white-house/our-government/the-judicial-branch/

CHAPTER 13

Political Parties and Interest Groups

Both political parties and interest groups are social bodies bound together by shared interests. Political parties are modern forms of factions in the sense that they seek goals particular to their interests. Interest groups have a shared vision to use the political system to attain their goals. Parties can develop higher degrees of cohesion in fragmented political systems. Interest groups use lobbying as a tool. Lobbying can be both direct and indirect; it is trying to persuade government officials to do something.

In countries with more than two parties, partisanship likely bows to practicalities and compromise. In the United States, it is challenging for third parties to get any relevant traction at the national level. There may be structural reasons that justify the maintenance of the two-party system in the United States. The Democrats and the Republicans dominate the national political spectrum today, which will likely remain so for the following years.

13.1 Parties and Interest Groups

Both political parties and interest groups are social bodies bound together by shared interests. They do their best to take advantage of the political system to accomplish their political goals. These are the factions James

Madison feared would be so destructive of democracy. The way they go about working the system to get political goals realized is very different.

Political parties are modern forms of factions in the sense that they seek goals particular to their interests. *Political parties* are groups bound by common interests which seek to use the political system to attain their goals from inside the system by controlling government. Different factors may affect and influence parties and interest groups' internal processes, such as choosing a favorite candidate and getting him elected. This form of *electioneering* is nominating and electing candidates to office. Once they are in office, they are *governing public officials* and run the political show.

Interest groups have a shared vision to use the political system to accomplish their goals. *Interest groups*, including corporations, are societies bound by common interests which endeavor to use the political system to achieve their policy goals by persuading inside people in power that will give them what they want. This form of action is known as lobbying. The act of persuading officials is a type of lobbying. It is typical for party representatives in government and interest group lobbyists outside the government to develop close working relationships where their interests overlap. These actions magnify their power.

13.2 The Role of Parties in a Democracy[148],[149]

What is involved with the duties of a political party? A political party must represent the interests of its members by gaining control of the

---

[148] For information on the role of political parties in socialist countries, see Corwin 11-24. Generally, in Cuba, as in China, only members of the Communist Party are allowed to vote or hold public office, and the party's most relevant members make all government decisions. Some exceptions to this rule may apply in China since the Asian country has a multiparty system, in which the Communist Party has authority over the rest.

[149] Under certain conditions, The Chinese political system allows for the participation of some non-CCP members (independents) and members of minor parties in the National People's Congress (NPC). The CCP is the only party that effectively holds power at the national level.

government. Parties have vital advantages and tools to strengthen and facilitate democracy in some crucial ways. Parties act as democracy-strengthening agents by providing a bridge and connection between voters and their elected officials.

Political parties also practice partisan politics. *Partisanship* is about identifying one's interests with a party's platform. Elected officials can be held accountable to the people who vote for them through re-election. *Accountability* is about ensuring our elected officials do what they say they are going to do. When a political party is helping to create accountability, they provide cohesion. Parties can develop higher degrees of cohesion in fragmented political systems. Parties also provide a voice to those in power, and they provide the opposition voice to those who are not in government.

13.3 Political Parties Create the Normality

Political parties create the normality that people countenance since they politically shape the social and cultural environment. The *responsible party model* is when political parties conform to paragons about how parties should ideally operate. One of these tools is the party platform. A *party platform* is a distinct set of policies based on a party's ideology, whose candidates align. People expect them to follow the party's platform and promises. If elected, citizens expect candidates to enact the values and policies of the party.

Voters make their choices based on the public policies political parties promote through their platforms; they are willing to vote against the party's candidates if they fail to keep their campaign promises successfully. Voters will likely reject party officials at the polls if party officials poorly carry out their partisan platforms' commitments. In the United States, the responsible party model is nothing but a yardstick against which actual parties can be measured.

United States parties can create unique party platforms different from each other in the political system. With several levels and branches, the national system offers many places where people and groups can engage the government. Candidates, in general, promise to support their party's platform if elected. People choose the political party they want to support through a process called partisan sorting. *Partisan sorting* identifies with the party because it most closely stands for their views and values and not for regional or other non-ideological reasons. Partisan sorting has historically been enforced by voters rather than by tight political party regulations. Increasingly, party members are not only partisan (that is, they identify with the political team); they are hyperpartisan.

Hyper-partisanship is when people are loyal to the party at all costs. Hyper-partisanship is an ideology that suggests that someone would choose their team over the other every time, even if it may require that they change their minds on policy priorities or values to do so. When voters are unwilling to vote against their party, even when it lets them down because the priority is to deny their opponents a win, they send a message to their party that it is acceptable not to keep promises.

To follow the dictates of the political party leaders to which they belong, House members and senators in the United States Congress may sometimes ignore the voters in their home states and the groups that represent them. For example, a member of the United States Congress from a state with a sizable elderly population may be inclined to vote in favor of legislation that will likely increase the benefits for retired people. However, their political party leaders, who disapprove of government spending on social programs, may ask for a vote against the legislation. The opposite can also occur, especially in the case of a legislator soon facing re-election. With two-year terms of office, it is more likely to see House members buck their party in favor of their constituents. (Corwin, 21)

13.4 Party Organization and Decision-Making

In liberal democratic countries, political parties no longer choose leaders in smoke-filled rooms behind the scenes. There is a formal and transparent process. Historically, *party machines* were organizations in which party leaders or "bosses" made the decisions and kept their voters' loyalty by providing them with services and support. Reforms included bringing party decisions, like whom to nominate, out of the proverbial "smoke-filled rooms." The way we are choosing political candidates today is in the smoke-free air of democratic transparency.

Political parties choose candidates through primaries and caucuses. *Primary elections*, often abbreviated to *primaries*, are processes by which voters can indicate their political preference for their party's candidate, or a general candidate, in an upcoming general election, local election, or by-election. *Primaries* are usually party-held preliminary elections.

A *caucus* is a meeting of political supporters or members (usually active) of a specific political party or movement. The definition of this term varies between countries and political cultures. *Caucuses* are the party gatherings where partisans debate candidate choices openly. While party officials still have a great deal of clout and resources, they are no longer "the boss."

Generally, political parties in the United States do not like nominating methods that allow non-party members to participate in selecting party nominees. In 2000, the United States Supreme Court heard a case brought by the California Democratic Party, the California Republican Party, and the California Libertarian Party. At the time, the parties argued that they had the right to determine who associated with the party and who participated in choosing the party nominee. The Supreme Court ultimately agreed to limit the states' choices for nomination methods to closed and open primaries.

13.5 A four-part party structure

The party structure rests in, more or less, four essential elements that make the party structure. The people in the electorate who identify with the party are people who vote party lines. These citizens are known as the *party followers* (1). On the other hand, *party activists* (2) are the party base, the most ideologically extreme of the party's voters. These activists are the ones that are the core group of people within the political party. *Party leaders* (3) are those who act as the official representatives of the political party.

The *party organization* is the official group, whose career party officials are part of it, that runs the party. This party organization is the functioning of the party within the state. Those who win an election are known as the *party-in-government members* (4) because they represent the people. *Party identification* is when people think of themselves as partisans (team members) and generally vote for the party. Identity politics are crucial to understanding national politics since political representation is, for some experts, rooted in the representatives' racial, ethnic, socioeconomic, gender, and sexual identity.

13.6 Why does the United States have a two-party political system?

In countries with more than two parties, partisanship likely bows to practicalities and compromise. If not, a party typically gets left out in the cold. In the United States, it is challenging for third parties to get any traction at the national level. There are structural reasons for the two-party system in the United States. The primary structural reason is that the United States does not have a proportional representation system, often found in parliamentary governments. The United States follows a *single member, first past the post district* model. These congressional districts in the United States have only one person elected—the person who gets the most votes.

The United States has made legal barriers to third parties to access federal funds. This situation implies that candidates are no longer dependent on the parties for their infrastructure. Third parties are vulnerable to the ability of social media to be manipulated and weaponized against them.

Third parties are cutting into fundraising against the major two parties. The parties are struggling to keep financial control in the age of the Internet. There is now much more opportunity for those not blessed by a major party's nomination to stage a campaign. Unlimited corporate and interest group funds are available to parties. A third-party candidate must get a certain number of signatures on a petition to get on the ballot in most states. Usually, when a third party begins to get traction, one of the parties will co-opt the winning issues.

13.7 The Parties Today

The Democrats and the Republicans dominate the United States political spectrum today. Democrats seek an activist government that believed it could and should solve economic and social problems at the national level. Republicans seek a hands-off, anti-regulatory business party. By the 1960s, Democrats had a solid hold on the United States Congress. *Richard Nixon's "southern strategy"* took advantage of race as a wedge issue to break conservative southern Democrats away from the Democrats and give the Republicans a majority.

Republicans seek a government that attends to its inherent responsibilities of maintaining a stable monetary and fiscal climate, encouraging a free and competitive economy, and enforcing law and order. Republicans seek a balance between the branches of government and every level. The Republican Party perceives that communism is the principal significant disturber of peace in the world today. Thus, they are reluctant to have relations with countries run by communist leaders and parties.[150]

The "new" Republican coalition began with the rise of evangelical Christian politics. Generally, traditional southerners were far more hierarchical, authoritarian, and evangelical-Christian than the average economic conservative Republican. The relationship between these two Republican groups ultimately led to considerable political friction because of broken promises and misunderstandings. For a time,

---

[150] For an in-depth analysis of the values of the two leading parties of the United States, see Donaldson, Robert. *Modern America: a Documentary History of the Nation Since 1945: A Documentary History of the Nation Since 1945*, 2014. London: Routledge. Internet resource.

economic conservatives paid lip service to social conservatives' concerns to keep the peace.

As one understands them today, national political parties did not exist in the United States during the republic's early years. At various points in the past 170 years in the United States history, national elites and voters have sought to create and foster alternatives to the existing party system. Political parties formed as alternatives to the Republican and Democratic parties are known as third parties or minor parties. Third parties, often born of frustration with the current political system, attract supporters from one or both of the existing and leading parties during an election but fail to attract enough votes to win. No third-party candidate has ever won the presidency, and historians still discuss why.

The Republican Party and the Democratic Party still have their economic and social left-right divisions. Trump's coalition's conservative social dimension is an interesting one, as critics argue that social conservatives seem to have set aside the traditional values that so motivated them in years past.

In the United States, two political movements formed fifteen years following John Kennedy's election: the American New Left and the American New Right. The New Left supports the call for social, economic, and political justice based on the equality of class, gender, and race rather than by the traditional leftist-Marxist dogma that socialism would replace the decadent capitalist system. On the other hand, the New Right focuses on downsizing the federal government, supporting state's rights, resisting communism, and reducing government regulations. Even if experts often describe both tendencies as radical movements, they are less orthodox than the traditional Left and the traditional Right.

13.8 Interest Groups' Basics

Madison's definition of factions can apply to both interest groups and political parties. Political parties and interest groups both work together and compete for social influence, although in different ways. Even though its writers did not mention the term interest group in the United States Constitution, the text's framers were aware that individuals would eventually band together in an attempt to use the governmental structure in their favor. One should especially consider that, while interest group activity often transcends political party lines, one can perceive many interests as more supportive of one party than the other. Thus, interest groups and political parties are related and may even closely work together as long as they support similar causes. For example, The American Conservative Union, Citizens United, the National Rifle Association, and National Right to Life will likely have relationships with Republican lawmakers than with Democratic ones.[151]

Interest groups do not need to be moderate—in fact, it is quite the opposite. The more stalwart and uncompromising interest groups stand on their positions, the better situated they are to draw a membership who shares their particular views. Individual citizens can join interest groups that promote and support the causes they favor.

Interest groups help provide representation to the people. The United States Constitution bases political representation almost entirely on geography. Interest groups give people a chance to get other interests they care about represented in government policy pursuing. Interest groups also help with political participation. *Political efficacy* is when people's sense of their ability to have a higher degree of control of their lives. Interest groups give people political participation opportunities that they would not typically have. Interest groups amplify the power of one. What one voice may not achieve, a chorus of multitudes may do much more quickly.

The role the interest groups provide in educating the public is essential. Interest groups usually provide information on their cause to

---

[151] Corwin, Edward. "The Basic Doctrine of American Constitutional Law." *Michigan Law Review*, vol. 12, no. 4, 1914, pp. 247–276. *JSTOR*, www.jstor.org/stable/1276027. Accessed 8 Mar. 2021.

policymakers by testifying in front of congressional committees, working with bureaucrats, or communicating directly with their members. Interest groups provide agenda building. By publicizing the values and interests they care about to the public and policymakers, interest groups can get onto their radar screens. This focus provides program alternatives and program monitoring.

13.9 Understanding Interest Groups

Interest groups can benefit society. Interest groups provide collective goods. *Collective goods* are benefits that, if the group is successful in obtaining them, can be enjoyed by everyone, whether they were members of the group and contributed to the purpose or not. There may be a problem with people who do not contribute to the interest group and only profit from it. *The free-rider problem is* a quandary with getting people to join an interest group if they enjoy the benefit? Does a member get *material benefits* provided of actual monetary worth, like insurance discounts or professional paybacks? Are there *solidary benefits* that appeal to one's desire to associate with other people who care about the same things one does? Are there *expressive benefits* which are the opportunity to do work for something that matters deeply to one? Does the interest group provide *selective incentives* which benefit offered to induce people to join up?

We can understand interest groups' politics best if we think about the kinds of interests that bind their members together into different groups. *Economic interest groups* are those which seek to influence policy for the pocketbook issues of their members. On the other hand, *equal opportunity interest groups* pretend to influence the policymaking process by politically targeting citizens who feel unrepresented. These are different from public interest groups which aspire to change policy according to values that they consider are good for every citizen. *Government interest groups* are groups hired by governments to lobby other governments.

13.10 Interest Group Politics

What does one mean by "interest group politics"—are lobbyists politicians? Interest groups and their lobbyists are political actors in that they can bring considerable power to bear on elected officials. Power is relative amongst interest groups. Power can come from strength in numbers and resources.

Interest groups use lobbying as a tool. Lobbying can be direct and indirect. *Lobbying* is trying to persuade government officials to do something. *Lobbyists* are professionals who promote agendas and persuade public officials. *Direct lobbying* impacts public officials directly, while *indirect lobbying* focuses on the public to get the public to put pressure on public officials.

Professional lobbyists come from the ranks of professional politicians. There is a *revolving door* between lobbyists and politicians. The revolving door theory explains how people move from the public to the private sector and then sometimes back to the public sector. With direct lobbying of Congress, the Congress member's lobbyists focus on the committees and subcommittees that deal with the policies they mind. Interest groups research and investigate policy options and bring their findings to Congress members who cannot become experts on every topic they pass a law on.

Interest groups give money. *Political action committees (PACs)* can raise money but are limited in their contributions to candidates. One practical way for interest groups to increase their power is to form coalitions with other groups conveniently. Interest groups are as interested in influencing the people who implement the laws as they are interested in determining who makes them. The result is the public being shut out of the policymaking process, known as the Iron Triangle. Often, lobbyists, bureaucrats, and Congress members end up working together closely on laws affecting a particular sector that they finally come to identify with each other's interests. *Iron triangles* are the close policymaking relationships between legislators, regulators, and state-regulated groups.

Interest groups provide direct and indirect lobbying. Direct lobbying of the courts happens at the state level. State judges are frequently elected and willing to take campaign contributions. Lobbyists also operate in the Supreme Court and carry out their political mission by writing and submitting amicus curiae briefs on behalf of groups with interest in a particular case. Challenging a law in court is one way of lobbying the court to change the law. Indirect lobbying occurs when groups find it more beneficial to stay concealed behind an ostensible social movement. In these cases, they attempt to persuade the public to put pressure on our representatives.

People outside the political culture can lobby as well. When citizens become lobbyists, they are known as grassroots. Groups that orchestrate *grassroots lobbying* are usually those that arise from spontaneous popular movements and revolts. Fake grassroots movements are known as *Astroturf lobbying*. This lobbying type occurs through an orchestrated effort by an established interest group dressed up to look like a genuine popular movement. Astroturf lobbying is made more convenient by the Supreme Court rulings that say that spending money by individuals, groups, or corporations is a form of *protected free speech*.

CHAPTER 14

Media and Political Communication

People make decisions throughout their lives according to their perceptions and biases, eventually shaped by the information they receive from the media. News agencies influence our actions, judgments, and beliefs. Depending on how critical citizens are, media corporations will alter their perception of the world more or less. In countries like the United States, the government controls the media by the use of licensing. Reporting is not only about accurately reporting facts but also about increasing advertiser revenues and audience shares. Media outlets are looking to make a profit. Real reporting means digging out nuggets of truth and stitching them together into a coherent story that accurately informs the public of what is happening in their world. Ideally, in the entertainment and media industry, stories, pieces, and narratives are both fact-based and fact-checked. Respectable journalists do not write or spread fake news. Journalists can lose sight of what is necessary and still ethically acceptable for the sake of media sales and revenues.

14.1 Introduction to Media and Political Communication

How politicians and governments communicate with people occurs in all types of forms, such as the internet, books, television, and advertisements in mass media. The media can influence the governmental implementation of public policies and the development of public opinion. The media uses established communication channels for transmitting news, as well as influencing human behavior. The powerful complex of media technology not only carries information to us, but it also collects information about us.

The way media companies monitor and collect data about us creates a narrative and empowers companies. A significant component of power-building is control of the information or how one assembles data into narratives that influence public opinion. The rise of both cable and satellite television audiences translates into more options for media dissemination.

The phenomenal increase in channels through which information can flow for the informed citizen has made understanding the relationships among power, narratives, and political communication all the more central. The media are all-encompassing, enormously powerful and invasive, and yet, at the same time, more porous and open to our influence than ever before. The past decades have witnessed dramatic changes in the media environment, which have deepened during the social media revolution.

By intending to democratize political participation, social media has changed the way politicians, journalists, and public figures interact with the citizens. In real-time, social media users can respond to each other and influence public opinion. Citizens deliberate about policy-making in social media networks such as Facebook, Twitter, Instagram, Reddit, and more. Social media have these days the potential to both shape political campaigns and influence power relations in political parties as they allow candidates to campaign with a higher degree of independence than before.

14.2 Media Sourcing

The origin of media and the stories reported is a relevant aspect to verify. The roots of our thoughts and beliefs can be very blurry. Some media channels create their own stories through scientific reporting methods, while other sources merely report other news stories. A *media aggregator* is a channel that only picks and chooses from the reporting of others. Media aggregators do not always verify facts. They disseminate stories, even if the narrative is false.

Competent media reporting rests on reporting up to standards. *Reporting* in the media is the process by which professional journalists track down facts, check them, and ask hard questions, not settling for easy answers and pushing until they have found the truth. When looking for truth, the truth is not relative—it is verifiable with empirical (real-world) evidence. More and more news sites rely on using others' work, including the wire services like the Associated Press. Without the reporting of skilled, assiduous, and persistent journalists, our system would be in serious trouble.

Even though traditional forms of international diplomacy persist, one can see that modern hybrid wars also take place in the media. In this context, global public opinion is the prize. Governments, business organizations, religious-related entities, terrorist groups, and large-scale international NGOs pursue their political objectives by using the media. Throughout the world, public opinion is essential to the welfare of every government. Publicists do their best to create powerful narratives that are convincing enough for people all around the globe.

14.3 How we get and consume our news

A hallmark of authoritarian political systems is the state's effort to control the narrative by managing the press[152]. When the government controls the story, then truth can be relative to the media producer. He who controls the narrative-setting process also regulates what people think and feel about something. Our media channels that seek out truth include word of mouth, print media, broadcast media, or electronic media sources.

---

[152] On media biases and political repression, see Davenport, Christian. *Media Bias, Perspective, and State Repression: The Black Panther Party.* Cambridge University Press, 2010.

Print media is in decline and it is struggling to figure out its role in the electronic world. The use of magazines and newspapers has evolved to appease today's audiences and advertisers. TV news, especially local news, still draws older generations, and its audience is dwindling. The internet is rapidly becoming the go-to place for people, predominantly the youth, to seek information.[153]

In today's busy world, we get in touch with the media from numerous sources and places. *Media convergence* is the process by which most of us get our news from many different sources. You may receive information from a multiplicity of news sources every day—paper, the internet, and television. People are becoming acclimatized to the media narrative in their life. A *mediated citizen*[154] is a citizen whose media dictate his lines of communication and thought. People live within a media bubble; however, it is possible to pop that bubble.

When people are comfortable in their information bubble, they are less likely to make changes. An *information bubble* is a person's media comfort zone, in which they listen to the news, curate social media, and meet new people, all of which reinforce the ideas they already have. Popping the bubble should be a fundamental goal of an educated person. We are vulnerable to manipulation tactics. Public opinion-influencing tactics leave us especially vulnerable to be controlled by those who guide the information we get. We live our lives according to the information we receive from the media. News agencies influence our actions, decisions, and beliefs. Depending on how critical we are, the media will more or less be able to alter our perception of the world. They have the adequate tools to do so.

---

[153] Newspaper revenues declined considerably between the years 2008 and 2018. Advertising revenue fell from $37.8 billion in 2008 to $14.3 billion in 2018, which evidences a 62% decline. For more information on this, see Grieco, Elizabeth. "Fast Facts about the Newspaper Industry's Financial Struggles as McClatchy Files for Bankruptcy." *Pew Research Center*, 14 Feb. 2020.

[154] On mass media depictions of citizens and the influence of those depictions, see Shumow, Moses. *Mediated Communities: Civic Voices, Empowerment and Media Literacy in the Digital Era.* Peter Lang, 2015.

14.4 Media Ownership and Government Regulations

In the United States, the government does not own the media and news sources. Who owns media agencies if the government does not own them? And how does the government regulate the media? The government controls the media by the use of licensing. The government sells licenses to radio and TV stations and is now questioning the role social media plays in national security-related issues. Because of that, policymakers carefully examine which threats the media represent and boost. News agencies are big businesses all around the world.

Only in the United States, six corporations own most of the major media outlets. What difference does that fact make? How important is media ownership for us? How having little to no diversity in media ownership can affect us? Those who control the media are known as gatekeepers. *Gatekeepers* are the people in charge of what information gets to us, and most importantly, how it does. Today, most news comes from—or at least through—massive, corporate-owned sources. One can these days see a *commercial bias* in the media toward what will increase advertiser revenues and audience shares. When taking news stories and information from the media in a context that could be considered reliable, one should adequately contextualize and understand the media bias nature and the outlets' ideological and political views.

Having money, however, does not necessarily help when building effective political communication. Innovation and creativity play a crucial role in political communication, as in other forms of cultural integration, and are not only a thing of the wealthy. Money certainly gives an advantage over the rest, but there are other factors that one should consider. Small and medium-sized news outlets can adjust to their budget and still create engaging and convincing narratives.

There is a continuous effort to get large audiences and keep them engaged. The media does that while also making way for increased advertising, which results in a reduced emphasis on political news, particularly for local television. Journalists lighten and dramatize the content of the information we get through the media. News is turned into *infotainment or soft news* to keep audiences tuned in and engaged.

Similarly, on the internet, infotainment is used to generate more news leads and story reads. *Clickbait* is the sensational headlines that tease you into clicking a link to find some intriguing-sounding information. By appealing to emotions and feelings, journalists aim to obtain more clicks from you. Today's media's corporate ownership means that the media outlets frequently face conflicts of interest in deciding what news to cover and how to cover it.

When doing their best to avoid getting "scooped" by another station or newspaper, reporters and editors alike sometimes jump the gun. Today, anyone can start a blog, a website, a podcast, or a YouTube Channel and start publishing his/her independent views. Social media networking has given voice to many new actors that influence public opinion.

If small media outlets and new-coming influencers look like they will be profitable, enterprising corporations likely have an incentive to scoop them up. Today, some outlets look like alternative media but have the funding of giants behind them. They are not independent at all. By appearing to be alternative or independent can attract new potential audiences that mistrust larger media outlets.

Media in the United States of America functions like a private enterprise system in which large businesses seek profit. The media in this country is almost entirely privately-owned, but they do not operate without some degree of public control. With fewer limitations on how many stations an owner can possess, the potential for media monopoly has become enormous over the years.[155]

The internet is known as a place in which the media can freely operate. However, that is only true as long as there is internet freedom in that

---

[155] On media monopoly and the hilling effects of corporate ownership and mass advertising on the nation's news, see Bagdikian, Ben. *The Media Monopoly.* Beacon Press, 2000.. Since 1983, the number of corporations controlling most of America's daily newspapers, magazines, radio and television stations, book publishers, and movie companies has dwindled from fifty to ten to six.

country. Should the internet be regulated? Is it time to consider internet connectivity a basic human right? And are we prepared if it turns against us? Supporters of net neutrality believe that the internet should be an open-access forum for innovation. In the aftermath of Russian hacking and social media manipulation during the 2016 election, the internet has been up for scrutiny in Congress.

It is important to note that U.S. Congress members are mostly not among the generations that are internet savvy. It comes as no surprise that they often don't seem to know what they are searching for. Even though there has been significant-tech adoption since 2012 among older generations, Millennials still stand out for their technology use. On the other hand, Gen Z's are tech native.

14.5 What Do Journalists Do?

Both reporters and journalists gather information to later present it as news stories, feature articles, or documentaries. Journalists usually work on the staff of news organizations, but they work freelance as well. Freelance journalism means that they write stories for whoever pays them. General reporters cover all kinds of news stories, while other journalists specialize in specific areas such as politics, business, or fashion.

Journalists play a relevant, far-reaching, and essential role in our political system because they chase the news and deliver information to the rest of society. Valid-reporting means seeking answers. Reporting means digging out nuggets of truth and stitching them together into a coherent story that truly informs the public of what is happening in their world. Self-claiming that one is a journalist is not enough to be an authentic journalist. Citizens have to keep a keen eye on whether they contribute valuable, high-quality, factual, and not-strongly biased information to the public debate.

Journalism falls into four principal journalistic roles. The first role is to be a *gatekeeper* of truth. Editors and high-authority reporters who decide about what should be covered and what should not are the gatekeepers of truth for society. The second role is to be a disseminator. A *disseminator* is a reporter who mainly focuses on getting out facts rather than opinions. The third role of a journalist is to be a *researcher/analyst*. This type of journalist is a person who digs for information and interprets both its transcendence and significance by contextualizing it. The fourth type of reporter is a *public mobilizer*. This journalist usually has an agenda, and it is part of their job to make citizens aware of what is going on around them and encourage them to take action.

Journalists do not only communicate about what is going on in the world but also influence public opinion. In his seminal study of *Public Opinion*, Walter Lippmann observed that political action mostly derived from voting rights and mass media communications rather than from the collectively arrived at the will of rational, enlightened men. Citizens politically decide, more or less, through the exercise of the vote and the influence of public opinion. Lippmann recognized in 1922 that public opinion was a constructed and manufactured thing that could be shaped and manipulated by those with the resources and interests in doing so[156]. Publicists, press agents, and journalists are part of a social class situated between political organizations and media institutions. Their job is often to influence the public opinion-building process according to the needs of their clients.[157]

14.6 Issues, challenges, and controversies professional journalism faces

Professional journalists are often in a position that does not allow them to earn money from their work. It is too easy to make money off their work without paying them for it. News aggregators pose a threat to journalism because high-quality reporting costs both time and money. If a

---

[156] On the role of news in the process of manufacturing public opinion, see Lipmann.

[157] For more information about how the press agents influence public opinion, see McNair, Brian. *An Introduction to Political Communication*. Routledge, Taylor & Francis Group, 2018. Political programs, policy agendas, electoral messages, pressure group campaigns, and acts of domestic and global terrorism have the potential for communicative effectiveness.

news source only retells another agency's story, the original story writer loses revenue for their work.

Another problem with professional journalism is that people have equated journalism with print journalism. Nowadays, people do not buy or subscribe to print outlets as they used to in the past. People object to paying for content online. There is a slow appreciation of electronic media. Major outlets are doing their best to maintain old business models based on subscription and print ad revenue while still successfully venturing into the digital world. As citizens distrust the media in general, it becomes more difficult for the public to trust the media. The public distrusts the media, which lacks credibility these days.

Respectable journalists do not write fake news. Fake news is out there, but credible journalists do their best to confront it. What is distinctive about good journalism is the reporters' commitment to accuracy, objectivity, and detail in telling their stories. Journalists have to properly research and verify their facts because they act as communicators who work in service of the truth, even if it is troublesome.

Low-quality journalism may allow disinformation and misinformation to originate in or leak into the news industry, which is likely to mislead public opinion. Strong ethical journalism and professional standards are required as antidotes to both disinformation and misinformation. As long as we do not control the avalanche of disinformation, the public may come to disbelieve all content, including journalism. Citizens are likely to take as credible whatever content their close friends and preferred influencers share in social networks. Disinformation campaigns do not necessarily aspire to convince the public to believe that its content is veracious but rather impact the agenda-setting. Fake news can shape what people think is relevant and what is not.

One should consider that when people use the phrase "fake news," for the most part, what they are trying to do is to control the narrative. Fake news accusations are used as a way of delegitimizing a journalist's work. Because of its popularity, the term has recently been weaponized to leverage attacks against the media. Citizens may use the term "fake news" to satisfy their need for structure in the world. Cognitively speaking, people need to satisfy their need to see the world around them as an orderly, coherent, and structured place rather than solely to express their political, cultural, or personal ideology. One can already see the negative impacts of this situation on public beliefs about health, science, and intercultural affairs.

News organizations in the United States recognize fake news as a sociopolitical problem while acknowledging the challenge in defining it because of its many uses and connotations depending on the context. In general, specialists consider fake news as a social media phenomenon thriving on political polarization driven by mostly ideological and partisan, but sometimes also cultural and financial motivations. It has become common throughout the world to blame for the rise of fake news to the current political environment, to technological platforms Google, Twitter and Facebook, and some particular audiences as well.

14.7 Media Shapes The Political Narrative

The media has historically played an integral role in influencing social trends. The information era, a new history term used to capture the way the world has recently developed to rely on information for most of the actions that people take, remains significantly different from all the other periods in the history of humankind.

More than ever, information and narratives now have significant powers to change and influence the way people think and act. Most importantly, the reasoning they help portray on various relevant topics in society. The media is essential to push for specific narratives and messages in the modern world.

The contemporary media industry has emerged as the most advanced system of communication that humanity has ever experienced. Unlike in the past, when information and narratives could take long periods to reach citizens, the situation is radically different in our times since information travels the world in seconds. Researchers have studied the role of the contemporary media in political driving narratives quite extensively. The media drives our social, economic, and political trends. Communication outlets influence the reasoning that people hold as truths.

The primary purpose of the mass media outlets is to tell convincing yet engaging stories. Ideally, in the media industry, stories and narratives are not only fact-based but also fact-checked. And who exactly are the storytellers? At the pinnacle of political reporting are the Washington press corporations. Some of them have been politicians or at least members of the political world. As politicians move from the political to the private sector, the list of government officials regularly changes. This *revolving door-like process* consists of moving from the political sector to the public or the private ones. Some journalists are ethically stellar, but others' loyalty may lie more toward their political allies than their audiences.

14.8 Media and politicians will try to create a narrative line and spin the facts that fit the narrative

When a politician *spins* a story, they are likely to purposely select pieces of information that fit their political narrative and intentionally interpret data to make things look different by distorting facts and ignoring relevant factors. In political journalism, spins are attempts to control communication to deliver one's preferred message and persuade audiences. The term is commonly used to refer to the sophisticated art of promoting one's agenda by selling and spreading specific messages in favor of one's interests and views. Political spins often imply a certain degree of deception. A person who offers to give their opinion or commentary to mass media outlets on a particular subject area (most typically *political analysis*) is a pundit. A *pundit* is a person who can sometimes fall into the "analyst" category of journalists and sometimes into the bloviator category. The journalist can spin a story through different methods.

Journalists can spin a tale by creating an agenda for their news source and creating an important story that people focus on. *Agenda setting* is what a journalist, editor, or producer decides is important, becomes news and ends up on the political agenda.[158] This agenda-setting can frame issues so that one or two topics become relevant in the national discussion for the day. *Framing* the political debate and public opinion is about telling people what matters the most and what to pay attention to when reading the news. There should be a reliance on skilled and professional communicators who stick to engaging, easy, and already existing narratives to shape and influence political debates.

Journalists can lose sight of what is necessary for the sake of media sales and revenues. A *feeding frenzy* is a process by which a scandal turns average journalists into sharks-like beings waiting for the next tidbit of news to drop. This situation can cause trouble when people focus on scandal and clickbait instead of seeking the truth. During election cycles, it is a common problem to only focus on the person winning a race. This *horse race-type of journalism* in election reporting focuses on who is ahead, who is losing support, and who is a surprisingly long shot, but not on the substance of what the election is really about. Much of the time, the end result is the *soundbite* generated, which is a short and snappy memorable line that commentators may repeat over and over. Often, they do so by taking facts out of context.

---

[158] See Zaller, John. *The Nature and Origins of Mass Opinion.* Cambridge University Press, 2011 for more information on the tactics to influence public opinion throughout history.

CHAPTER 15

Domestic Policy

15.1 Introduction to Policy

A **policy** is a prescribed course of action for those who work for the government. It creates a set of operational principles through which to accomplish desired goals.

Setting **domestic policy** creates standard operational procedures by which a government operates. Policies are put in place to guide the bureaucratic agencies that work under the Executive Branch.

When governments create laws and policies, either domestic or foreign, it is called policymaking. **Policymaking** is the process by which the Congress creates public policies. A **public policy** is a government plan of action to solve a problem that people share collectively or that they cannot solve on their own. These public policies are meant to create solutions to problems for the greater good of society. We can understand public policy as a purposeful course of action intended by officials to solve problems of society.

15.2 Making Public Policy

The power to make public policy in the United States begins with Congress. Policies are usually created by legislators in the form of new proposals or bills, which are passed by both the House and Senate and signed into law by the president. The role of influencing and creating public policy also resides in limited form within the Executive Branch.

A president may also create policy through multiple pathways: by placing an issue on the public agenda, including in their budget proposal, vetoing a law passed by Congress, or issuing an **executive order** that establishes a new policy or augments an existing one. Executive orders are directed only to government bureaucracies at the federal, state, or local levels. These agencies can wield enormous control over policy through how they enforce such orders.

The court system also can make public policy. When a court rules on what the government can, should or should not do, it is clearly taking an active policy making role. The courts, especially the **Supreme Court**, can create public policy by hearing cases that change policy adoption, allow for policy to be formulated, or create standards by which we interpret public law.

15.3 Types of domestic public policy

Scholars have come up with a typology of domestic problems that require different kinds of policies to solve them. These categories help determine the types of social and economic policies that the nation adopts.

The method by which a policy is implemented may vary according to the type of economic and political policy. Some policies are considered redistributive in nature. These **redistributive policies** use resources from affluent segments of society to provide benefits for those less likely to participate in the political sector. Redistributive policies are less likely to occur in more capitalistic market systems.

Domestic policies that are equally taxing on all of the population are called distributive in nature. A **distributive policy** is one whose costs are borne by the entire population. An example would be a flat-based tax system that is the same across all income brackets.

Some domestic policies, however, do not deal with the allocation of goods and resources in society. A domestic policy that does not distribute resources but exerts control within society through behaviors it requires is called a regulatory policy. **Regulatory policies** control behavior rather than distributing resources.

15.4 Social Policy

Many domestic policies are designed as social policies. **Social policies** are primarily distributive and redistributive policies that improve Americans' quality of life. If a social policy is distributive or redistributive for social welfare needs, it is a **social welfare policy,** a government program designed to provide for those who cannot, or sometimes will not, provide for themselves. Those programs that care for those who cannot care for themselves are the most redistributive in nature. Often there are rules and requirements, usually based on income potential.

Social policies that filter who is eligible or not for the redistribution of wealth often utilize means-tested programs. **Means-tested programs** require that beneficiaries prove they lack the necessary income or resources to provide for themselves, according to the government's definitions of eligibility. This is usually based on income-earning potential. In the United States, these types of programs often carry a social stigma and are contentious during elections.

Certain types of means-tested social programs are designed to help families in need. One example is the **Temporary Assistance to Needy Families (TANF)** program that replaced AFDC. This program provides block grants to state governments, giving states greater control over how they spend their money. The TANF program caps the amount that the federal government will pay for welfare and requires work in exchange for time-limited benefits. Other requirements may include recipients finding jobs within two years, then removing them from welfare rolls after a total of five years or less, depending on the state.

Another domestic policy program for helping people who make less than a federally legislated income level is the **Supplemental Nutrition Assistance Program (SNAP).** SNAP is the largest United States food assistance program for low-income families, providing vouchers to purchase food. This program helps those without enough resources for food and sustenance. In modern times, many Americans are unaware that the policy we have referred to for years as "welfare" is mostly gone.

One of the best-known social policies is Social Security Insurance. **Social insurance policies** are longer-term distributive programs that provide benefits to a specific segment of the population. **Social Security** is a program born in the Great Depression to provide retirement funding for the elderly. It works through an economic input, or buy-in, when workers pay into the federally backed program. People contribute to Social Security during their working lives in order to receive benefits after they retire. Current workers pay the Social Security of retirees, with any leftover money going into the Social Security trust fund. Most people, at least those who are older, see Social Security as something they have earned and to which they are entitled, not as a government handout.

Still, there are problems with Social Security. With longer life spans, most people end up getting much more back from Social Security and Medicare than they may have contributed.   Many workers who have paid into the system see Social Security as an entitlement. **Entitlement programs** require benefits to be paid to people who are entitled to receive them. They are not needs-based nor do they follow a means-tested approval system. Even though there is talk of the Social Security system going insolvent, it could be made sustainable. Some potential remedies, however, are politically unpalatable and vigorously opposed by interest groups, including the American Association of Retired People (AARP).

Domestic policies to ensure the health care of people are increasing. The **Patient Protection and Affordable Care Act** established and made access to health insurance more available and affordable for most Americans. The United States stands out among industrialized nations as the only one that doesn't have a universal health-care system guaranteeing minimum basic care to all. Historically, healthcare in America pre-2010 utilized Medicare (covering old people) and Medicaid (covering the poorest people) for health care coverage of those without insurance. The consequences were that many uninsured people fell through the cracks.

Medicare was a social insurance program designed to help the elderly pay their medical costs. This program has been modified since the inception, however, it is still focused on elderly care. Medicare has become an extraordinarily expensive program. **Medicaid** is a means-tested welfare program designed to assist the poor -- especially children -- with their medical costs. This program undergoes adjustments when domestic policies allow for increased coverage and care for different segments of society.

15.4 Economic Policy

Government creates economic policies to keep the economy stable, growing, and functioning smoothly. **Economic policies** include all the different strategies that government officials, elected and appointed, employ to solve economic problems, to protect economic rights, and to provide procedural guarantees to keep the financial markets running smoothly. The government can control and regulate the marketplace or allow it to go mostly unregulated, with each approach depending on the political policy and party in power.

The consequences of a largely unregulated market vary. More regulation of the commerce of food and energy can increase the cost of goods and services for consumers. Traditionally, policymakers have felt that the government should pursue a hands-off economic policy. This allows for consumers to decide how much they are willing to pay for goods and services. Since the Great Depression, the goal of economic policymakers has been to even out the dramatic cycles of inflation and recession without undermining the vitality and productivity of a market-driven economy. America has gone through various series of recessions, depressions, and economic growth, often influenced by the domestic policies set by the government.

Economic policies are complicated, so for the sake of brevity we will provide a short and simple description. The government uses fiscal policy to grow or shrink the economy through taxation. **Fiscal policy** is the government's power to tax and spend with the aim of stabilizing the economy. This is done to create both surpluses and deficits in national spending. A **surplus** is money saved after spending on the government's domestic policy. A **deficit** is money owed after spending beyond what is actually available.

There are many tools available to create a healthy fiscal policy. One power of the government is known as monetary policy. **Monetary policy** is the power to control the money supply by manipulating interest rates. When interest rates are low, people can borrow money at a lower cost, spurring more business activity. The monetary policy of the United States is run by the **Federal Reserve System (the Fed)**. The Federal Reserve System is a group of 12 banks run by a board of governors whose chair is appointed by the president. It sets interest rates for the nation and is autonomous of the Executive Branch or Congress.

The government has the power to take from every citizen and business a share of their revenue for the purpose of ensuring the national interest. Taxation is the power to charge people a percentage of their income for the domestic and foreign policy needs of the government. **Tax policy** is the way in which the government requires that individuals and businesses contribute to collective costs. Taxation levels may be different for people depending on their income levels. A **progressive income tax** is a tax on people with more money at a higher rate than the rate applied to people with less money. This is different from a **regressive tax.,**. A regressive tax may take a higher percentage of a poorer person's gross resources, like sales taxes or value-added taxes (VATs) or some proposals for a flat income tax. There are other types of taxes as well, including **capital gains taxes**, a controversial tax that may be levied on the return from capital investments.

15.5 Environmental Policy

President Richard Nixon in 1970 signed a National Environmental Policy Act that a year later became the **Environmental Protection Agency,** or EPA. During the 1970s, laws were passed regarding clean air and clean water, as well as protections for endangered species. With these, sources of air and water pollutants came under federal regulation. Environmental policy attempts to balance the protection and conservation of natural resources with economic growth and jobs. Industries are required to follow federal and state rules designed to protect the natural environment. The rigor with which these regulations are enforced often depends on the political party in power at any particular time. For example, President Ronald Reagan in 1982 cut EPA funding by 30 percent.

The **Department of the Interior** was established in 1849 to manage natural resources, and oversees energy development on federal lands as well as offshore leases. A division, the **Bureau of Land Management**, was formed in 1946 to manage the federal lands that total almost 250 million acres.

15.6 Energy Policy

U.S **energy policy** is sometimes connected to environmental policy, especially when energy production and consumption involves the exploitation of natural resources and creates pollutants. Legislation, regulations, international treaties, subsidies and taxation are all modes of policy implementation. Coal, oil, natural gas, hydroelectric and nuclear power, and more recently renewables including wind and solar power have powered America through the years and been subjects of energy policies. Fossil fuels still account for most United States energy consumption. Federal tax policies and subsidies can be used as incentives for the development of specific energy sources.

There is concern in the United States and worldwide over greenhouse gas emissions that are related to climate change. China and the United States are the biggest carbon polluters, and many nations and industries are taking steps to reduce such emissions and move toward energy efficiencies and renewable sources, though there has been no firm global agreement on such policies as yet.

15.7 Health Policy

America's massive and complex health-care industry accounts for about 17 percent of all spending, mostly on medical services to diagnose and treat illnesses and injuries, both physical and mental. **Health policy** has therefore become a contentious issue between political parties and is often adjusted, depending on who is in power. The United States system is a third-party payer arrangement in which health insurance companies reimburse medical providers a portion of the cost of services to patients. Almost half of Americans participate in private health insurance plans through their employers. Medicare (15 percent), for people over 65, and Medicaid (16 percent), for low-income people, are public programs touched on earlier under social policies. While the Affordable Care Act, also known as Obamacare, has helped expand coverage since its passage in 2010, there are still about 30 million (13 percent) of Americans who are uninsured, mostly because of the high costs of healthcare. Soaring costs have also driven employers to reduce the reimbursements paid to medical providers and to increase the burden of insurance premium payments on their employees.

15.8 Transportation Policy

The Department of Transportation (DOT) plans and coordinates federal transportation projects to enhance national economic competitiveness, facilitating the movement of people and goods and also setting safety regulations for all major modes of transport, including air, water, and land – both roads and railways. **National Transport Policy** also attempts to reduce negative impacts on the environment. The Federal Aviation Administration, Highway Administration, Railroad Administration, Transit Administration and other agencies are related to the DOT.

Many federal infrastructure programs and policies have failed to modernize in recent decades, according to DOT research, leading to five major challenges, which involve crumbling infrastructure, congestion, climate change, injuries and fatalities as well as unequal economic opportunity.

Transportation is the biggest source of United States greenhouse gas emissions, with more than 100 million people living amid pollution that exceeds health-based air quality standards. Traffic congestion costs the economy more than $165 billion in wasted productivity and fuel each year. Additionally, many infrastructure assets including highways, public transit and rail systems have come to the end of their useful lives and require repair or replacement. New modes of transport will also be necessary to handle the demands of both the economy and the environment in the future.

CHAPTER 16

Foreign Policy

16.1 Foreign policy

Foreign policy determines how the United States reacts and responds to governments and non-governmental groups beyond its borders. **Foreign policy** is the official policy designed to solve problems that occur between the United States and actors from abroad. It is important to have successful policies for national self-preservation. Without a strong and effective foreign policy, America's security as a rich and peaceful country could come under threat. Although the United States has little control over the other actors involved. its foreign policy is generally carried out for the good of American citizens or in the interest of national security.

16.2 Two fundamental perspectives on our relationship with the world

Relationships with other nations can be seen through two distinct perspectives: isolationism and interventionism. **Isolationism** is a foreign policy view holding that Americans should put themselves and their problems first and not interfere in global concerns. The United States pursued an isolationist policy after World War I, but this experiment was seen largely as a failure. The second fundamental perspective is **interventionism**, which holds that to keep the republic safe, the United States must be actively engaged in shaping the global environment and willing to intervene in order to create desired outcomes.

16.3 Foreign policy and external actors

Many organizations are external actors within the current foreign policy environment. Intergovernmental organizations are bodies that have countries as members, including the United Nations, NATO, OPEC, and the EU. These international bodies work together to create agreements among nations regarding international policies. American foreign policy relies on the concept of **American Exceptionalism**, which teaches that the United States is unique, marked by a distinct set of ideas including equality, self-rule, and limited government. The aim of foreign policy is to create a commonly held theory of democratic peace teaching that democratic nations are less likely to engage in wars with one another

The president is the chief negotiator for the United States, and any treaty negotiated must then be ratified by the Senate. The president has ample resources available to fulfill the obligations of the office. The **National Security Council (NSC)** is the president's inner circle that advises on matters of foreign policy and is coordinated by the national security adviser. Foreign policy is negotiated through the **Department of State, which** is charged with managing foreign affairs. The secretary of state is part of the president's cabinet and fulfills a variety of foreign policy roles, including maintaining diplomatic and consular posts around the world, sending delegates and missions (groups of government officials) to a variety of international organization meetings, and negotiating treaties and executive agreements with other countries. The **Department of Defense (DOD)** manages the United States military and its equipment in order to protect the nation. It is headed by the secretary of defense, and under that office are the **Joint Chiefs of Staff**, service chiefs of the Army, Navy, Marine Corps, Air Force, Space Force, and the National Guard Bureau. While the chief of the Coast Guard is not an official member of the Joint Chiefs, a Coast Guard admiral routinely meets with the group.

The Defense Department is the government's biggest agency and accounts for a large portion of the national budget, along with health spending and Social Security. It employs almost 3 million service members and civilians in more than 160 countries and is headquartered in the iconic Pentagon building in Arlington, Virginia, just outside Washington DC.

16.4 Trade policy

United States **trade policy** objectives in recent decades have included reducing protections both at home and abroad, opening foreign markets for American exports, and increasing global economic integration. While there has much success in integrating the world's economies, the United States has seen its share of the gross world product (GWP) plummet since the post-war period, and its position as the world's biggest economy challenged first by Japan in the 1990s and now by China, which is expected to overtake it in the future. America's international trade deficit now routinely exceeds $600 billion annually, as the United States buys far more foreign goods and services than it sells.

The **Department of Commerce** is charged by the president with helping the economy expand through working to ensure fair trade and providing the data necessary to support commerce. It also helps negotiate bilateral trade agreements, enforces laws and issues sanctions that attempt to ensure a level playing field for United States businesses.

Even more directly concerned with trade policy is the office of the **United States Trade Representative** (USTR), which is responsible for developing and recommending trade policy to the president. It also conducts trade negotiations for the executive branch and participates in the World Trade Organization (WTO).

Tariffs are customs duties levied on imported and exported goods and services. They are typically used to protect domestic industries or as leverage in trade negotiations and disputes. While Congress originally had the power to levy tariffs granted by the Constitution, the president has the power to negotiate international agreements, so Congress has partially delegated to the executive the latitude to negotiate trade agreements and set **tariff policy**. The United States has been a member of the WTO since 1995, and as such makes tariff policies within the regulatory context of the global trading system.

Tariffs are actually a type of tax paid on goods sourced from other countries and usually paid to United States customs authorities by importing companies. While tariffs may offer some protection to domestic industries by raising prices of competing imported goods, they are ultimately paid by United States consumers to whom cost increases are passed by importers.

APPENDIX A

Declaration of Independence

When in the Course of human events, it becomes necessary for one people to dissolve the political bands which have connected them with another, and to assume among the powers of the earth, the separate and equal station to which the Laws of Nature and of Nature's God entitle them, a decent respect to the opinions of mankind requires that they should declare the causes which impel them to the separation.

We hold these truths to be self-evident, that all men are created equal, that they are endowed by their Creator with certain unalienable Rights, that among these are Life, Liberty and the pursuit of Happiness. —That to secure these rights, Governments are instituted among Men, deriving their just powers from the consent of the governed, —That whenever any Form of Government becomes destructive of these ends, it is the Right of the People to alter or to abolish it, and to institute new Government, laying its foundation on such principles and organizing its powers in such form, as to them shall seem most likely to effect their Safety and Happiness. Prudence, indeed, will dictate that Governments long established should not be changed for light and transient causes; and accordingly all experience hath shewn, that mankind are more disposed to suffer, while evils are sufferable, than to right themselves by abolishing the forms to which they are accustomed. But when a long train of abuses and usurpations, pursuing invariably the same Object evinces a design to reduce them under absolute Despotism, it is their right, it is their duty, to throw off such Government, and to provide new Guards for their future security. —Such has been the patient sufferance of these Colonies; and such is now the necessity which constrains them to alter their former Systems of Government. The history of the present King of Great Britain is a history of repeated injuries and usurpations, all having in direct object the establishment of an absolute Tyranny over these States. To prove this, let Facts be submitted to a candid world.

He has refused his Assent to Laws, the most wholesome and necessary for the public good. He has forbidden his Governors to pass Laws of immediate and pressing importance, unless suspended in their operation till his Assent should be obtained; and when so suspended, he has utterly neglected to attend to them.

He has refused to pass other Laws for the accommodation of large districts of people, unless those people would relinquish the right of Representation in the Legislature, a right inestimable to them and formidable to tyrants only.

He has called together legislative bodies at places unusual, uncomfortable, and distant from the depository of their public Records, for the sole purpose of fatiguing them into compliance with his measures.

He has dissolved Representative Houses repeatedly, for opposing with manly firmness his invasions on the rights of the people.

He has refused for a long time, after such dissolutions, to cause others to be elected; whereby the Legislative powers, incapable of Annihilation, have returned to the People at large for their exercise; the State remaining in the mean time exposed to all the dangers of invasion from without, and convulsions within.

He has endeavoured to prevent the population of these States; for that purpose obstructing the Laws for Naturalization of Foreigners; refusing to pass others to encourage their migrations hither, and raising the conditions of new Appropriations of Lands.

He has obstructed the Administration of Justice, by refusing his Assent to Laws for establishing Judiciary powers.

He has made Judges dependent on his Will alone, for the tenure of their offices, and the amount and payment of their salaries.

He has erected a multitude of New Offices, and sent hither swarms of Officers to harrass our people, and eat out their substance.

He has kept among us, in times of peace, Standing Armies without the Consent of our legislatures.

He has affected to render the Military independent of and superior to the Civil power.

He has combined with others to subject us to a jurisdiction foreign to our constitution, and unacknowledged by our laws; giving his Assent to their Acts of pretended Legislation:

For Quartering large bodies of armed troops among us:

For protecting them, by a mock Trial, from punishment for any Murders which they should commit on the Inhabitants of these States:

For cutting off our Trade with all parts of the world:

For imposing Taxes on us without our Consent:

For depriving us in many cases, of the benefits of Trial by Jury:

For transporting us beyond Seas to be tried for pretended offences

For abolishing the free System of English Laws in a neighbouring Province, establishing therein an Arbitrary government, and enlarging its Boundaries so as to render it at once an example and fit instrument for introducing the same absolute rule into these Colonies:

For taking away our Charters, abolishing our most valuable Laws, and altering fundamentally the Forms of our Governments:

For suspending our own Legislatures, and declaring themselves invested with power to legislate for us in all cases whatsoever.

He has abdicated Government here, by declaring us out of his Protection and waging War against us.

He has plundered our seas, ravaged our Coasts, burnt our towns, and destroyed the lives of our people.

He is at this time transporting large Armies of foreign Mercenaries to compleat the works of death, desolation and tyranny, already begun with circumstances of Cruelty & perfidy scarcely paralleled in the most barbarous ages, and totally unworthy the Head of a civilized nation.

He has constrained our fellow Citizens taken Captive on the high Seas to bear Arms against their Country, to become the executioners of their friends and Brethren, or to fall themselves by their Hands.

He has excited domestic insurrections amongst us, and has endeavoured to bring on the inhabitants of our frontiers, the merciless Indian Savages, whose known rule of warfare, is an undistinguished destruction of all ages, sexes and conditions.

In every stage of these Oppressions We have Petitioned for Redress in the most humble terms: Our repeated Petitions have been answered only by repeated injury. A Prince whose character is thus marked by every act which may define a Tyrant, is unfit to be the ruler of a free people.

Nor have We been wanting in attentions to our Brittish brethren. We have warned them from time to time of attempts by their legislature to extend an unwarrantable jurisdiction over us. We have reminded them of the circumstances of our emigration and settlement here. We have appealed to their native justice and magnanimity, and we have conjured them by the ties of our common kindred to disavow these usurpations, which, would inevitably interrupt our connections and correspondence. They too have been deaf to the voice of justice and of consanguinity. We must, therefore, acquiesce in the necessity, which denounces our Separation, and hold them, as we hold the rest of mankind, Enemies in War, in Peace Friends.

We, therefore, the Representatives of the united States of America, in General Congress, Assembled, appealing to the Supreme Judge of the world for the rectitude of our intentions, do, in the Name, and by Authority of the good People of these Colonies, solemnly publish and declare, That these United Colonies are, and of Right ought to be Free and Independent States; that they are Absolved from all Allegiance to the

British Crown, and that all political connection between them and the State of Great Britain, is and ought to be totally dissolved; and that as Free and Independent States, they have full Power to levy War, conclude Peace, contract Alliances, establish Commerce, and to do all other Acts and Things which Independent States may of right do. And for the support of this Declaration, with a firm reliance on the protection of divine Providence, we mutually pledge to each other our Lives, our Fortunes and our sacred Honor.

The 56 signatures on the Declaration appear in the positions indicated:

Column 1
Georgia:
Button Gwinnett
Lyman Hall
George Walton

Column 2
North Carolina:
William Hooper
Joseph Hewes
John Penn
South Carolina:
Edward Rutledge
Thomas Heyward, Jr.
Thomas Lynch, Jr.
Arthur Middleton

Column 3
Massachusetts:
John Hancock
Maryland:
Samuel Chase
William Paca

Thomas Stone
Charles Carroll of Carrollton
Virginia:
George Wythe
Richard Henry Lee
Thomas Jefferson
Benjamin Harrison
Thomas Nelson, Jr.
Francis Lightfoot Lee
Carter Braxton

Column 4
Pennsylvania:
Robert Morris
Benjamin Rush
Benjamin Franklin
John Morton
George Clymer
James Smith
George Taylor
James Wilson
George Ross
Delaware:
Caesar Rodney
George Read
Thomas McKean

Column 5
New York:
William Floyd
Philip Livingston
Francis Lewis
Lewis Morris

New Jersey:
Richard Stockton
John Witherspoon
Francis Hopkinson
John Hart
Abraham Clark

Column 6
New Hampshire:
Josiah Bartlett
William Whipple
Massachusetts:
Samuel Adams
John Adams
Robert Treat Paine
Elbridge Gerry
Rhode Island:
Stephen Hopkins
William Ellery
Connecticut:
Roger Sherman
Samuel Huntington
William Williams
Oliver Wolcott
New Hampshire:
Matthew Thornton

APPENDIX B

The Constitution of the United States

We the People of the United States, in Order to form a more perfect Union, establish Justice, insure domestic Tranquility, provide for the common defence, promote the general Welfare, and secure the Blessings of Liberty to ourselves and our Posterity, do ordain and establish this Constitution for the United States of America.

Article. I.

Section. 1.

All legislative Powers herein granted shall be vested in a Congress of the United States, which shall consist of a Senate and House of Representatives.

Section. 2.

The House of Representatives shall be composed of Members chosen every second Year by the People of the several States, and the Electors in each State shall have the Qualifications requisite for Electors of the most numerous Branch of the State Legislature.

No Person shall be a Representative who shall not have attained to the Age of twenty five Years, and been seven Years a Citizen of the United

States, and who shall not, when elected, be an Inhabitant of that State in which he shall be chosen.

Representatives and direct Taxes shall be apportioned among the several States which may be included within this Union, according to their respective Numbers, which shall be determined by adding to the whole Number of free Persons, including those bound to Service for a Term of Years, and excluding Indians not taxed, three fifths of all other Persons. The actual Enumeration shall be made within three Years after the first Meeting of the Congress of the United States, and within every subsequent Term of ten Years, in such Manner as they shall by Law direct. The Number of Representatives shall not exceed one for every thirty Thousand, but each State shall have at Least one Representative; and until such enumeration shall be made, the State of New Hampshire shall be entitled to chuse three, Massachusetts eight, Rhode-Island and Providence Plantations one, Connecticut five, New-York six, New Jersey four, Pennsylvania eight, Delaware one, Maryland six, Virginia ten, North Carolina five, South Carolina five, and Georgia three.

When vacancies happen in the Representation from any State, the Executive Authority thereof shall issue Writs of Election to fill such Vacancies.

The House of Representatives shall chuse their Speaker and other Officers; and shall have the sole Power of Impeachment.

Section. 3.

The Senate of the United States shall be composed of two Senators from each State, chosen by the Legislature thereof, for six Years; and each Senator shall have one Vote.

Immediately after they shall be assembled in Consequence of the first Election, they shall be divided as equally as may be into three Classes. The Seats of the Senators of the first Class shall be vacated at the Expiration of the second Year, of the second Class at the Expiration of the fourth Year, and of the third Class at the Expiration of the sixth Year, so that one third may be chosen every second Year; and if Vacancies happen by Resignation, or otherwise, during the Recess of the Legislature of any State, the Executive thereof may make temporary Appointments until the next Meeting of the Legislature, which shall then fill such Vacancies.

No Person shall be a Senator who shall not have attained to the Age of thirty Years, and been nine Years a Citizen of the United States, and who shall not, when elected, be an Inhabitant of that State for which he shall be chosen.

The Vice President of the United States shall be President of the Senate, but shall have no Vote, unless they be equally divided.

The Senate shall chuse their other Officers, and also a President pro tempore, in the Absence of the Vice President, or when he shall exercise the Office of President of the United States.

The Senate shall have the sole Power to try all Impeachments. When sitting for that Purpose, they shall be on Oath or Affirmation. When the President of the United States is tried, the Chief Justice shall preside: And no Person shall be convicted without the Concurrence of two thirds of the Members present.

Judgment in Cases of Impeachment shall not extend further than to removal from Office, and disqualification to hold and enjoy any Office of honor, Trust or Profit under the United States: but the Party convicted shall nevertheless be liable and subject to Indictment, Trial, Judgment and Punishment, according to Law.

Section. 4.

The Times, Places and Manner of holding Elections for Senators and Representatives, shall be prescribed in each State by the Legislature thereof; but the Congress may at any time by Law make or alter such Regulations, except as to the Places of chusing Senators.

The Congress shall assemble at least once in every Year, and such Meeting shall be on the first Monday in December, unless they shall by Law appoint a different Day.

Section. 5.

Each House shall be the Judge of the Elections, Returns and Qualifications of its own Members, and a Majority of each shall constitute a Quorum to do Business; but a smaller Number may adjourn from day to day, and may be authorized to compel the Attendance of absent Members, in such Manner, and under such Penalties as each House may provide.

Each House may determine the Rules of its Proceedings, punish its Members for disorderly Behaviour, and, with the Concurrence of two thirds, expel a Member.

Each House shall keep a Journal of its Proceedings, and from time to time publish the same, excepting such Parts as may in their Judgment require Secrecy; and the Yeas and Nays of the Members of either House on any question shall, at the Desire of one fifth of those Present, be entered on the Journal.

Neither House, during the Session of Congress, shall, without the Consent of the other, adjourn for more than three days, nor to any other Place than that in which the two Houses shall be sitting.

Section. 6.

The Senators and Representatives shall receive a Compensation for their Services, to be ascertained by Law, and paid out of the Treasury of the United States. They shall in all Cases, except Treason, Felony and Breach of the Peace, be privileged from Arrest during their Attendance at the Session of their respective Houses, and in going to and returning from the same; and for any Speech or Debate in either House, they shall not be questioned in any other Place.

No Senator or Representative shall, during the Time for which he was elected, be appointed to any civil Office under the Authority of the United States, which shall have been created, or the Emoluments whereof shall have been encreased during such time; and no Person holding any Office under the United States, shall be a Member of either House during his Continuance in Office.

Section. 7.

All Bills for raising Revenue shall originate in the House of Representatives; but the Senate may propose or concur with Amendments as on other Bills.

Every Bill which shall have passed the House of Representatives and the Senate, shall, before it become a Law, be presented to the President of the United States; If he approve he shall sign it, but if not he shall return it, with his Objections to that House in which it shall have originated, who shall enter the Objections at large on their Journal, and proceed to reconsider it. If after such Reconsideration two thirds of that House shall agree to pass the Bill, it shall be sent, together with the Objections, to the other House, by which it shall likewise be reconsidered, and if approved by two thirds of that House, it shall become a Law. But in all such Cases the Votes of both Houses shall be determined by yeas and Nays, and the Names of the Persons voting for and against the Bill shall be entered on the Journal of each House respectively. If any Bill shall not be returned by the President within ten Days (Sundays excepted) after it shall have been presented to him, the Same shall be a Law, in like Manner as if he had signed it, unless the Congress by their Adjournment prevent its Return, in which Case it shall not be a Law.

Every Order, Resolution, or Vote to which the Concurrence of the Senate and House of Representatives may be necessary (except on a question of Adjournment) shall be presented to the President of the United States; and before the Same shall take Effect, shall be approved by him, or being disapproved by him, shall be repassed by two thirds of the Senate and House of Representatives, according to the Rules and Limitations prescribed in the Case of a Bill.

Section. 8.

The Congress shall have Power To lay and collect Taxes, Duties, Imposts and Excises, to pay the Debts and provide for the common Defence and general Welfare of the United States; but all Duties, Imposts and Excises shall be uniform throughout the United States;

To borrow Money on the credit of the United States;

To regulate Commerce with foreign Nations, and among the several States, and with the Indian Tribes;

To establish an uniform Rule of Naturalization, and uniform Laws on the subject of Bankruptcies throughout the United States;

To coin Money, regulate the Value thereof, and of foreign Coin, and fix the Standard of Weights and Measures;

To provide for the Punishment of counterfeiting the Securities and current Coin of the United States;

To establish Post Offices and post Roads;

To promote the Progress of Science and useful Arts, by securing for limited Times to Authors and Inventors the exclusive Right to their respective Writings and Discoveries;

To constitute Tribunals inferior to the supreme Court;

To define and punish Piracies and Felonies committed on the high Seas, and Offences against the Law of Nations;

To declare War, grant Letters of Marque and Reprisal, and make Rules concerning Captures on Land and Water;

To raise and support Armies, but no Appropriation of Money to that Use shall be for a longer Term than two Years;

To provide and maintain a Navy;

To make Rules for the Government and Regulation of the land and naval Forces;

To provide for calling forth the Militia to execute the Laws of the Union, suppress Insurrections and repel Invasions;

To provide for organizing, arming, and disciplining, the Militia, and for governing such Part of them as may be employed in the Service of the United States, reserving to the States respectively, the Appointment of the Officers, and the Authority of training the Militia according to the discipline prescribed by Congress;

To exercise exclusive Legislation in all Cases whatsoever, over such District (not exceeding ten Miles square) as may, by Cession of particular States, and the Acceptance of Congress, become the Seat of the

Government of the United States, and to exercise like Authority over all Places purchased by the Consent of the Legislature of the State in which the Same shall be, for the Erection of Forts, Magazines, Arsenals, dock-Yards, and other needful Buildings;—And

To make all Laws which shall be necessary and proper for carrying into Execution the foregoing Powers, and all other Powers vested by this Constitution in the Government of the United States, or in any Department or Officer thereof.

Section. 9.

The Migration or Importation of such Persons as any of the States now existing shall think proper to admit, shall not be prohibited by the Congress prior to the Year one thousand eight hundred and eight, but a Tax or duty may be imposed on such Importation, not exceeding ten dollars for each Person.

The Privilege of the Writ of Habeas Corpus shall not be suspended, unless when in Cases of Rebellion or Invasion the public Safety may require it.

No Bill of Attainder or ex post facto Law shall be passed.

No Capitation, or other direct, Tax shall be laid, unless in Proportion to the Census or enumeration herein before directed to be taken.

No Tax or Duty shall be laid on Articles exported from any State.

No Preference shall be given by any Regulation of Commerce or Revenue to the Ports of one State over those of another: nor shall Vessels bound to, or from, one State, be obliged to enter, clear, or pay Duties in another.

No Money shall be drawn from the Treasury, but in Consequence of Appropriations made by Law; and a regular Statement and Account of the Receipts and Expenditures of all public Money shall be published from time to time.

No Title of Nobility shall be granted by the United States: And no Person holding any Office of Profit or Trust under them, shall, without the Consent of the Congress, accept of any present, Emolument, Office, or Title, of any kind whatever, from any King, Prince, or foreign State.

Section. 10.

No State shall enter into any Treaty, Alliance, or Confederation; grant Letters of Marque and Reprisal; coin Money; emit Bills of Credit; make any Thing but gold and silver Coin a Tender in Payment of Debts; pass any Bill of Attainder, ex post facto Law, or Law impairing the Obligation of Contracts, or grant any Title of Nobility.

No State shall, without the Consent of the Congress, lay any Imposts or Duties on Imports or Exports, except what may be absolutely necessary for executing it's inspection Laws: and the net Produce of all Duties and Imposts, laid by any State on Imports or Exports, shall be for the Use of the Treasury of the United States; and all such Laws shall be subject to the Revision and Controul of the Congress.

No State shall, without the Consent of Congress, lay any Duty of Tonnage, keep Troops, or Ships of War in time of Peace, enter into any Agreement or Compact with another State, or with a foreign Power, or engage in War, unless actually invaded, or in such imminent Danger as will not admit of delay.

Article. II.

Section. 1.

The executive Power shall be vested in a President of the United States of America. He shall hold his Office during the Term of four Years, and, together with the Vice President, chosen for the same Term, be elected, as follows

Each State shall appoint, in such Manner as the Legislature thereof may direct, a Number of Electors, equal to the whole Number of Senators and Representatives to which the State may be entitled in the Congress: but no Senator or Representative, or Person holding an Office of Trust or Profit under the United States, shall be appointed an Elector.

The Electors shall meet in their respective States, and vote by Ballot for two Persons, of whom one at least shall not be an Inhabitant of the same State with themselves. And they shall make a List of all the Persons voted for, and of the Number of Votes for each; which List they shall sign and certify, and transmit sealed to the Seat of the Government of the United States, directed to the President of the Senate. The President of the Senate shall, in the Presence of the Senate and House of Representatives, open all the Certificates, and the Votes shall then be counted. The Person having the greatest Number of Votes shall be the President, if such Number be a Majority of the whole Number of Electors appointed; and if there be more than one who have such Majority, and have an equal Number of Votes, then the House of Representatives shall immediately chuse by Ballot one of them for President; and if no Person have a Majority, then from the five highest on the List the said House shall in like Manner chuse the President. But in chusing the President, the Votes shall be taken by States, the Representation from each State having one Vote; A quorum for this Purpose shall consist of a Member or Members from two thirds of the States, and a Majority of all the States shall be necessary to a Choice. In every Case, after the Choice of the President, the Person having the greatest Number of Votes of the Electors shall be the Vice President. But if there should remain two or more who have equal Votes, the Senate shall chuse from them by Ballot the Vice President.

The Congress may determine the Time of chusing the Electors, and the Day on which they shall give their Votes; which Day shall be the same throughout the United States.

No Person except a natural born Citizen, or a Citizen of the United States, at the time of the Adoption of this Constitution, shall be eligible to the Office of President; neither shall any Person be eligible to that

Office who shall not have attained to the Age of thirty five Years, and been fourteen Years a Resident within the United States.

In Case of the Removal of the President from Office, or of his Death, Resignation, or Inability to discharge the Powers and Duties of the said Office, the Same shall devolve on the Vice President, and the Congress may by Law provide for the Case of Removal, Death, Resignation or Inability, both of the President and Vice President, declaring what Officer shall then act as President, and such Officer shall act accordingly, until the Disability be removed, or a President shall be elected.

The President shall, at stated Times, receive for his Services, a Compensation, which shall neither be encreased nor diminished during the Period for which he shall have been elected, and he shall not receive within that Period any other Emolument from the United States, or any of them.

Before he enter on the Execution of his Office, he shall take the following Oath or Affirmation:—"I do solemnly swear (or affirm) that I will faithfully execute the Office of President of the United States, and will to the best of my Ability, preserve, protect and defend the Constitution of the United States."

Section. 2.

The President shall be Commander in Chief of the Army and Navy of the United States, and of the Militia of the several States, when called into the actual Service of the United States; he may require the Opinion, in writing, of the principal Officer in each of the executive Departments, upon any Subject relating to the Duties of their respective Offices, and he shall have Power to grant Reprieves and Pardons for Offences against the United States, except in Cases of Impeachment.

He shall have Power, by and with the Advice and Consent of the Senate, to make Treaties, provided two thirds of the Senators present concur; and he shall nominate, and by and with the Advice and Consent of the Senate, shall appoint Ambassadors, other public Ministers and Consuls,

Judges of the supreme Court, and all other Officers of the United States, whose Appointments are not herein otherwise provided for, and which shall be established by Law: but the Congress may by Law vest the Appointment of such inferior Officers, as they think proper, in the President alone, in the Courts of Law, or in the Heads of Departments.

The President shall have Power to fill up all Vacancies that may happen during the Recess of the Senate, by granting Commissions which shall expire at the End of their next Session.

Section. 3.

He shall from time to time give to the Congress Information of the State of the Union, and recommend to their Consideration such Measures as he shall judge necessary and expedient; he may, on extraordinary Occasions, convene both Houses, or either of them, and in Case of Disagreement between them, with Respect to the Time of Adjournment, he may adjourn them to such Time as he shall think proper; he shall receive Ambassadors and other public Ministers; he shall take Care that the Laws be faithfully executed, and shall Commission all the Officers of the United States.

Section. 4.

The President, Vice President and all civil Officers of the United States, shall be removed from Office on Impeachment for, and Conviction of, Treason, Bribery, or other high Crimes and Misdemeanors.

Article III.

Section. 1.

The judicial Power of the United States, shall be vested in one supreme Court, and in such inferior Courts as the Congress may from time to time ordain and establish. The Judges, both of the supreme and inferior

Courts, shall hold their Offices during good Behaviour, and shall, at stated Times, receive for their Services, a Compensation, which shall not be diminished during their Continuance in Office.

Section. 2.

The judicial Power shall extend to all Cases, in Law and Equity, arising under this Constitution, the Laws of the United States, and Treaties made, or which shall be made, under their Authority;—to all Cases affecting Ambassadors, other public Ministers and Consuls;—to all Cases of admiralty and maritime Jurisdiction;—to Controversies to which the United States shall be a Party;—to Controversies between two or more States;—between a State and Citizens of another State,—between Citizens of different States, —between Citizens of the same State claiming Lands under Grants of different States, and between a State, or the Citizens thereof, and foreign States, Citizens or Subjects.

In all Cases affecting Ambassadors, other public Ministers and Consuls, and those in which a State shall be Party, the supreme Court shall have original Jurisdiction. In all the other Cases before mentioned, the supreme Court shall have appellate Jurisdiction, both as to Law and Fact, with such Exceptions, and under such Regulations as the Congress shall make.

The Trial of all Crimes, except in Cases of Impeachment, shall be by Jury; and such Trial shall be held in the State where the said Crimes shall have been committed; but when not committed within any State, the Trial shall be at such Place or Places as the Congress may by Law have directed.

Section. 3.

Treason against the United States, shall consist only in levying War against them, or in adhering to their Enemies, giving them Aid and Comfort. No Person shall be convicted of Treason unless on the Testimony of two Witnesses to the same overt Act, or on Confession in open Court.

The Congress shall have Power to declare the Punishment of Treason, but no Attainder of Treason shall work Corruption of Blood, or Forfeiture except during the Life of the Person attainted.

Article. IV.

Section. 1.

Full Faith and Credit shall be given in each State to the public Acts, Records, and judicial Proceedings of every other State. And the Congress may by general Laws prescribe the Manner in which such Acts, Records and Proceedings shall be proved, and the Effect thereof.

Section. 2.

The Citizens of each State shall be entitled to all Privileges and Immunities of Citizens in the several States.

A Person charged in any State with Treason, Felony, or other Crime, who shall flee from Justice, and be found in another State, shall on Demand of the executive Authority of the State from which he fled, be delivered up, to be removed to the State having Jurisdiction of the Crime.

No Person held to Service or Labour in one State, under the Laws thereof, escaping into another, shall, in Consequence of any Law or Regulation therein, be discharged from such Service or Labour, but shall be delivered up on Claim of the Party to whom such Service or Labour may be due.

Section. 3.

New States may be admitted by the Congress into this Union; but no new State shall be formed or erected within the Jurisdiction of any other State; nor any State be formed by the Junction of two or more States, or Parts of States, without the Consent of the Legislatures of the States concerned as well as of the Congress.

The Congress shall have Power to dispose of and make all needful Rules and Regulations respecting the Territory or other Property belonging to the United States; and nothing in this Constitution shall be so construed as to Prejudice any Claims of the United States, or of any particular State.

Section. 4.

The United States shall guarantee to every State in this Union a Republican Form of Government, and shall protect each of them against Invasion; and on Application of the Legislature, or of the Executive (when the Legislature cannot be convened), against domestic Violence.

Article. V.

The Congress, whenever two thirds of both Houses shall deem it necessary, shall propose Amendments to this Constitution, or, on the Application of the Legislatures of two thirds of the several States, shall call a Convention for proposing Amendments, which, in either Case, shall be valid to all Intents and Purposes, as Part of this Constitution, when ratified by the Legislatures of three fourths of the several States, or by Conventions in three fourths thereof, as the one or the other Mode of Ratification may be proposed by the Congress; Provided that no Amendment which may be made prior to the Year One thousand eight hundred and eight shall in any Manner affect the first and fourth Clauses in the Ninth Section of the first Article; and that no State, without its Consent, shall be deprived of its equal Suffrage in the Senate.

Article. VI.

All Debts contracted and Engagements entered into, before the Adoption of this Constitution, shall be as valid against the United States under this Constitution, as under the Confederation.

This Constitution, and the Laws of the United States which shall be made in Pursuance thereof; and all Treaties made, or which shall be made, under the Authority of the United States, shall be the supreme Law of the Land; and the Judges in every State shall be bound thereby, any Thing in the Constitution or Laws of any State to the Contrary notwithstanding.

The Senators and Representatives before mentioned, and the Members of the several State Legislatures, and all executive and judicial Officers, both of the United States and of the several States, shall be bound by Oath or Affirmation, to support this Constitution; but no religious Test shall ever be required as a Qualification to any Office or public Trust under the United States.

Article. VII.

The Ratification of the Conventions of nine States, shall be sufficient for the Establishment of this Constitution between the States so ratifying the Same.

Done in Convention by the Unanimous Consent of the States present the Seventeenth Day of September in the Year of our Lord one thousand seven hundred and Eighty seven and of the Independance of the United States of America the Twelfth In witness whereof We have hereunto subscribed our Names,

G. Washington
Presidt and deputy from Virginia
Delaware
Geo: Read
Gunning Bedford jun
John Dickinson
Richard Bassett
Jaco: Broom
Maryland

James McHenry
Dan of St Thos. Jenifer
Danl. Carroll
Virginia
John Blair
James Madison Jr.
North Carolina
Wm. Blount
Richd. Dobbs Spaight
Hu Williamson
South Carolina
J. Rutledge
Charles Cotesworth Pinckney
Charles Pinckney
Pierce Butler
Georgia
William Few
Abr Baldwin
New Hampshire
John Langdon
Nicholas Gilman
Massachusetts
Nathaniel Gorham
Rufus King
Connecticut
Wm. Saml. Johnson
Roger Sherman
New York
Alexander Hamilton
New Jersey
Wil: Livingston
David Brearley
Wm. Paterson

Jona: Dayton
Pensylvania
B Franklin
Thomas Mifflin
Robt. Morris
Geo. Clymer
Thos. FitzSimons
Jared Ingersoll
James Wilson
Gouv Morris

Constitutional Amendments

The U.S. Bill of Rights (Amendments 1–10)

The Preamble to The Bill of Rights

Congress of the United States begun and held at the City of New-York, on Wednesday the fourth of March, one thousand seven hundred and eighty nine.

The Conventions of a number of the States, having at the time of their adopting the Constitution, expressed a desire, in order to prevent misconstruction or abuse of its powers, that further declaratory and restrictive clauses should be added: And as extending the ground of public confidence in the Government, will best ensure the beneficent ends of its institution.

Resolved by the Senate and House of Representatives of the United States of America, in Congress assembled, two thirds of both Houses concurring, that the following Articles be proposed to the Legislatures of the several States, as amendments to the Constitution of the United States, all, or any of which Articles, when ratified by three fourths of the said Legislatures, to be valid to all intents and purposes, as part of the said Constitution; viz.

Articles in addition to, and Amendment of the Constitution of the United States of America, proposed by Congress, and ratified by the

Legislatures of the several States, pursuant to the fifth Article of the original Constitution.

Note: The following text is a transcription of the first ten amendments to the Constitution in their original form. These amendments were ratified December 15, 1791, and form what is known as the "Bill of Rights."

Amendment I

Congress shall make no law respecting an establishment of religion, or prohibiting the free exercise thereof; or abridging the freedom of speech, or of the press; or the right of the people peaceably to assemble, and to petition the Government for a redress of grievances.

Amendment II

A well regulated Militia, being necessary to the security of a free State, the right of the people to keep and bear Arms, shall not be infringed.

Amendment III

No Soldier shall, in time of peace be quartered in any house, without the consent of the Owner, nor in time of war, but in a manner to be prescribed by law.

Amendment IV

The right of the people to be secure in their persons, houses, papers, and effects, against unreasonable searches and seizures, shall not be violated, and no Warrants shall issue, but upon probable cause, supported by Oath or affirmation, and particularly describing the place to be searched, and the persons or things to be seized.

Amendment V

No person shall be held to answer for a capital, or otherwise infamous crime, unless on a presentment or indictment of a Grand Jury, except in cases arising in the land or naval forces, or in the Militia, when in actual service in time of War or public danger; nor shall any person be subject for the same offence to be twice put in jeopardy of life or limb; nor shall be compelled in any criminal case to be a witness against himself, nor be deprived of life, liberty, or property, without due process of law; nor shall private property be taken for public use, without just compensation.

Amendment VI

In all criminal prosecutions, the accused shall enjoy the right to a speedy and public trial, by an impartial jury of the State and district wherein the crime shall have been committed, which district shall have been previously ascertained by law, and to be informed of the nature and cause of the accusation; to be confronted with the witnesses against him; to have compulsory process for obtaining witnesses in his favor, and to have the Assistance of Counsel for his defence.

Amendment VII

In Suits at common law, where the value in controversy shall exceed twenty dollars, the right of trial by jury shall be preserved, and no fact tried by a jury, shall be otherwise re-examined in any Court of the United States, than according to the rules of the common law.

Amendment VIII

Excessive bail shall not be required, nor excessive fines imposed, nor cruel and unusual punishments inflicted.

Amendment IX

The enumeration in the Constitution, of certain rights, shall not be construed to deny or disparage others retained by the people.

Amendment X

The powers not delegated to the United States by the Constitution, nor prohibited by it to the States, are reserved to the States respectively, or to the people.

Amendment XI

The Judicial power of the United States shall not be construed to extend to any suit in law or equity, commenced or prosecuted against one of the United States by Citizens of another State, or by Citizens or Subjects of any Foreign State.

Amendment XII

The Electors shall meet in their respective states and vote by ballot for President and Vice-President, one of whom, at least, shall not be an inhabitant of the same state with themselves; they shall name in their ballots the person voted for as President, and in distinct ballots the person voted for as Vice-President, and they shall make distinct lists of all persons voted for as President, and of all persons voted for as Vice-President, and of the number of votes for each, which lists they shall sign and certify, and transmit sealed to the seat of the government of the United States, directed to the President of the Senate; — the President of the Senate shall, in the presence of the Senate and House of Representatives, open all the certificates and the votes shall then be counted; — The person having the greatest number of votes for President, shall be the President, if such number be a majority of the whole number of Electors appointed; and if no person have such majority, then from the persons having the highest numbers not exceeding three on the list of those voted for as President, the House of Representatives shall choose immediately, by ballot, the President. But in choosing the President, the votes shall be taken by states, the representation from each state having one vote; a quorum for this purpose shall consist of a member or members from two-thirds of the states, and a majority of all the states shall be necessary to a choice. [And if the House of Representatives shall not choose a President whenever the right of choice shall devolve upon them, before the fourth day of March next following, then the Vice-President shall act as President, as in case of the death or other constitutional disability of the President. —]* The person having the greatest number of votes as Vice-President, shall be the Vice-President, if such number be a majority of the whole number of Electors appointed, and if no person have a majority, then from the two highest numbers on the list, the Senate shall choose the Vice-President; a quorum for the purpose shall consist of twothirds of the whole number of Senators, and a majority of the whole number shall be necessary to a choice. But no person constitutionally ineligible to the office of President shall be eligible to that of Vice-President of the United States.

*Superseded by Section 3 of the 20th amendment.

Amendment XIII

Section 1.

Neither slavery nor involuntary servitude, except as a punishment for crime whereof the party shall have been duly convicted, shall exist within the United States, or any place subject to their jurisdiction.

Section 2.

Congress shall have power to enforce this article by appropriate legislation.

Amendment XIV

Section 1.

All persons born or naturalized in the United States, and subject to the jurisdiction thereof, are citizens of the United States and of the State wherein they reside. No State shall make or enforce any law which shall abridge the privileges or immunities of citizens of the United States; nor shall any State deprive any person of life, liberty, or property, without due process of law; nor deny to any person within its jurisdiction the equal protection of the laws.

Section 2.

Representatives shall be apportioned among the several States according to their respective numbers, counting the whole number of persons in each State, excluding Indians not taxed. But when the right to vote at any election for the choice of electors for President and Vice-President of the United States, Representatives in Congress, the Executive and Judicial officers of a State, or the members of the Legislature thereof, is denied to any of the male inhabitants of such State, being twenty-one years of age,* and citizens of the United States, or in any way abridged, except for participation in rebellion, or other crime, the basis of representation therein shall be reduced in the proportion which the number of such male citizens shall bear to the whole number of male citizens twenty-one years of age in such State.

Section 3.

No person shall be a Senator or Representative in Congress, or elector of President and Vice-President, or hold any office, civil or military, under the United States, or under any State, who, having previously taken an oath, as a member of Congress, or as an officer of the United States, or as a member of any State legislature, or as an executive or judicial officer of any State, to support the Constitution of the United States, shall have engaged in insurrection or rebellion against the same, or given aid or comfort to the enemies thereof. But Congress may by a vote of two-thirds of each House, remove such disability.

Section 4.

The validity of the public debt of the United States, authorized by law, including debts incurred for payment of pensions and bounties for services in suppressing insurrection or rebellion, shall not be questioned. But neither the United States nor any State shall assume or pay any debt or obligation incurred in aid of insurrection or rebellion against the

United States, or any claim for the loss or emancipation of any slave; but all such debts, obligations and claims shall be held illegal and void.

Section 5.

The Congress shall have the power to enforce, by appropriate legislation, the provisions of this article.

*Changed by Section 1 of the 26th amendment.

Amendment XV
Section 1.

The right of citizens of the United States to vote shall not be denied or abridged by the United States or by any State on account of race, color, or previous condition of servitude—

Section 2.

The Congress shall have the power to enforce this article by appropriate legislation.

Amendment XVI

The Congress shall have power to lay and collect taxes on incomes, from whatever source derived, without apportionment among the several States, and without regard to any census or enumeration.

Amendment XVII

The Senate of the United States shall be composed of two Senators from each State, elected by the people thereof, for six years; and each Senator shall have one vote. The electors in each State shall have the qualifications requisite for electors of the most numerous branch of the State legislatures.

When vacancies happen in the representation of any State in the Senate, the executive authority of such State shall issue writs of election to fill such vacancies: Provided, That the legislature of any State may empower the executive thereof to make temporary appointments until the people fill the vacancies by election as the legislature may direct.

This amendment shall not be so construed as to affect the election or term of any Senator chosen before it becomes valid as part of the Constitution.

Amendment XVIII

Section 1.

After one year from the ratification of this article the manufacture, sale, or transportation of intoxicating liquors within, the importation thereof into, or the exportation thereof from the United States and all territory subject to the jurisdiction thereof for beverage purposes is hereby prohibited.

Section 2.

The Congress and the several States shall have concurrent power to enforce this article by appropriate legislation.

Section 3.

This article shall be inoperative unless it shall have been ratified as an amendment to the Constitution by the legislatures of the several States, as provided in the Constitution, within seven years from the date of the submission hereof to the States by the Congress.

Amendment XIX

The right of citizens of the United States to vote shall not be denied or abridged by the United States or by any State on account of sex.

Congress shall have power to enforce this article by appropriate legislation.

Amendment XX

Section 1.

The terms of the President and the Vice President shall end at noon on the 20th day of January, and the terms of Senators and Representatives at noon on the 3d day of January, of the years in which such terms would have ended if this article had not been ratified; and the terms of their successors shall then begin.

Section 2.

The Congress shall assemble at least once in every year, and such meeting shall begin at noon on the 3d day of January, unless they shall by law appoint a different day.

Section 3.

If, at the time fixed for the beginning of the term of the President, the President elect shall have died, the Vice President elect shall become President. If a President shall not have been chosen before the time fixed for the beginning of his term, or if the President elect shall have failed to qualify, then the Vice President elect shall act as President until a President shall have qualified; and the Congress may by law provide for the case wherein neither a President elect nor a Vice President elect shall have qualified, declaring who shall then act as President, or the manner in which one who is to act shall be selected, and such person shall act accordingly until a President or Vice President shall have qualified.

Section 4.

The Congress may by law provide for the case of the death of any of the persons from whom the House of Representatives may choose a

President whenever the right of choice shall have devolved upon them, and for the case of the death of any of the persons from whom the Senate may choose a Vice President whenever the right of choice shall have devolved upon them.

Section 5.

Sections 1 and 2 shall take effect on the 15th day of October following the ratification of this article.

Section 6.

This article shall be inoperative unless it shall have been ratified as an amendment to the Constitution by the legislatures of threefourths of the several States within seven years from the date of its submission.

Amendment XXI

Section 1.

The eighteenth article of amendment to the Constitution of the United States is hereby repealed.

Section 2.

The transportation or importation into any State, Territory, or possession of the United States for delivery or use therein of intoxicating liquors, in violation of the laws thereof, is hereby prohibited.

Section 3.

This article shall be inoperative unless it shall have been ratified as an amendment to the Constitution by conventions in the several States, as provided in the Constitution, within seven years from the date of the submission hereof to the States by the Congress.

Amendment XXII

Section 1.

No person shall be elected to the office of the President more than twice, and no person who has held the office of President, or acted as President, for more than two years of a term to which some other person was elected President shall be elected to the office of the President more than once. But this Article shall not apply to any person holding the office of President when this Article was proposed by the Congress, and shall not prevent any person who may be holding the office of President, or acting as President, during the term within which this Article becomes operative from holding the office of President or acting as President during the remainder of such term.

Section 2.

This article shall be inoperative unless it shall have been ratified as an amendment to the Constitution by the legislatures of threefourths of the several States within seven years from the date of its submission to the States by the Congress.

Amendment XXIII

Section 1.

The District constituting the seat of Government of the United States shall appoint in such manner as the Congress may direct:

A number of electors of President and Vice President equal to the whole number of Senators and Representatives in Congress to which the District would be entitled if it were a State, but in no event more than the least populous State; they shall be in addition to those appointed by the States, but they shall be considered, for the purposes of the election of President and Vice President, to be electors appointed by a State; and they shall meet in the District and perform such duties as provided by the twelfth article of amendment.

Section 2.

The Congress shall have power to enforce this article by appropriate legislation.

Amendment XXIV

Section 1.

The right of citizens of the United States to vote in any primary or other election for President or Vice President, for electors for President or Vice President, or for Senator or Representative in Congress, shall not be denied or abridged by the United States or any State by reason of failure to pay any poll tax or other tax.

Section 2.

The Congress shall have power to enforce this article by appropriate legislation.

Amendment XXV

Section 1.

In case of the removal of the President from office or of his death or resignation, the Vice President shall become President.

Section 2.

Whenever there is a vacancy in the office of the Vice President, the President shall nominate a Vice President who shall take office upon confirmation by a majority vote of both Houses of Congress.

Section 3.

Whenever the President transmits to the President pro tempore of the Senate and the Speaker of the House of Representatives his written declaration that he is unable to discharge the powers and duties of his office, and until he transmits to them a written declaration to the contrary, such powers and duties shall be discharged by the Vice President as Acting President.

Section 4.

Whenever the Vice President and a majority of either the principal officers of the executive departments or of such other body as Congress may by law provide, transmit to the President pro tempore of the Senate and the Speaker of the House of Representatives their written declaration that the President is unable to discharge the powers and duties of his office, the Vice President shall immediately assume the powers and duties of the office as Acting President.

Thereafter, when the President transmits to the President pro tempore of the Senate and the Speaker of the House of Representatives his written declaration that no inability exists, he shall resume the powers and duties of his office unless the Vice President and a majority of either the principal officers of the executive department or of such other body as Congress may by law provide, transmit within four days to the President pro tempore of the Senate and the Speaker of the House of Representatives their written declaration that the President is unable to discharge the powers and duties of his office. Thereupon Congress shall decide the issue, assembling within forty-eight hours for that purpose if not in session. If the Congress, within twenty-one days after receipt of the latter written declaration, or, if Congress is not in session, within twenty-one days after Congress is required to assemble, determines by two-thirds vote of both Houses that the President is unable to discharge the powers and duties of his office, the Vice President shall continue to discharge the same as Acting President; otherwise, the President shall resume the powers and duties of his office.

Amendment XXVI

Section 1.

The right of citizens of the United States, who are eighteen years of age or older, to vote shall not be denied or abridged by the United States or by any State on account of age.

Section 2.

The Congress shall have power to enforce this article by appropriate legislation.

Amendment XXVII

No law, varying the compensation for the services of the Senators and Representatives, shall take effect, until an election of Representatives shall have intervened.

APPENDIX C

Federalist 10 and 51

Federalist Papers #10 and #51
From the New York Packet.
Friday, November 23, 1787.
Author: James Madison

To the People of the State of New York:

AMONG the numerous advantages promised by a well-constructed Union, none deserves to be more accurately developed than its tendency to break and control the violence of faction. The friend of popular governments never finds himself so much alarmed for their character and fate, as when he contemplates their propensity to this dangerous vice. He will not fail, therefore, to set a due value on any plan which, without violating the principles to which he is attached, provides a proper cure for it. The instability, injustice, and confusion introduced into the public councils, have, in truth, been the mortal diseases under which popular governments have everywhere perished; as they continue to be the favorite and fruitful topics from which the adversaries to liberty derive their most specious declamations. The valuable improvements made by the American constitutions on the popular models, both ancient and modern, cannot certainly be too much admired; but it would be an unwarrantable partiality, to contend that they have as effectually obviated the danger on this side, as was wished and expected. Complaints are everywhere heard from our most considerate and virtuous citizens, equally the friends of public and private faith, and of public and personal liberty, that our governments are too unstable, that the public good is disregarded in the conflicts of rival parties, and that measures are too often decided, not according to the rules of justice and the rights of the minor party, but by the superior force of an interested and overbearing majority. However anxiously we may wish that these complaints had no foundation, the evidence, of known facts will not permit us to deny that they are in some degree true. It will be found, indeed, on a candid review of our situation, that some of the distresses under which we labor have been erroneously charged on the operation of our governments; but it will be found, at the same time, that other causes will not alone account for many of our heaviest misfortunes; and, particularly, for that prevailing and increasing distrust of public engagements, and alarm for private rights, which are echoed from one end of the continent to the other. These must be chiefly, if not wholly, effects of the unsteadiness and injustice with which a factious spirit has tainted our public administrations.

By a faction, I understand a number of citizens, whether amounting to a majority or a minority of the whole, who are united and actuated by some common impulse of passion, or of interest, adversed to the rights of other citizens, or to the permanent and aggregate interests of the community.

There are two methods of curing the mischiefs of faction: the one, by removing its causes; the other, by controlling its effects.

There are again two methods of removing the causes of faction: the one, by destroying the liberty which is essential to its existence; the other, by giving to every citizen the same opinions, the same passions, and the same interests.

It could never be more truly said than of the first remedy, that it was worse than the disease. Liberty is to faction what air is to fire, an aliment without which it instantly expires. But it could not be less folly to abolish liberty, which is essential to political life, because it nourishes faction, than it would be to wish the annihilation of air, which is essential to animal life, because it imparts to fire its destructive agency.

The second expedient is as impracticable as the first would be unwise. As long as the reason of man continues fallible, and he is at liberty to exercise it, different opinions will be formed. As long as the connection subsists between his reason and his self-love, his opinions and his passions will have a reciprocal influence on each other; and the former will be objects to which the latter will attach themselves. The diversity in the faculties of men, from which the rights of property originate, is not less an insuperable obstacle to a uniformity of interests. The protection of these faculties is the first object of government. From the protection of different and unequal faculties of acquiring property, the possession of different degrees and kinds of property immediately results; and from the influence of these on the sentiments and views of the respective proprietors, ensues a division of the society into different interests and parties.

The latent causes of faction are thus sown in the nature of man; and we see them everywhere brought into different degrees of activity, according to the different circumstances of civil society. A zeal for different opinions concerning religion, concerning government, and many other points, as well of speculation as of practice; an attachment to different leaders ambitiously contending for pre-eminence and power; or to persons of other descriptions whose fortunes have been interesting to the human passions, have, in turn, divided mankind into parties, inflamed them with mutual animosity, and rendered them much more disposed to vex and oppress each other than to co-operate for their common good. So strong is this propensity of mankind to fall into mutual animosities, that where no substantial occasion presents itself, the most frivolous and fanciful distinctions have been sufficient to kindle their unfriendly passions and excite their most violent conflicts. But the most common and durable source of factions has been the various and unequal distribution of property. Those who hold and those who are without property have ever formed distinct interests in society. Those who are creditors, and

those who are debtors, fall under a like discrimination. A landed interest, a manufacturing interest, a mercantile interest, a moneyed interest,
with many lesser interests, grow up of necessity in civilized nations, and
divide them into different classes, actuated by different sentiments and
views. The regulation of these various and interfering interests forms the
principal task of modern legislation, and involves the spirit of party and
faction in the necessary and ordinary operations of the government.

No man is allowed to be a judge in his own cause, because his interest would certainly bias his judgment, and, not improbably, corrupt his
integrity. With equal, nay with greater reason, a body of men are unfit
to be both judges and parties at the same time; yet what are many of the
most important acts of legislation, but so many judicial determinations,
not indeed concerning the rights of single persons, but concerning the
rights of large bodies of citizens? And what are the different classes of
legislators but advocates and parties to the causes which they determine?
Is a law proposed concerning private debts? It is a question to which the
creditors are parties on one side and the debtors on the other. Justice
ought to hold the balance between them. Yet the parties are, and must be,
themselves the judges; and the most numerous party, or, in other words,
the most powerful faction must be expected to prevail. Shall domestic
manufactures be encouraged, and in what degree, by restrictions on foreign manufactures? are questions which would be differently decided by
the landed and the manufacturing classes, and probably by neither with
a sole regard to justice and the public good. The apportionment of taxes
on the various descriptions of property is an act which seems to require
the most exact impartiality; yet there is, perhaps, no legislative act in
which greater opportunity and temptation are given to a predominant
party to trample on the rules of justice. Every shilling with which they
overburden the inferior number, is a shilling saved to their own pockets.

It is in vain to say that enlightened statesmen will be able to adjust
these clashing interests, and render them all subservient to the public
good. Enlightened statesmen will not always be at the helm. Nor, in
many cases, can such an adjustment be made at all without taking into

view indirect and remote considerations, which will rarely prevail over the immediate interest which one party may find in disregarding the rights of another or the good of the whole.

The inference to which we are brought is, that the CAUSES of faction cannot be removed, and that relief is only to be sought in the means of controlling its EFFECTS.

If a faction consists of less than a majority, relief is supplied by the republican principle, which enables the majority to defeat its sinister views by regular vote. It may clog the administration, it may convulse the society; but it will be unable to execute and mask its violence under the forms of the Constitution. When a majority is included in a faction, the form of popular government, on the other hand, enables it to sacrifice to its ruling passion or interest both the public good and the rights of other citizens. To secure the public good and private rights against the danger of such a faction, and at the same time to preserve the spirit and the form of popular government, is then the great object to which our inquiries are directed. Let me add that it is the great desideratum by which this form of government can be rescued from the opprobrium under which it has so long labored, and be recommended to the esteem and adoption of mankind.

By what means is this object attainable? Evidently by one of two only. Either the existence of the same passion or interest in a majority at the same time must be prevented, or the majority, having such coexistent passion or interest, must be rendered, by their number and local situation, unable to concert and carry into effect schemes of oppression. If the impulse and the opportunity be suffered to coincide, we well know that neither moral nor religious motives can be relied on as an adequate control. They are not found to be such on the injustice and violence of individuals, and lose their efficacy in proportion to the number combined together, that is, in proportion as their efficacy becomes needful.

From this view of the subject it may be concluded that a pure democracy, by which I mean a society consisting of a small number of citizens, who assemble and administer the government in person, can admit of no cure for the mischiefs of faction. A common passion or interest will, in almost every case, be felt by a majority of the whole; a communication and concert result from the form of government itself; and there is nothing to check the inducements to sacrifice the weaker party or an obnoxious individual. Hence it is that such democracies have ever been spectacles of turbulence and contention; have ever been found incompatible with personal security or the rights of property; and have in general been as short in their lives as they have been violent in their deaths. Theoretic politicians, who have patronized this species of government, have erroneously supposed that by reducing mankind to aperfect equality in their political rights, they would, at the same time, be perfectly equalized and assimilated in their possessions, their opinions, and their passions.

A republic, by which I mean a government in which the scheme of representation takes place, opens a different prospect, and promises the cure for which we are seeking. Let us examine the points in which it varies from pure democracy, and we shall comprehend both the nature of the cure and the efficacy which it must derive from the Union.

The two great points of difference between a democracy and a republic are: first, the delegation of the government, in the latter, to a small number of citizens elected by the rest; secondly, the greater number of citizens, and greater sphere of country, over which the latter may be extended.

The effect of the first difference is, on the one hand, to refine and enlarge the public views, by passing them through the medium of a chosen body of citizens, whose wisdom may best discern the true interest of their country, and whose patriotism and love of justice will be least likely to sacrifice it to temporary or partial considerations. Under such a regulation, it may well happen that the public voice, pronounced by the representatives of the people, will be more consonant to the public good than if pronounced by the people themselves, convened for the purpose. On the other hand, the effect may be inverted. Men of factious tempers, of local prejudices, or of sinister designs, may, by intrigue, by corruption, or by other means, first obtain the suffrages, and then betray the interests, of the people. The question resulting is, whether small or extensive republics are more favorable to the election of proper guardians of the public weal; and it is clearly decided in favor of the latter by two obvious considerations:

In the first place, it is to be remarked that, however small the republic may be, the representatives must be raised to a certain number, in order to guard against the cabals of a few; and that, however large it may be, they must be limited to a certain number, in order to guard against the confusion of a multitude. Hence, the number of representatives in the two cases not being in proportion to that of the two constituents, and being proportionally greater in the small republic, it follows that, if the proportion of fit characters be not less in the large than in the small republic, the former will present a greater option, and consequently a greater probability of a fit choice.

In the next place, as each representative will be chosen by a greater number of citizens in the large than in the small republic, it will be more difficult for unworthy candidates to practice with success the vicious arts by which elections are too often carried; and the suffrages of the people being more free, will be more likely to centre in men who possess the most attractive merit and the most diffusive and established characters.

It must be confessed that in this, as in most other cases, there is a mean, on both sides of which inconveniences will be found to lie. By enlarging too much the number of electors, you render the representatives too little acquainted with all their local circumstances and lesser interests; as by reducing it too much, you render him unduly attached to these, and too little fit to comprehend and pursue great and national objects. The federal Constitution forms a happy combination in this respect; the great and aggregate interests being referred to the national, the local and particular to the State legislatures.

The other point of difference is, the greater number of citizens and extent of territory which may be brought within the compass of republican than of democratic government; and it is this circumstance principally which renders factious combinations less to be dreaded in the former than in the latter. The smaller the society, the fewer probably will be the distinct parties and interests composing it; the fewer the distinct parties and interests, the more frequently will a majority be found of the same party; and the smaller the number of individuals composing a majority, and the smaller the compass within which they are placed, the more easily will they concert and execute their plans of oppression. Extend the sphere, and you take in a greater variety of parties and interests; you make it less probable that a majority of the whole will have a common motive to invade the rights of other citizens; or if such a common motive exists, it will be more difficult for all who feel it to discover their own strength, and to act in unison with each other. Besides other impediments, it may be remarked that, where there is a consciousness of unjust or dishonorable purposes, communication is always checked by distrust in proportion to the number whose concurrence is necessary.

Hence, it clearly appears, that the same advantage which a republic has over a democracy, in controlling the effects of faction, is enjoyed by a large over a small republic,--is enjoyed by the Union over the States composing it. Does the advantage consist in the substitution of representatives whose enlightened views and virtuous sentiments render them superior to local prejudices and schemes of injustice? It will not be denied that the representation of the Union will be most likely to possess these requisite endowments. Does it consist in the greater security afforded by a greater variety of parties, against the event of any one party being able to outnumber and oppress the rest? In an equal degree does the increased variety of parties comprised within the Union, increase this security. Does it, in fine, consist in the greater obstacles opposed to the concert and accomplishment of the secret wishes of an unjust and interested majority? Here, again, the extent of the Union gives it the most palpable advantage.

The influence of factious leaders may kindle a flame within their particular States, but will be unable to spread a general conflagration through the other States. A religious sect may degenerate into a political faction in a part of the Confederacy; but the variety of sects dispersed over the entire face of it must secure the national councils against any danger from that source. A rage for paper money, for an abolition of debts, for an equal division of property, or for any other improper or wicked project, will be less apt to pervade the whole body of the Union than a particular member of it; in the same proportion as such a malady is more likely to taint a particular county or district, than an entire State.

In the extent and proper structure of the Union, therefore, we behold a republican remedy for the diseases most incident to republican government. And according to the degree of pleasure and pride we feel in being republicans, ought to be our zeal in cherishing the spirit and supporting the character of Federalists.

Federalist Paper #51: The Structure of the Government Must Furnish the Proper Checks and Balances Between the Different Departments

From the New York Packet.
Friday, February 8, 1788.

Author: Alexander Hamilton or James Madison To the People of the State of New York:

TO WHAT expedient, then, shall we finally resort, for maintaining in practice the necessary partition of power among the several departments, as laid down in the Constitution? The only answer that can be given is, that as all these exterior provisions are found to be inadequate, the defect must be supplied, by so contriving the interior structure of the government as that its several constituent parts may, by their mutual relations, be the means of keeping each other in their proper places. Without presuming to undertake a full development of this important idea, I will hazard a few general observations, which may perhaps place it in a clearer light, and enable us to form a more correct judgment of the principles and structure of the government planned by the convention. In order to lay a due foundation for that separate and distinct exercise of the different powers of government, which to a certain extent is admitted on all hands to be essential to the preservation of liberty, it is evident that each department should have a will of its own; and consequently should be so constituted that the members of each should have as little agency as possible in the appointment of the members of the others. Were this principle rigorously adhered to, it would require that all the appointments for the supreme executive, legislative, and judiciary magistracies should be drawn from the same fountain of authority, the people, through channels having no communication whatever with one another. Perhaps such a plan of constructing the several departments would be less difficult in practice than it may in contemplation appear. Some difficulties, however, and some additional expense would attend the execution of it. Some deviations, therefore, from the principle must be admitted. In the constitution of the judiciary department in particular, it might be inexpedient to insist rigorously on the principle: first, because peculiar qualifications being essential in the members, the primary consideration ought to be to select that mode of choice which best secures these qualifications; secondly, because the permanent tenure by which the appointments are held in that department, must soon destroy all sense of dependence on the authority conferring them. It is equally evident, that the members of each department should be as little dependent as possible on those of the others, for the emoluments annexed to their offices. Were the executive magistrate, or the judges, not independent of the legislature in this particular, their independence in every other would be merely nominal. But the great security against a gradual concentration of the several powers in the same department, consists in giving to those who administer each department the necessary constitutional means and personal motives to resist encroachments of the others. The provision for defense must in this, as in all other cases, be made commensurate to the danger of attack. Ambition must be made to counteract ambition. The interest of the man must be connected with the constitutional rights of the place. It may be a reflection on human nature, that such devices should be necessary to control the abuses of government. But what is government itself, but the greatest of all reflections on human nature? If men were angels, no government would be necessary. If angels were to govern men, neither external nor internal controls on government would be necessary. In framing a government which is to be administered by men over men, the great difficulty lies in this: you must first enable the government to control the governed; and in the next place oblige it to control itself. A dependence on the people is, no doubt, the primary control on the government; but experience has taught mankind the necessity of auxiliary precautions. This policy of supplying, by opposite and rival interests, the defect of better motives, might be traced through the whole system of human affairs, private as well as public. We see it particularly displayed in all the subordinate distributions of power, where the constant aim is to divide and arrange the several offices in such a manner as that each may be a check on the other that the private interest of every individual may be a sentinel over the public rights. These inventions of prudence cannot be less requisite in the distribution of the supreme powers of the State. But it is not possible to give to each department an equal power of self-defense. In republican government, the legislative authority necessarily predominates. The remedy for this inconveniency is to divide the legislature into different branches; and to render them, by different modes of election and different principles of action, as little connected with each other as the nature of their common functions and their common dependence on the society will admit. It may even be necessary to guard against dangerous encroachments by still further precautions. As the weight of the legislative authority requires that it should be thus divided, the weakness of the executive may require, on the other hand, that it should be fortified. An absolute negative on the legislature appears, at first view, to be the natural defense with which the executive magistrate should be armed. But perhaps it would be neither altogether safe nor alone sufficient. On ordinary occasions it might not be exerted with the requisite firmness, and on extraordinary occasions it might be perfidiously abused. May not this defect of an absolute negative be supplied by some qualified connection between this weaker department and the weaker branch of the stronger department, by which the latter may be led to support the constitutional rights of the former, without being too much detached from the rights of its own department? If the principles on which these observations are founded be just, as I persuade myself they are, and they be applied as a criterion to the several State constitutions, and to the federal Constitution it will be found that if the latter does not perfectly correspond with them, the former are infinitely less able to bear such a test. There are, moreover, two considerations particularly applicable to the federal system of America, which place that system in a very interesting point of view. First. In a single republic, all the power surrendered by the people is submitted to the administration of a single government; and the usurpations are guarded against by a division of the government into distinct and separate departments. In the compound republic of America, the power surrendered by the people is first divided between two distinct governments, and then the portion allotted to each subdivided among distinct and separate departments. Hence a double security arises to the rights of the people. The different governments will control each other, at the same time that each will be controlled by itself. Second. It is of great importance in a republic not only to guard the society against the oppression of its rulers, but to guard one part of the society against the injustice of the other part. Different interests necessarily exist in different classes of citizens. If a majority be united by a common interest, the rights of the minority will be insecure. There are but two methods of providing against this evil: the one by creating a will in the community independent of the majority that is, of the society itself; the other, by comprehending in the society so many separate descriptions of citizens as will render an unjust combination of a majority of the whole very improbable, if not impracticable. The first method prevails in all governments possessing an hereditary or self-appointed authority. This, at best, is but a precarious security; because a power independent of the society may as well espouse the unjust views of the major, as the rightful interests of the minor party, and may possibly be turned against both parties. The second method will be exemplified in the federal republic of the United States. Whilst all authority in it will be derived from and dependent on the society, the society itself will be broken into so many parts, interests, and classes of citizens, that the rights of individuals, or of the minority, will be in little danger from interested combinations of the majority. In a free government the security for civil rights must be the same as that for religious rights. It consists in the one case in the multiplicity of interests, and in the other in the multiplicity of sects. The degree of security in both cases will depend on the number of interests and sects; and this may be presumed to depend on the extent of country and number of people comprehended under the same government. This view of the subject must particularly recommend a proper federal system to all the sincere and considerate friends of republican government, since it shows that in exact proportion as the territory of the Union may be formed into more circumscribed Confederacies, or States oppressive combinations of a majority will be facilitated: the best security, under the republican forms, for the rights of every class of citizens, will be diminished: and consequently the stability and independence of some member of the government, the only other security, must be proportionately increased. Justice is the end of government. It is the end of civil society. It ever has been and ever will be pursued until it be obtained, or until liberty be lost in the pursuit. In a society under the forms of which the stronger faction can readily unite and oppress the weaker, anarchy may as truly be said to reign as in a state of nature, where the weaker individual is not secured against the violence of the stronger; and as, in the latter state, even the stronger individuals are prompted, by the uncertainty of their condition, to submit to a government which may protect the weak as well as themselves; so, in the former state, will the more powerful factions or parties be gradually induced, by a like motive, to wish for a government which will protect all parties, the weaker as well as the more powerful. It can be little doubted that if the State of Rhode Island was separated from the Confederacy and left to itself, the insecurity of rights under the popular form of government within such narrow limits would be displayed by such reiterated oppressions of factious majorities that some power altogether independent of the people would soon be called for by the voice of the very factions whose misrule had proved the necessity of it. In the extended republic of the United States, and among the great variety of interests, parties, and sects which it embraces, a coalition of a majority of the whole society could seldom take place on any other principles than those of justice and the general good; whilst there being thus less danger to a minor from the will of a major party, there must be less pretext, also, to provide for the security of the former, by introducing into the government a will not dependent on the latter, or, in other words, a will independent of the society itself. It is no less certain than it is important, notwithstanding the contrary opinions which have been entertained, that the larger the society, provided it lie within a practical sphere, the more duly capable it will be of self-government. And happily for the REPUBLICAN CAUSE, the practicable sphere may be carried to a very great extent, by a judicious modification and mixture of the FEDERAL PRINCIPLE.

PUBLIUS.

APPENDIX D

Selected Supreme Court Cases

Selected Supreme Court Cases

A. L. A. Schechter Poultry Corp. v. United States, 295 U.S. 495 (1935). This case represented a challenge to the constitutionality of a law called the National Industrial Recovery Act. This law was a major part of President Franklin D. Roosevelt's attempt to rebuild the nation's economy during the Great Depression. Major industries in the United States, however, objected to the way the law empowered the president to regulate aspects of American industry, such as labor conditions and even pay. In the unanimous decision, the court determined that the act was unconstitutional because it shifted the power to regulate commerce from the legislative branch to the executive branch.

Arizona v. United States, 567 U.S. 387 (2012). This case involved federal attempts to prevent an Arizona state immigration law (S.B. 1070) from being enforced. The United States brought suit, arguing that immigration law is exclusively in the federal domain. Agreeing with the federal government, a federal district court enjoined specific provisions in the law. Arizona appealed to the Supreme Court to overturn the decision. In a 5–3 decision, the court found that specific provisions in the law did conflict with federal law, while others were constitutional.

Brown v. Board of Education of Topeka, 347 U.S. 483 (1954). This case represented a challenge to the principle of "separate but equal" established by *Plessy v. Ferguson* in 1896. The case was brought by students who were denied admittance to certain public schools based exclusively on race. The unanimous decision in *Brown v. Board* determined that the existence of racially segregated public schools violated the equal protection clause of the Fourteenth Amendment. The court decided that schools segregated by race perpetrated harm by giving legal sanction to the idea that African Americans were inherently inferior. The ruling effectively overturned *Plessy v. Ferguson* and removed the legal supports for segregated schools nationwide.

Buckley v. Valeo, 424 U.S. 1 (1976). This case concerned the power of the then recently created Federal Election Commission to regulate the financing of political campaigns. These restrictions limited the amount of contributions that could be made to candidates and required political contributions to be disclosed, among other things. In 1975, Senator James Buckley filed suit, arguing that these limits amounted to a violation of First Amendment protections on free speech and free association. In a series of decisions in this complex case, the court determined that these restrictions did not violate the First Amendment.

Burwell v. Hobby Lobby Stores, Inc., 573 U.S. 682 (2014). This case involved a challenge to the mandate in the Patient Protection and Affordable Care Act that required that all employment-based group health care plans provide coverage for certain types of contraceptives. The law, however, allowed exemptions for religious employers such as churches that held a religious-based opposition to contraception. The plaintiffs in the case argued that Hobby Lobby, a large family-owned chain of arts and crafts stores, was run based on Christian principles and therefore should be exempt as well because of the Religious Freedom Restoration Act of 1993 (RFRA). The 5–4 decision in *Burwell v. Hobby Lobby* agreed with the plaintiffs and declared that RFRA permits for- profit companies like

Hobby Lobby to deny coverage for contraception in their health plans when that coverage violates a religious belief.

Bush v. Gore, 531 U.S. 98 (2000). Following voting in the November 2000 presidential election, observers recognized that the outcome of the very close national election hinged on the outcome of the election in Florida. Because the Florida election was so close, manual recounts were called for by the state's supreme court. Then-governor George W. Bush, who was ahead in the initial count, appealed to the U.S. Supreme Court to halt the manual recount and to declare that the method of manual recount being used violated his rights to equal protection and due process. The court issued a two-part *per curiam* opinion on the case. (In a *per curiam* opinion, the court makes it clear that the decision in the case is not intended to set a legal precedent.) In the first part, the court ruled in a 7–2 decision that the manual recount did violate the plaintiff's right to equal protection. In the second part, decided by a smaller 5–4 margin, the court ruled that there was not sufficient time to adjust the recount procedure and conduct a full recount. The effect of this ruling gave the Florida electoral votes, and thus the presidency, to George W. Bush.

Citizens United v. Federal Election Commission, 558 U.S. 310 (2010). In 2007, the nonprofit corporation Citizens United was prevented by the Federal Election Commission (FEC) from showing a movie about then-presidential candidate Hillary Clinton. The FEC noted that showing the movie violated the Bipartisan Campaign Reform Act (BCRA). BCRA prohibited campaign communications one month before a primary election and two months before a general election, required donors to be disclosed, and prohibited corporations from using their general funds for campaign communications. The plaintiffs argued that these restrictions constituted a violation of the First Amendment. The 5–4 decision in *Citizens United v. FEC* agreed with the plaintiffs and concluded that the restrictions imposed by BCRA and enforced by the FEC violated the corporation's First Amendment right to free expression.

Dobbs v. Jackson Women's Health Organization, 597 U.S. ___ (2022)
Supreme Court case that reversed *Roe v. Wade* and *Planned Parenthood of Southeastern Pennsylvania v. Casey*, the decisions that originally asserted the fundamental right to an abortion prior to the viability of the fetus. *Dobbs v. Jackson* states that the Constitution does not confer a right to abortion; and, the authority to regulate abortion is "returned to the people and their elected representatives."

***Dred Scott v. Sandford,* 60 U.S. 393 (1856).** This case concerned the constitutionality of the Missouri Compromise, which declared that certain states would be entirely free of slavery. Dred Scott, an enslaved person, was brought by his owner into free territories. When the owner brought him back to Missouri, a slave state, Dred Scott sued claiming that his time living in free territory made him free. After failing in his attempts in Missouri, Scott appealed to the Supreme Court. In a 7–2 decision, the court declared that the relevant parts of the Missouri Compromise were unconstitutional, and that Scott remained enslaved as a result.

***Gideon v. Wainwright,* 372 U.S. 335 (1963).** In 1961, Clarence E. Gideon was arrested and accused of breaking into a poolroom and stealing money from a cigarette machine. Not being able to afford a lawyer, and being denied a public defender by the judge, Gideon defended himself and was subsequently found guilty. Gideon appealed to the Supreme Court declaring that the denial by the trial judge constituted a violation of his constitutional right to representation. The unanimous decision by the court in *Gideon v. Wainwright* agreed that the Sixth Amendment required that those facing felony criminal charges be supplied with legal representation.

***King v. Burwell,* 576 U.S. 473 (2015).** When Congress wrote and passed the Patient Protection and Affordable Care Act in 2010, lawmakers intended for states to create exchanges through which residents in those states could purchase health care insurance plans. For those residents who could not afford the premiums, the law also allowed for tax credits to help reduce the cost. If states didn't create an exchange, the federal government created the exchange for the state. While the intention of the lawmakers was for the tax credits to apply to the federally created exchanges as well, the language of the law was somewhat unclear on this point. Residents in Virginia brought suit against the law arguing that the law should be interpreted in a way that withholds tax credits from those participating in the federally created exchange. In the 6–3 decision, the court disagreed, stating that viewing the law in its entirety made it clear that the intent of the law was to provide the tax credits to those participating in either exchange.

L. A. Schechter Poultry Corp. v. United States, 295 U.S. 495 (1935). This case represented a challenge to the constitutionality of a law called the National Industrial Recovery Act. This law was a major part of President Franklin D. Roosevelt's attempt to rebuild the nation's economy during the Great Depression. Major industries in the United States, however, objected to the way the law empowered the president to regulate aspects of American industry, such as labor conditions and even pay. In the unanimous decision, the court determined that the act was unconstitutional because it shifted the power to regulate commerce from the legislative branch to the executive branch.

***Lawrence v. Texas*, 539 U.S. 558 (2003).** This case concerned two men in Houston who in 1998 were prosecuted and convicted under a Texas law that forbade certain types of intimate sexual relations between two persons of the same sex. The men appealed to the Supreme Court arguing that their Fourteenth Amendment rights to equal protection and privacy were violated when they were prosecuted for consensual sexual intimacy in their own home. In the 6–3 decision in *Lawrence v. Texas*, the court concluded that while so-called anti-sodomy statutes like the law in Texas did not violate one's right to equal protection, they did violate the due process clause of the Fourteenth Amendment. The court stated that the government had no right to infringe on the liberty of persons engaging in such private and personal acts.

***Marbury v. Madison*, 5 U.S. 137 (1803).** This case involved the nomination of justices of the peace in Washington, DC, by President John Adams at the end of his term. Despite the Senate confirming the nominations, some of the commissions were not delivered before Adams left office. The new president, Thomas Jefferson, decided not to deliver the commissions. William Marbury, one of the offended justices, sued, saying that the Judiciary Act of 1789 empowered the court to force Secretary of State James Madison to deliver the commissions. In the unanimous decision in *Marbury v. Madison*, the court declared that while Marbury's rights were violated when Madison refused to deliver the commission, the court did not have the power to force the secretary to do so despite what the Judiciary Act says. In declaring that the law conflicted with the U.S. Constitution, the case established the principle of judicial review wherein the Supreme Court has the power to declare laws passed by Congress and signed by the president to be unconstitutional.

***McDonald v. Chicago*, 561 U.S. 742 (2010).** This case developed as a consequence of the decision in *District of Columbia v. Heller*, 554 U.S. 570 (2008), which dismissed a Washington, DC, handgun ban as a violation of the Second Amendment. In *McDonald v. Chicago*, the plaintiffs argued that the Fourteenth Amendment had the effect of applying the Second Amendment to the states, not just to the federal government. In a 5–4 decision, the court agreed with the plaintiffs and concluded that rights like the right to keep and bear arms are important enough for maintaining liberty that the Fourteenth Amendment rightly applies them to the states.

***Miranda v. Arizona*, 384 U.S. 436 (1966).** When Ernesto Miranda was arrested, interrogated, and confessed to kidnapping in 1963, the arresting officers neglected to inform him of his Fifth Amendment right not to self-incriminate. After being found guilty at trial, Miranda appealed to the Supreme Court, insisting that the officers violated his Fifth Amendment rights. The 5–4 decision in *Miranda v. Arizona* found that the right to not incriminate oneself relies heavily on the suspect's right to be informed of these rights at the time of arrest. The opinion indicated that suspects must be told that they have the right to an attorney and the right to remain silent in order to ensure that any statements they provide are issued voluntarily.

***National Federation of Independent Business v. Sebelius*, 567 U.S. 519 (2012).** This case represented a challenge to the constitutionality of the Patient Protection and Affordable Care Act. The suing states argued that the Medicare expansion and the individual mandate that required citizens to purchase health insurance or pay a fine were both unconstitutional. The 5–4 decision found that the Medicare expansion was permissible, but that the federal government could not withhold all Medicare funding for states that refused to accept the expansion. More importantly, it found that Congress had the power to apply the mandate to purchase health insurance under its enumerated power to tax.

***New York Times Co. v. Sullivan*, 376 U.S. 254 (1964).** This case began when the *New York Times* published a full-page advertisement claiming that the arrest of Martin Luther King, Jr. in Alabama was part of a concerted effort to ruin him. Insulted, an Alabama official filed a libel suit against the newspaper. Under Alabama law, which did not require that persons claiming libel have to show harm, the official won a judgment. The *New York Times* appealed to the Supreme Court, arguing that the ruling violated its First Amendment right to free speech. In a unanimous decision, the court declared that the First Amendment protects even false statements by the press, as long as those statements are not made with actual malice.

***Obergefell v. Hodges*, 576 U.S. 644 (2015).** This case concerned groups of same-sex couples who brought suits against a number of states and relevant agencies that refused to recognize same-sex marriages created in states where such marriages were legal. In the 5–4 decision, the court found that not only did the Fourteenth Amendment provision for equal protection under the law require that states recognize same-sex marriages formed in other states, but that no state could deny marriage licenses to same-sex couples if they also issued them to other types of couples.

***Plessy v. Ferguson*, 163 U.S. 537 (1896).** When Homer Plessy, a man of mixed racial heritage, sat in a Whites-only railroad car in an attempt to challenge a Louisiana law that required railroad cars be segregated, he was arrested and convicted. Appealing his conviction to the Supreme Court, he argued that the segregation law was a violation of the principle of equal protection under the law in the Fourteenth Amendment. In a 7–1 decision, the court disagreed, indicating that the law was not a violation of the equal protection principle because the different train cars were separate but equal. Plessy v. Ferguson's "separate but equal" remained a guiding principle of segregation until *Brown v. Board of Education* (1954).

***Roe v. Wade*, 410 U.S. 113 (1973).** This case involved a pregnant woman from Texas who desired to terminate her pregnancy. At the time, Texas only allowed abortions in cases where the woman's life was in danger. Using the pseudonym "Jane Roe," the woman appealed to the Supreme Court, arguing that the Constitution provides women the right to terminate an abortion. The 7–2 decision in *Roe v. Wade* sided with the plaintiff and declared that the right to privacy upheld in the decision in *Griswold v. Connecticut* (1965) included a woman's right to an abortion. In balancing the rights of the woman with the interests of the states to protect human life, the court created a trimester framework. In the first trimester, a pregnant woman could seek an abortion without restriction. In the second and third trimesters, however, the court asserted that states had an interest in regulating abortions, provided that those regulations were based on health needs.

Schechter Poultry Corp. v. United States. See ***A. L. A. Schechter Poultry Corp. v. United States.***

***Shelby County v. Holder,* 570 U.S. 529 (2013).** After decades in which African Americans encountered obstacles to voting, particularly in southern states, Congress passed the Voting Rights Act of 1965. Among other things, the law prohibited certain congressional districts from changing election laws without federal authorization. In 2010, Shelby County in Alabama brought a suit against the U.S. attorney general, claiming that both section five of the act, which required districts to seek preapproval, and section four, which determined which districts had to seek preapproval, were unconstitutional. In a 5–4 decision, the court found that both sections violated the Tenth Amendment.

***United States v. Windsor,* 570 U.S. 744 (2013).** When Thea Clara Spyer died in 2009, she left her estate to her wife, Edith Windsor, with whom she had been legally married in Canada years before. Because of a 1996 U.S. law called the Defense of Marriage Act (DOMA), this marriage was not recognized by the federal government. As a result, Windsor was compelled to pay an enormous tax on the inheritance, which she would not have had to pay had the federal government recognized the marriage. Appealing to the Supreme Court, Windsor argued that DOMA was unconstitutional because it deprives same-sex couples of their Fifth Amendment right to equal protection. In the 5–4 decision, the court agreed with Windsor, stating that DOMA was intended to treat certain married couples differently in blatant violation of their Fifth Amendment rights.

APPENDIX E

Electoral College Map

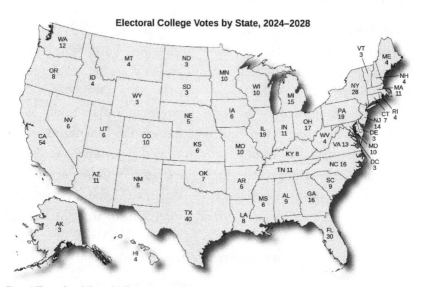

Electoral College Votes by State, 2024–2028

Figure **1** The number of Electoral College votes granted to each state equals the total number of representatives and senators that state has in the U.S. Congress or, in the case of Washington, DC, as many electors as it would have if it were a state. The number of representatives may fluctuate based on state population, which is determined every ten years by the U.S. Census, mandated by Article I, Section 2 of the Constitution. The most recent census was conducted in 2020.

About the Author

Rodgir Cohen, PhD, is a University lecturer residing in Redlands, California. As a combat veteran and community activist, his research focuses on psychology, political science, and religious studies. His recent books include topics in California government, American political science, and world religions. Cohen is driven by a passion for social justice and creating a better world through actions and words. When he is not lecturing, he often can be found, cruising on his boat in San Diego.